Jews and Freemasons in Europe

Jews and Freemasons in Europe 1723-1939

Jacob Katz   *Translated from the Hebrew by Leonard Oschry*

Harvard University Press, Cambridge, Massachusetts, 1970

© Copyright 1970 by the President and Fellows of Harvard College
All rights reserved

Distributed in Great Britain by Oxford University Press, London

Library of Congress Catalog Card Number 71-115475
SBN 674-47480-5

Printed in the United States of America

To the memory of Yonina Talmon

Preface to the English Edition

The theme of this book—the relation between Jews and Freemasons—has been the subject of countless books written, mainly in German and French, by propagandists of anti-Jewish or anti-Masonic leanings or by apologists in counterargument. Historians, however, have paid little if any attention to this subject. This is not surprising, for to the scholar presumed connection between Jews and Freemasons seemed little more than myth; any sources that could have clarified the assumption were hidden in the libraries and archives of the Masons, and usually inaccessible to the probing historian.

My own interest in this subject arose from studying the emergence of Jews into modern society, and my attempts to trace the routes by which these former ghetto-dwellers found their way into the social circles of their neighbors. It occurred to me that the semi-clandestine societies of the eighteenth and nineteenth centuries might have been among these. My initial inquiries indicated that I had come upon an important but unknown facet of a social process; but only later investigations, which took me from country to country, library to library, and archive to archive, revealed the wealth of material on the subject and its significance to modern Jewish history—indeed, to the history of modern Europe.

My work on this subject was begun in 1962–63 when I was a visiting professor at Harvard University. The treasures of Widener Library afforded me the first clues on the subject. I thank the personnel of this and of many other libraries where I pursued my research. I should like to make special mention of the Masonic libraries of Berne, Zurich, Frankfurt, and Paris, which assisted me with great courtesy. Most significant was my acquisition from the library of the Grand Lodge of Holland in The Hague, where I was graciously admitted and where I spent many fruitful hours in research. I extend my gratitude to Mr. B. Croiset Van Uchelen, the Curator of the Library, a great expert in Masonic bibliography, who assisted me in solving many problems related to my work.

The translation of the text from the Hebrew was done by Rabbi Aryeh Oschry, whose sensitivity to the intricacies of both languages made this translation true to the original.

The Hebrew University of Jerusalem   Jacob Katz
Jerusalem, Israel
January 1, 1970

Contents

Jews and Freemasons in Europe

The Problem and Its Background

The two names, Jews and Freemasons, joined together will most likely arouse different associations in different minds, each association reflecting the individual's cultural and national background. Although almost everyone has heard of the name "Freemasons," only to a few will the term denote more than the image of a selective secret society, active at one time or another in history, and still claiming the allegiance of some individuals. Yet, if the Freemasons themselves constitute a puzzle, their being coupled with Jews seems even more astonishing. Are the two in any way connected? Any person of European extraction (Polish, Rumanian, Hungarian, German, or French)—or anyone familiar with the recent history of these countries during the rise of anti-Semitism in Eastern Europe and Germany in the years between the two World Wars, and before and during the Dreyfus Affair in France, will recall that the combination of the two names became a popular slogan. Anti-Semites kept reiterating it in their speeches, in the press, and in inflammatory tracts. They tried to convey the impression that the Jews and the Freemasons had formed an alliance to endanger the states where they happened to live. A special notoriety was achieved by the brochure *The Protocols of the Elders of Zion,* which purported to contain the proceedings of a session of the elders of the Jews, who were plotting, in league with the Masonic lodges, to seize control of the world. This pamphlet, which first appeared in Russia, circulated widely in a German translation prepared in 1919, and subsequently was disseminated in millions of copies in a variety of languages.[1]

As for the German Freemasons, their outcry was motivated by a special consideration. Hitherto they had been more readily suspected of an aversion to, rather than a sympathy for, Jews. For the most part, their lodges were considered hives of anti-Semitism—and not without reason. Indeed, with the rise of political anti-Semitism in Germany during the 1880's, Jews found their position in the Masonic lodges becoming precarious. Even such lodges which had heretofore been accustomed to accepting Jews as members or admitting them as visitors now barred them. Actually Jews had never gained free access to the German lodges—not even during the period of

greatest social advances, the sixties and seventies of the nineteenth
century. In some lodges, membership was made conditional upon
adherence to the Christian faith. Nor was the stipulation rescinded
during the years when liberalism reached its peak. Such were the
lodges of Prussia, for the most part, with their centers in Berlin and
their branches extending beyond its borders. Starting at the beginning of the nineteenth century, a long and protracted struggle, a
war of words and ideas reflecting a social conflict, raged incessantly
between the upholders of the Christian restriction and their opponents. Among the participants were, firstly, all those Jews who had
been initiated into Masonry in other countries, or who had themselves founded lodges in Germany under the auspices of the French
and English branches of the movement. They were joined by non-
Jews as well and, during the thirties and forties, by entire lodges
who argued that Masonry stood above all religious differences. The
upholders of this principle enjoyed the support of the Masonic associations abroad: in Holland, England, France, and even the United
States of America. From this fact, it becomes evident that the Masons of those countries never acquiesced in any restriction based on
religion. In fact, if we trace the history of the Freemasons back to
its very inception, we find that the principle of religious toleration
was already incorporated in the very first constitution compiled in
England in the 1720's. Historical research will have to find the answer to the question: how far was this principle enforced in the
areas where it was accepted in theory, and how and why was it rejected in other areas, in both theory and practice?

This brief survey has proceeded in the reverse direction, from the
present to the past. It has brought to light the changes and transformations in the attitudes of Freemasons to Jews. That the Masons
found it necessary to take a stand against Jews shows that the latter
kept on pressing to enter the order. We should bear in mind that
the first, the London Grand Lodge, was founded in 1717, and that
lodges in the continental countries sprang up from 1730 to 1750. At
that time a new type of Jew was emerging, one who had acquired
some Western education and had adjusted his behavior to conform
to the standards accepted among gentiles, to the extent that he now
could aspire to full membership in their society. This new Jew first
made his appearance among the Sephardim of England, Holland,

2

and France and afterward among the Ashkenazim of all Western countries. After the 1780's he became a permanent feature of European social life [2] as becomes evident from the number of Jews who kept knocking at the doors of the Masonic lodges. From then onward, the stream of entry seekers flowed incessantly. All the efforts to block their admission failed to deter them. As a result, struggles and conflicts ensued between those clamoring for the lodge doors to be opened and those who strove to keep the doors closed.

As far as the history of the relations between Jews and the Freemasons is concerned, there can be no doubt where the topic belongs. Here we have an unobserved sideshow of the process of Jews becoming absorbed in European society. One aspect of this phenomenon is the desire of Jews to find a common social framework uniting them with non-Jews, usually referred to as assimilation. Nor was this in truth the unilateral aim of Jews. No assimilation can be effective unless the absorbing body is willing to assimilate the foreign body. Indeed, many segments of the surrounding society encouraged the assimilation of Jews, and exemplary instances of this attitude can be found among the Freemasons. Yet the readiness to accept Jews into European society was not universal, and even Freemasons imposed restrictions, often showing distinct reserve and even open hostility. This aspect of the phenomenon belongs in the category usually referred to as social anti-Semitism which, as is common knowledge, consists of many types and varying degrees of intensity. In our account of the relations between Jews and Freemasons, we shall encounter various forms of reservations against Jews, ranging from outright rejection, the utter refusal to establish any social contact with them, to avoidance of them on account of the religious attitudes separating Jews and Christians. Religious antagonism produced its effects, even though both groups had, at that time, abandoned the dogmatic and behavioral patterns of their churches and congregations.

The acceptance of Jews into European society was conditioned by the change in their civil status. Previously regarded as foreigners who were granted residence privileges by special decree, Jews had now, as a result of the emancipation, acquired civil rights. Yet such rights were not conferred upon them automatically. In most localities, Jews were forced to engage in a protracted struggle. They achieved full citizenship step by step, having to wrest each new posi-

3

tion in turn. Surprisingly, the Jewish effort to secure emancipation ran parallel with the history of their relations with the Freemasons. It could not by any means have been foreseen that methods suited to the state—an institution which coerces by the authority of law—should also make their appearance within the framework of a voluntary movement, where membership in the association of affiliated societies was a matter of free choice. Historical facts, however, defy reason, and our description will show that there was a close and far-reaching correspondence between the struggle of the Jewish community to acquire civil rights and Jews striving for equality among the Freemasons. We can discern the initial explanation for this phenomenon if we keep the nature of the Masonic order in mind. Although the association is basically voluntary, nevertheless its laws and regulations are absolutely binding upon all its members. Since the original constitution had laid down that in the lodges no man could be discriminated against on the grounds of his religion, the striving for the implementation of the rule, wherever it was assailed or violated, was fully justified. On the other hand, that this principle, permanently recorded in the written constitution, *could* be violated, shows what obstacles lay in the path of its practical implementation. In all these respects, there is a close resemblance between Masonic emancipation—a term coined and used by the Masons themselves, in their time—and the over-all civil emancipation. The history of Masonic emancipation is a mirror clearly reflecting the problems inherent in civil emancipation.

If we have spoken of assimilation, anti-Semitism, and emancipation in the general community and in the Masonic society as manifesting similarities, we can also speak of a fourth phenomenon in which a direct, reciprocal influence was exerted by both. We refer here to the Reform movement, which rose and developed at the same time as an ever-increasing number of Jews directed their steps toward the Masonic lodges. Are these two movements, then, connected by some common bond? Indeed, the Masonic lodges did not merely constitute some mere social framework; they represented a *weltanschauung* bordering on religion. The humanistic lodges, which had opened the doors to Jews, adopted a universalistic position, claiming that there was fundamentally only one religion common to all mankind. This view coincided to some extent with the tenets of the Reform movement. The question arises whether some of the adherents, in word and deed, of the movement were not also active in the Masonic lodges. To this question my book will give an unequivocal answer.

From what I have written so far, we find that the history of Jewish-Freemason relations will lead us into the thick of all the problems claiming the attention of the historians of Jewry's recent past: assimilation, the Reform movement, emancipation, anti-Semitism.[3] A complete literature dealing with these topics has been produced; yet, their connection with the Masonic movement has hardly been paid any notice. This curious fact may be accounted for by the peculiar circumstances affecting the bibliography of Masonic literature, a consequence of the nature of the movement itself. Since the lodges conducted their activities in complete, or semi-secrecy, their affairs did not attract the attention of research scholars. As for the existing histories of certain, specific lodges, as well as the accounts of the movement as a whole, these were compiled, for the most part, by lodge members who alone possessed free access to the relevant source material. Most of these writers were amateur historians. Only very few of the studies in the history of the movement were written by scholars of any competence and in accordance with the canons of scientific, historical criticism. Furthermore, like other works on Masonry, these history books have not been disclosed to the scrutiny of ordinary readers. Most Masonic works contain the note that they "have been published as manuscripts for breathren"—not for distribution in the book market, but for circulation among the members of the Masonic lodges only. From time to time Freemasons published works explaining the nature of the movement, designed for the general reading public. These writings, however, were apologetic in nature, aiming only to refute adverse criticism. Both the attacks and the rebuttals are available to anyone interested in tracing the history of the Freemasons. Yet both are rather dubious sources for the construction of an authentic historical account. No wonder that most, and especially Jewish, historians have overlooked the problems connected with the history of this movement. With the exception of a small book in Russian,[4] describing the first encounters between Jews and Freemasons at the end of the eighteenth and beginning of the nineteenth century, no book on modern Jewish history has ever grappled with this problem.

The same difficulties encountered in the past continue to impede research to this very day. True, the comprehensive bibliography prepared by August Wolfstieg in 1923,[5] which alone contains 23,000 entries, is at the disposal of the research scholar. It has been enlarged by several supplements since then. Yet, for the reasons mentioned above, the works listed in the bibliography have not been placed in public libraries. Even the largest collections, as, for instance, in the Berlin Staatsbibliothek (now housed in Marburg) or the Cornell University Library, are far from complete. The person desirous of studying any topic in Masonic affairs must of necessity have recourse to the Masonic libraries themselves and the archives of the lodges. These sources are usually totally barred to non-Masons. Furthermore, in the last generation the quantity of extant Masonic material has been greatly reduced, especially in Germany. The Nazis confiscated the libraries on the pretext that they were going to expose the historic truth hidden in these sources. They failed to accomplish very much, even in the carrying out of this design.[6] In the meantime, the materials were scattered far and wide; no one knows whether they were destroyed during the war or hidden away somewhere. A more favorable situation obtains in France. The Grand Orient archive has been entrusted to the Bibliothèque Nationale and is open to readers. A number of scholarly works on various aspects of the History of the Freemasons in France could therefore be written, although in that country, even now, the subject arouses strong feelings between the ardent adherents and the vehement opponents of Masonry. In England the archives of the Grand Lodge are still closed to outsiders.[7] Among the Freemasons of that country, however, there are a number of genuine historians, or at least individuals who have acquired some proficiency in historical research. These members have joined together in a single lodge and their publications approach proper professional standards.[8]

Holland, among all the countries, provides the outstanding exception. The lodge library located in The Hague, which comprises a large collection of books and manuscripts, is open to the inspection of scholars. This library was confiscated during the Nazi occupation, but by far the major portion of the material was subsequently recovered. Among these items is the "Kloss Collection," the legacy of George Kloss (1787–1854) of Frankfurt, one of the great Masonic historians of the nineteenth century. Kloss participated actively in the struggle between the humanistic and Christian currents in masonry and collected the documents pertaining to the controversy.[9] Complete chapters of this book are based on materials discovered in his collection; nor could it have been written altogether had not the rich resources of the library of the Grand Lodge of Holland been available.

The materials for this work have been culled from sources scattered abroad in several countries. For the most part, these materials touch upon the history of one particular country, Germany. Although the Jews constituted a problem in the lodges of all countries —and we shall investigate the underlying, compelling causes— nowhere did it reach such a pitch of intensity or create such disturbances as in Germany. In England and Holland the problem was solved in principle when the first candidates applied for admission. From then on the question, though not disappearing entirely, only arose at intervals. In France, the Revolution had inculcated the ideal of equality among the Masons as well, and the problem vanished almost entirely. On the other hand, the Jewish problem claimed the attention of the German lodges throughout their entire existence, created wide schisms among them, and at times erupted into fierce, disruptive controversy. The object of their concern was whether Jews were fit to be accepted as members, or else admitted as visitors once they had been accepted as Masons elsewhere. Generation after generation in Germany continued to debate the question and an entire literature, pro and con, accumulated. Now, just as the German attitude is the exception among the countries in Jewish-Masonic relations, so is it unique, too, in the second topic coming into the purview of this book, the spurious Jewish-Masonic plot. The allegation that such a plot existed gained wide credence in many countries. Yet in none was the belief so widespread or so decisively influential as in Germany. Only in that country did a movement arise and adopt the slogan "Jews and Freemasons" as the point of departure in a campaign to destroy both.

The historian is not justified in projecting from the present to the past. Hence he cannot regard the fate of the Freemasons and especially the Jews in the Third Reich as an indication of an inherent weakness in their position in earlier times. When the historian does seek to explain later events by their roots in the past, he must

7

first uncover the roots as they existed before, and then proceed to
show the causal connection between earlier and later events. The
questions of how such events could take place in Germany during
the thirties and forties of the twentieth century, and whether they
were conditioned by past German-Jewish relations will occupy the
attention of historians for many generations to come. No well-
grounded answer can be given without a prior, meticulous examination of the relations that arose when Jews were first becoming absorbed in German society. Apparently the history of these relations
in the Masonic movement could provide a not insignificant contribution to the understanding of the problem from two different
points of approach. On the one hand, the Jewish struggle to gain
entry to the Masonic lodges exemplifies the difficulties encountered
by Jews in becoming absorbed in Germany, as compared with the
rest of Western society. On the other hand, a similar, though not
identical, fate suffered by Freemasons in the Third Reich shows
that here a profound revolution transformed German society itself,
to the extent that wheels of fortune turned on a group like the
Freemasons which had been hostile to Jews, and now the Masons
were attacked and, in great measure, crushed along with the Jews.

8

The abundance of topics touched by the subject of this book requires a careful balancing of the material so as to avoid the omis-
sion, as far as possible, of relevant details, and yet permit the establishing of certain generalizations. My presentation is chronological.
In the end, however, we shall have to return, sum up our findings,
and place them in proper perspective, and at the same time analyze
their historical significance.

I shall first present the problem arising from the confrontation of
Jews and Freemasons. We have already established that the emergence of the Freemasons and the entry of Jews into European society took place almost simultaneously. The question is whether this
was a pure coincidence of discrete social events, or whether the two
processes were in some way connected. The two events—the founding of a new society, a community of lodges; and the acceptance of
a rejected group, namely Jews—are the symptoms of the growing
transformation of the old European society. The mind of eighteenth-century man could no longer acquiesce in the rigid division
of society into estates. Similarly, to evaluate man by reference to his

origin or religion seemed absurd. Eighteenth-century man, therefore, proceeded to found lodges open to members of all groups. The individual Jew—or the Jewish group—had now acquired a new defender, and was here and there even welcomed into the surrounding society.

These developments were not mere fortuitous events. They were logically justified by the principle which holds, as its main theme, that man is to be judged by his individual worth and not by the social collective to which he belongs. This appraisal of a person in accordance with his individual, human characteristics is the point of origin for the establishment of universal rules valid for every man as man. The principle of universality was the justification for most of the social transformations of the eighteenth century, among them the founding of the Masonic lodges and the opening to Jews of the doors of European society.

Had the principle of universality been applied with complete consistency, Jews would have been granted free access to all sectors of society and above all to the Masonic lodges. In reality, the doctrine only provided Jews with the opportunity to *demand* the practical implementation of a principal accepted by all in theory. The narrative of this book will show how formidable were the obstacles obstructing the attainment of this goal. The survival power of preconceived ideas and the burden of the religious heritage of the recent and distant past, and on the part of both Christian and Jew, combined to impede the fulfillment of the principle. The key to understanding the subsequent events lies in the fact that even in the age when the doctrine of universality received general assent it was not converted into a practical guideline for public conduct.

9

The characteristic feature of the latest period—the topic of my final chapter—is the retrogression occurring on the plane of social reality and, even more so, on the ideological plane. In Germany the direction was reversed and even such lodges as had previously admitted Jews now barred them. Jews who had considered themselves socially integrated were thrust back into their own confines. Conditions were different in France. There the Masonic movement maintained its allegiance to the ideal of universality. No barriers were erected in the way of Jews seeking to enter the lodges. Yet a directional change occurred in both countries. In the broad stretches of public life, a halt was called to the progress of the ideal of absolute universality. Here and there its validity, by virtue of which Jews were, at least formally, integrated into the community, was now challenged. In France, as in Germany, demands to abolish the emancipation of Jews and to abandon its underlying principle of universality made themselves heard. Within this context, however, Jewish-Freemason relations differed in both countries. The Freemasons in Germany were divided among themselves; there were the proponents and opponents of the principle of universality. In France, by contrast, Freemasons formed a united front in favor of absolute universality. There, clearly, the Masons stood together on the side of the Jews.

This is the background, then, for the cry, "Jews and Freemasons." In tracing its rise we will be concerned with the conscious exploitation of a political instrument. If, in the first part of the book, attention is concentrated on what transpired between Jews and Freemasons inside the lodges, our attention, in the last section, will be directed outward to the public, political arena where the subject of Jews and Freemasons had been dragged by the propagandist's brutal hand.

Early Encounters

Masonic literature devotes considerable attention to the history of the movement. Here legend, wild speculation, and serious historical studies are mixed indiscriminately.[1] The Masonic expositors were interested in tracing the movement back to some genealogical tree rooted in the human past. They attached their movement to similar groups, like the Templars, which had emerged in the Middle Ages, or even ascribed its beginnings to antiquity, to early Biblical times; King Solomon, the *builder* of the Temple and Hiram, King of Tyre, who assisted in its construction, became central figures in Masonic history. Yet factual historical considerations as well gave rise to numerous discussions and investigations. After all, the Freemasons did not constitute the first exclusive society ever to be formed; societies, more or less secret, beginning with the craft guilds and ending with the Alchemists, Theosophists, and Rosicrucians in the seventeenth century had preceded them. Whether the Freemasons were no more than a variation of these groups was a question that could quite seriously be asked. The answers, however, were not always based on serious research or factual studies, but stemmed instead from individual preferences for a particular point of view. Some attempted to blacken the movement by associating it with former groups like the Alchemists or Theosophists. The Freemasons themselves were interested at times in discovering or inventing some ties binding them to guilds previously existing in their own country, thereby demonstrating that the movement was a local outgrowth, French or German as the case might be, and not a transplant from a foreign country, namely England.

Historically, the truth is that the movement did originate in England, the year 1717, from which the annals of the Freemasons are normally counted, being particularly significant. Obviously certain noteworthy events had occurred prior to that date, events which were the precursors of what took place in that year.[2] Long before them, craftsmen in the building as in other trades had banded together to promote higher standards of workmanship and to protect their common interests. At the same time, these associations or lodges served as the framework for the cultivation of social relations, education, and discipline which were not without some spiritual significance.

These masons were divided into three classes or degrees: apprentices, fellow-crafts, and masters. Their respective rights and obligations were defined by the constitutions of their societies. Members of the same class would assist one another, and be recognized by one another through certain secret signs and passwords. Here and there, too, opportunities presented themselves for spiritual and religious edification by the transmission of specific traditions, legends, and concepts and by the observance of ceremonies on certain, appointed occasions.

In the seventeenth century events occurred which decisively influenced the history of these guilds. Attracted by the side benefits of the associations, individuals who were not craftsmen sought and gained admission to the guilds. These new members were accorded a special designation: speculative, as distinct from the regular or operative Masons. Apparently circumstances inherent in the technological or economic history of England, but which are not quite clear to us, influenced the guilds progressively to reduce their professional functions and benefits to the extent that the speculative Masons outnumbered and finally completely displaced the operative Masons.

Then, in 1717, the four lodges of London met together and elected an over-all executive, known as the Grand Lodge. All four had previously divested themselves of any professional character and had become Freemason lodges in the later denotation of the term. Dignitaries of the city of London, including clergy and noblemen, were among the members. The Master of the Grand Lodge was John, Duke of Montague, and he appointed, four years later, the Rev. James Anderson to frame a new, Masonic constitution which would become binding upon all the lodges. This work was completed in 1723 and the results were published in the same year. The existence of a printed constitution ratified by the Grand Lodge of London induced other lodges to accept its rules, and new lodges, conforming to these by-laws, were established first in England and, during the thirties and forties, in continental countries as well. The Grand Lodge of London was recognized as the body empowered to authorize new lodges. It was referred to as the Mother Lodge; those founded under its auspices, as daughter lodges. In the course of time, Grand Lodges were established in other countries as well. Occasionally several Grand Lodges existed side by side, each granting independent authorization to individual daughter lodges.

The constitution compiled by Anderson was not entirely invented by him and the colleagues collaborating with him. Much of what had been incorporated in it was part of the tradition preserved in the lodges, and this tradition, in turn, was permeated with Christian concepts and symbols. So, for instance, June 24, John the Baptist's day, was appointed a Masonic holiday on which the members were to assemble, perform certain rites, and partake of a common meal.[3] Nevertheless, the influence of ideas current in England at the time is perceptible, and this is clearly evident in the opening paragraph, "The First Charge," where the relation of the Freemason to God and religion is defined. Since the controversy on whether Jews were or were not fit to become Freemasons later hinged on this clause, its text should be examined.

> I. Concerning GOD and RELIGION. A Mason is obliged by his Tenure, to obey the moral Law: and if he rightly understands the Art, he will never be a stupid Atheist, nor an irreligious Libertine. But though in ancient Times Masons were charg'd in every Country to be of the Religion of that country or Nation, whatever it was, yet it's now thought more expedient only to oblige them to that religion in which all Men agree, leaving their particular opinions to themselves; That is, to be good Men and true, or Men of Honour and Honesty, by whatever Denominations or Persuasions they may be distinguished; whereby Masonry becomes the Center of Union, and the Means of conciliating true Friendship among Persons that must have remain'd at a perpetual Distance.[4]

13

At first sight, this paragraph appears to place Freemasonry beyond the confines of any particular, positive religion. The moral law based on the "religion in which all Men agree" was to be the sole condition determing the worthiness of any individual to become a Freemason. Such a formulation rests upon the premise that belief in God is the natural heritage of every man and is a sufficient guarantee of his obedience to the moral law. Here we find ourselves within the atmosphere of eighteenth-century deism which adopted an attitude of indifference to the particular, historical religion claiming the allegiance of any specific individual.[5] The author of the constitution assumed that Freemasons had belonged to various religions in the past, and so Freemasons could belong to any religion, including the Jewish, at present as well.

This last conclusion is a logical consequence of the wording of the paragraph. Yet there is no explicit proof, or even an allusion, in the words of the author that he had such an idea in mind at the time of writing. His purpose was to transcend the individual differences of the Anglo-Christian sects: Anglicans, Catholics, and Puritans, and their various denominations. He wanted them to join together in a single association which would overlook individual dogmas and rites. Hence his formulation was couched in the terminology current in deistic thinking which claimed that not only the Christian denominations, but all religions, possessed a common foundation. At that time Jews had been living in England for the past two generations. Their numbers were small and they lived as recently arrived immigrants on the fringe of British society. Yet, even if some of them did aspire to become integrated in English society, it must not be assumed that an exclusive group like the Freemasons regarded Jews as constituting a problem which required the wording of the constitution to be adjusted to accommodate them.

That certain doubts did arise concerning the deistic basis of the constitution is evident from the amended version of the second edition published in 1738. I shall quote the sentences in which the original formulation has been changed:

> A Mason is obliged by his Tenure to observe the Moral Law as a true *Noachide* . . . In ancient Times the *Christian Masons* were charged to comply with the Christian *Usages* of each Country where they travell'd or work'd: But *Masonry* being found in all Nations, even of diverse Religions, they are now only charged to adhere to that Religion in which all Men agree (leaving each Brother to his own particular Opinions) that is, to be Good Men and True Men of Honour and Honesty, by whatever Names, Religions or Persuasions they may be distinguished: For they all agree in the 3 great *Articles of Noah,* enough to preserve the Cement of the Lodge.[6]

The "Religion of that country" is now replaced by "the Christian Usages of each Country" with which Christian Masons had been obliged to comply in the past. Yet even this second formulation assumes the existence of non-Christian Masonic lodges. The author regards the adherents of all religions as being subject to the moral law but, in the later versions, these religions are held to subscribe to a common concept: the three "great Articles of Noah." The author responsible for the wording of the constitutions of 1738 wrote as if the concept, "Noachide" and the "great Articles of Noah," were universally known. As the learned opponents of the Masons in the nineteenth century pointed out, however, these terms were culled from John Selden's *De jure naturali et gentium juxta disciplinam Ebraeorum,*[7] which had described the seven Noachide laws as part of the ancient Jewish legal heritage. Christian tradition had never known of any such concept as Noachide commandments. It was, however, current in Talmudic and medieval Judaism as the grounds for tolerance toward such gentiles as Jews considered deserving of respect. If a prior revelation had occurred in the time of Noah and this revelation was vouchsafed to all mankind, then all who acknowledged and obeyed the commandments given at the time would attain salvation.[8] Christianity lacked a principle of this nature and so found difficulty in according any positive religious status to those beyond its pale. The introduction of this concept, culled from ancient Jewish jurisprudence, into European thought by identifying it with the law of nature provided non-Jewish thinkers with an intellectual instrument which allowed them to justify toleration without abandoning their belief in divine revelation. Here is the train of thought behind the amended text of the Masonic constitutions.

Far removed as these constitutions were from any intention of making provision for Jews, they nevertheless, consciously or unconsciously, absorbed some traces of Jewish teaching. The amended formulation provided the basis for the German version prepared in 1741. On the other hand, the later English editions of the constitutions restored the original text, which was based on pure, formal, deistic foundations and was no longer tied to any particular, theological concepts.

As has been stated, there is no reason to assume that the authors of the English constitutions intended, in their universal tolerance, to provide for Jewish candidates in the flesh. Yet, when such candidates did apply for admission, the principle was followed in prac-

15

tice. The first instance of a Jew's being admitted to a Masonic lodge took place, as far as we know, in 1732. One, Edward Rose, was initiated into the London lodge in the presence of Jews and non-Jews. This event was a novelty and excited attention. Soon afterward the lodges began debating the propriety or otherwise of admitting this Jew.[9] That the final decision was not unfavorable is conclusively proved by the fact that Jews in significant numbers were admitted to membership in the ensuing years. Obviously Jewish names are found among the participants in the affairs of the Grand Lodge of London even before 1740, and several of these individuals rose to high office.[10] One, Allegri by name, declared before a lodge in Frankfurt that he had been initiated in London as early as in 1735.[11] In 1759 a petition was presented to the same Grand Lodge asking that authorization be granted to a new lodge; about half of the twenty-three signatures on the petition seem to have been Jewish names.[12]

It is evident that at least some of these Jews sought to retain their own religious principles within the framework of the lodges. In 1756 an anthology of Masonic prayers appeared in print, among them one to be recited "at the opening of the lodge meeting and the like for the use of Jewish Freemasons." [13] While the other prayers were addressed to the Father, the Son, and the Holy Ghost, the Jewish prayers contained nothing at variance with the Jewish tradition. Moses is referred to here as the Master of a Lodge in his time, teaching the Torah to Aaron, his sons, and the elders—an allusion to a Talmudic passage.[14] Clearly the prayer was composed by a Jew. The title page of the book containing the prayer offers the information that this prayer was intended for the use of "Jewish lodges." This would indicate that the number of Jewish Masons had increased so greatly that they had already formed a lodge of their own by that date. Another source reveals the existence of a Jewish lodge some ten years later.[15]

One of the first countries where the Masonic movement gained a foothold and then spread was Holland. There the local lodges followed British leadership and adopted the same attitude toward Jews as had prevailed in England. In principle, the lodges were open to Jews, and Jewish members were accepted in practice.[16] Some evidence, by no means sufficiently clear and belonging to a later date, seems to indicate that a Jewish lodge did exist in Holland.[17]

The earliest Jewish Freemasons in both Holland and England were Sephardim. The participants in the Grand Lodge of London, mentioned above, included the Mendez, De Medina, De Costa, Alvares, and Baruch (the last named may possibly have been an Ashkenazi) families. Among the petitioners of 1759, such names appear as Jacub Moses, Lazars Levy, and Jacub Arons,[18] all of whom may have been Ashkenazim. We know the exact text of a membership certificate, dated 1756, of a Jew, Emanuel Harris, a native of Halle, Germany, who had changed his name from Menachem Mendel Herz Wolff. The text of this certificate was published in 1769 by the research scholar Olof Gerhard Tychsen, who mentioned as a commonly known fact that in England, as contrasted with Germany, Jews were admitted to the Masonic lodges as a matter of course. Tychsen was even able to relate that one of the affiliates of the Grand Lodge of London was referred to as "The Jewish Lodge" on account of the composition of its membership.[19]

The admission of Jews into the lodges of England and Holland is a sign that tensions between Jews and their surrounding environment, at least for some segments of both populations, were abating. Rational principles had not entirely eliminated the Christian elements in Masonry, but had so tempered extremism that the brethren were now ready and accustomed to allowing Jews to mix in their company. Naturally, Jews also were affected by similar processes.[20] Participants in the predominantly Christian lodges and especially those who shared in the common meals were forced to make compromises at the expense of their Jewish traditions. They were able to justify their behavior as conforming to the mood prevailing among the Christians—and this was one of the main forces impelling the spread of Masonry—the feeling that the specific precepts of a particular religion did not constitute its significant feature, nor its ideological content its exclusive possession. Membership in a Masonic lodge, on the other hand, offered great advantages. It was surely worthwhile to belong to an association composed of prominent members of society. Belonging in their company would enhance one's prestige, and sometimes even confer tangible benefits. It afforded opportunities to be introduced to, and establish contact with, circles which Jews could never otherwise have reached. Membership was especially desirable for those whose business affairs took them to other cities and even abroad. Wherever the Mason might happen to be, his membership in one lodge opened

17

the doors of all the others to him. These social considerations must certainly have contributed to the spread of Freemasonry throughout Europe.[21] And all these incentives were especially attractive to Jews.

Nevertheless, the existence of separate Jewish lodges indicates some hesitancy which presumably was felt on both sides. The existence of a principle as such that admission should not be denied to Jews did not guarantee that no restraints would be imposed in practice. The application of any candidate for admission had to be voted on by the members of the particular lodge, and they enjoyed the right to reject his application without stating any reason for their action. An individual's Jewishness could conceivably have provided the pretext for his rejection without any objection being raised in principle against Jews as such. It is difficult to believe that French and Dutch Masons always stood above the prevailing anti-Jewish prejudices, and not in respect of religion alone. We do find that a lodge in London decided in 1793 not to allow the recommendation of any Jew for membership since there was no possibility of his being accepted.[22] We also learn of an explicit complaint emanating from Holland at the beginning of the nineteenth century against anti-Jewish discrimination in the admission practices of certain lodges.[23]

Alleged or real discrimination, however, did not imply that complete rejection or discrimination was enforced. In principle, the British and Dutch lodges still remained open to Jews as the occasion required.

A sudden change turned the development of the Masonic movement in France in a new direction. There, too, the first lodges founded in the 1730's [24] followed the English example, and as long as they adhered to original Masonic conceptions they could not cast any doubt upon the acceptability of Jews as members. Within the first generation of the penetration of Freemasonry into that country, however, a new attitude became evident in France, one which sought to find the basis of Masonic ideology in Christian foundations. The upholders of this view tried to trace the genealogical roots of Freemasonry back to the medieval Christian orders, and argued that the lodges were only a reincarnation of the Knights of Saint John of crusader times. A new, Christian element was introduced into Masonry, and a new rule stated that only Christians

were worthy of being brethren in the lodges. In 1742, a book entitled *Apologie pour l'ordre des Franc-Maçons* [25] appeared. One of its
paragraphs asserts: "The order is open to Christians only. It is neither possible nor permissible to accept any person outside the Christian church as a Freemason. Hence Jews, Moslems and pagans are
excluded as nonbelievers." [26] The constitution of the Grand Lodge
of France, which was ratified in 1755, contained an explicit passage
which made baptism a prerequisite for membership.[27]

This identification of Freemasonry with the Christian faith
emerged from a group which owed allegiance both to Freemasonry
and the Church, and sought to effect some compromise between
them. The very title, *Apologie,* indicates the point of departure of
the book; its underlying motive was the need of Freemasons to defend themselves against the charges leveled at them by churchmen.
In fact, from the very inception of the movement, Freemasons had
been subjected to severe attacks. They were suspected of harboring
intentions to subvert the foundations of the Church. The neutrality
of their first constitution to the patterns of positive religion, even if
this was interpreted as indifference to the variations of dogma and
modes of worship, was sufficient of itself to provoke antagonism, especially by the Catholic church. Nor was the reaction slow in coming: on April 28, 1738, Pope Clemens XII issued his bull against
the Freemasons. Their principal transgression was their willingness
to accept members of all religions and sects, and their adoption of
"natural righteousness" as a substitute for the true faith.[28] The
Church regarded the banding together of a group in membership
based on pure humanistic principles as threatening to remove the
individual Catholic from the sphere of influence of his Church.
Hence it forbade its adherents to join the association under pain of
excommunication.

If the above-mentioned *Apologie,* which appeared four years
later, was not actually a direct reply to the Papal bull, it did at least
answer the arguments presented in that document. The book's emphasis on the Christian character of Freemasonry was intended to
dull the edge of the contention that the Masons were drawn from
diverse religions. On the contrary, the movement was declared to be
exclusively Christian. Jews being non-Christians, it was possibly on
these, not on personal, grounds that they were denied admission. It
is difficult to conceive that Jews should have constituted any real

19

problem in France at the time with regard to Freemasonry—any more than could Moslems or pagans. It may be assumed that the three religions were declared unacceptable only to emphasize the Christian character of the brotherhood. Even during the succeeding decades we hear nothing about Jews struggling to enter, or of efforts to bar them from entering, Masonic lodges. Instead we find one source upholding the Christian character of the movement and at the same time declaring Jews acceptable in exceptional cases. Masons were obliged, at least, to be "familiar with the sacred mysteries of the Christian faith." "Only as an exception, as an expression of deference to the Old Testament, is a Jew able, on rare occasions, to take part in it." These observations appeared in the first Masonic encyclopedia to be published in France in 1766 [29] and convey the impression of being an attempt to justify the fact—infrequently as the phenomenon may have occurred—of Jewish membership in the lodges, a fact which was in conflict with the basic principles of Freemasonry, as it was now interpreted in France.

The question of Jewish acceptability assumed much more serious proportions in Germany. Its cities, at least some of the larger centers, had larger Jewish populations than the English or French (though not as large as the Dutch). Had many Jews begun all at once to knock on the gates of the lodges, then granting them membership would have constituted a grave problem for the Masons. This did happen at a later date, as we shall see in due course, when the process of social change had mass-produced a type of Jew who sought to enter Christian or Judeo-Christian society. Yet during the first decades of the widespread emergence of Masonic lodges in Germany (that is, until the 1770's), German Jews were, with few exceptions,[30] too securely tied to and concentrated within their own society and culture. We hear of three Jews visiting one of the Hamburg lodges in 1749,[31] that is to say, they came armed with membership certificates acquired elsewhere and were permitted to take part in the proceedings of the lodge. They were "Portuguese Jews," presumably belonging to lodges in England or Holland, like those cases referred to earlier.[32]

We must, however, revert to those instances since they afford an indication of the infrequency of such occurrences. That same Allegri, who claimed to have been admitted to membership in London in 1735, spent some time in Germany in the sixties. He recounted that he had visited lodges in Mannheim and other German cities, but had refrained from doing so in Frankfurt because of the "prejudices of the German Jews."[33] Similarly, O. G. Tychsen noted in 1769 that the few Jews who had become Freemasons were constrained to hide the fact from their coreligionists for fear of being branded as "heretics."[34] He likewise remarked that, when the Jewish Freemason who had printed his certificate passed through his city of Bützow, his religiosity was questioned by local Jews.[35] His Masonic affiliation had rendered him suspect in their eyes. Apparently, in the sixties, membership in the movement was still regarded as a breach of the Jewish faith, and this fact is both the reason for, as well as an indication of, the rarity of the phenomenon.

It may reasonably be assumed that Jewish candidates for admission to the movement appeared more frequently in Germany than in France. Yet no need had arisen as yet to treat them differently there than in France. The German movement had also stemmed from English roots; Anderson's constitutions had been translated into German in 1743 and this version was reprinted several times thereafter. An appendix had been added to the by-laws, but this was nothing more than a German translation of the French *Apologie*. The two documents, as we have seen, diverged from one another in their aims, and were in direct contradiction in their respective attitudes to the candidate's loyalty to a particular religion. In its original, English version the constitutions had laid down that adherence to any particular positive religion was a matter of no consequence. Yet the supplement asserted that adherence to the Christian religion was an essential precondition for membership. The incompatibility of the two statements now brought together in the same volume did not escape the notice of some of the members.[36] Nevertheless, in those times the problem did not loom so large as to require an authoritative and decisive solution, as Jews were only admitted here and there into Masonic membership. With the passage of time, however, the tendency grew increasingly stronger to regard Freemasonry as a Christian institution where a Jew had no business to be found.

The oldest and the pre-eminent Berlin lodge was the Grosse National-Mutterloge zu den drei Weltkugeln. Together with the Grosse Landesloge von Deutschland, it later waged a bitter and unre-

21

lenting struggle to bar the entry of Jews. At first, however, no definite policy was adopted. On February 7, 1763, the application of a Jew, Bruck by name, was considered and rejected. In spite of—or perhaps on account of—his offer to pay 100 guilders to the lodge treasury, some blemish in his character or conduct was discovered. His Jewishness was not held to disqualify him. The by-laws which were adopted three years later set down the same qualifications for membership stipulated in the French *Apologie:* "Only a Christian is eligible for membership in our respectable [*ehrwürdigen*] order, but on no account Jews, Moslems, or pagans. Lodges which have admitted any of these to their community have thereby clearly proved that they have no knowledge of the nature of the Freemasons." [37] The last sentence is polemical in tone and is directed against those lodges who had shown leniency in practice and had admitted Jews. Actually I have evidence that the Royal York, the lodge competing in Berlin with the Mutterloge, accepted a Jew a year later. His name was Moses Tobias, and the minutes we have report his initiation, noting that the candidate swore his Masonic oath on the Pentateuch. This precise designation was obviously meant to exclude the New Testament, the book used for this purpose at the initiation of gentile candidates. Tobias, who subsequently left Berlin, was presented with his membership certificate by the Royal York as late as in June 1774 with the express approval of the other Mother Lodge, the Landesloge, with which it had been connected for some time. In the course of time, the Royal York too succumbed to the prevailing anti-Jewish pressure, even though in theory it still maintained the principle of Jewish acceptability. In 1784 its Essingen affiliate inquired of the leaders of the Berlin lodge whether it was permissible to grant entry to wealthy Jews as members, in the same way as they were being admitted in England. The Berlin lodge replied that it was true that Jews from England bearing membership cards had made their appearance at intervals, for indeed there were Jews worthy to be admitted to all lodges, were it not for the prejudice against Jews in general which was not entirely baseless. The advice offered to the inquirers was that the Jewish applicants should be most carefully scrutinized and that, in any event, appropriate initiation fees should be levied on them. Another precondition for the admission of Jews was that they be clean-shaven.[38]

There were similar divisions of opinion in Frankfurt and vicinity at that very time. A lodge founded in Kassel applied for authorization to the Zur Einigkeit lodge in Frankfurt, which, in turn, acted on behalf of the Grand Lodge of London. One of the signatories to the application was a Jew—a clear indication that his townsmen found him worthy to mix in their company. His name, however, provided the Frankfurt lodge with the pretext to deny the lodge the authorization it sought.[39] Two Jews, Baruch and Tonsica, were admitted to membership in a *Winkelloge* (one not officially recognized by the Mother Lodge) in 1758. When this lodge finally received its authorization, the Jews were forced to resign.[40]

These examples reflect the state of affairs that came into being and continued until the 1780's. A description written by one of the leading German Masons sums up the events of those years. The author, Johann August Strack, compiled this apologetic work in 1770 and republished it in an enlarged edition in 1778. Replying to the accusation of indifference on the part of the Masons to the Christian faith, Strack repeated the answer already advanced in the French *Apologie:* that Masons adhere to the Christian religion is attested to by the fact that no member of any other faith, be he Jew, Moslem, or pagan, is accepted by them. "And even if examples are cited of Jews who were Freemasons, no responsibility devolves on us. It should fall instead upon those spurious [*unächte*] lodges which have, at times, formed such unnatural connections. It is essentially impossible for any persons other than Christians to be Freemasons."[41] Those lodges, then, which sought to represent the main or official outlook of Freemasonry expressed their uniqueness by emphasising their Christian exclusiveness. Evidence to this effect is found in the contemporaneous Masonic classic, Lessing's *Ernst und Falk* (1778–1780), whose contents will be examined in some detail further on. "Allow enlightened Jews to come and seek admission?" The author aims this challenge at the Freemasons. He himself formulates the answer: "A Jew? The Freemason is at least obliged to be a Christian."[42] Jews striving for admission were forced to content themselves with membership in one of the nonauthorized lodges, which by their very nature never acquired more than a marginal and doubtful status by the side of the central and Grand Lodges.

In the same period Jews aspiring to Masonic membership occu-

23

pied a marginal status in their own community. The Jewish names listed in the Masonic rosters of those days are not known to us from any other source. We must assume that, if they were not doubtful and unprincipled characters, like some mentioned before, they were at least unconventional persons who were anxious to find their way individually into the non-Jewish world. Socially, the vast majority of Jews were at this stage certainly confined within their own community. Yet, by the seventies at the latest, a circle of enlightened Jews becomes discernible, concentrated especially round Moses Mendelssohn, a group of people who looked longingly for some social and intellectual contact with the surrounding society. The Masonic lodges, however, hardly seemed to suggest themselves as the suitable and effective instrument for social integration. Mendelssohn was somewhat critical of his friend Lessing's membership in the Masonic movement. It is related that Mendelssohn taunted his friend, whether seriously or in jest, about the secrets he had unlocked as a result of the revelations vouchsafed to him as a Mason. "From our earliest youth, we have been seeking for the truth. From the beginning of our acquaintance, we have searched together with all the effort and earnestness such a search fittingly requires. Yet, is it now possible that truths exist which Lessing has solemnly sworn not to divulge to the person who has been his faithful friend for these twenty-five years?" [43] Apparently Mendelssohn resented his friend's presuming, as a Freemason, to possess certain knowledge which he was not permitted to share with one who had been his faithful ally in the very search for truth.

In his written remarks on Lessing's *Ernst und Falk,* Mendelssohn dealt with the more serious issue of principle. The book itself is apologetic and consists of the conversations of the two friends whose names form its title. Here Freemasonry is presented, at times, as the area where universal brotherhood in all its purity is aspired to in theory; and at others, as it exists in reality, as an association of persons belonging to a specific class and religion, as a society protected against intrusion from without and embroiled within, and as a group the members of which are more interested in satisfying their mystic curiosity and craving for alchemistic adventure rather than in cultivating human perfection. Yet, despite Lessing's inclusion of such criticisms in his work, his intention was, understandably, to judge Freemasonry by its lofty ideals and not as it existed in prac-

24

tice. Mendelssohn accordingly pointed out that here Lessing resembled the modern Berlin theologians, and all the criticism leveled at them applied to him as well.[44] The implication of the analogy was apparently that Freemasonry was similar to rational theology, in proclaiming universal principles without following them in practice.

Whether Mendelssohn's critique was expressing the resentment of the Jew at having been excluded from the Masonic association is not clear. His philosophical detachment kept him from aspiring to goals beyond his reach. In any event, he remained outside, while all his friends belonged—as did anyone who had made a name for himself in the intellectual world—to some Masonic lodge or other. Whatever motives may have inspired Mendelssohn were unique to him and could not furnish any example for the many in the succeeding generations.

25

III   The Order of the Asiatic Brethren

The generation growing up in the shadow of Mendelssohn accepted his ideal of the removal of all barriers separating Jews from Christians, but did not inherit his virtues of patience and moderation. His disciples and followers desired to attain in practice what they had been taught to believe in, and sought to hasten the process of absorption into the cells of their social environment—and here the Masonic cells were held to be of basic importance. Although these individuals were unable to crush the opposition, they would support every effort on the part of the Freemasons to create new frameworks where the principle of equality of Jews and non-Jews would be upheld. Three or four such attempts took place around the end of Mendelssohn's lifetime (1786), the period of the enactment of the first laws aimed at the removal of civil disabilities from Jews and of the first agitation for the integration of Jews into the general society. The initial attempt led to the flaring up of the first controversy over the acceptance of Jews in Masonic lodges.

The earliest attempt to found a Masonic order with the avowed purpose of accepting both Jews and Christians in its ranks was the formation of the Order of the Asiatic Brethren or, to give it its full name, Die Brüder St. Johannes des Evangelisten aus Asien in Europa. We are fully familiar with the history of this society [1] which was more important than all the others because of the scope of its activities and its influence. Founded in Vienna in 1780–81,[2] its central figure and promoter was Hans Heinrich von Ecker und Eckhoffen, of Bavarian extraction. He and his younger brother Hans Carl (whom we shall meet again) had behind them a rich past in the history of the Masonic societies in Germany. The Eckers were of the type of aristocrats who had lost their property and forefeited the economic support of their class. Yet, because of their illustrious name, their family connections, and their confident bearing they had succeeded, at least outwardly, in preserving their associations with the ruling classes. They were not at all discriminating in their choice of occupation—so long as it allowed them to maintain their standard of living. This could best be achieved through association with those who wielded the real power in the states: the absolute princes, and the rising capitalists who enjoyed their patronage. Members of Masonic societies were at times drawn from the upper and propertied classes, but because these organizations often had need of individuals ready to perform remunerative functions, they also served as a refuge for those searching an easy, but not always honest, livelihood. Heinrich was a man of this type. He had been active among the Rosicrucians in Bavaria and Austria, whose dabbling in alchemy served as confidence schemes to swindle money out of the naive and reckless. As a result of some quarrel, he severed his connections with them and, in 1781, published a book denouncing them.[3] At that very time he was busy forming a new order, later to become renowned as the Order of the Asiatic Brethren but known in its first manifestation as Die Ritter vom wahren Licht.

I have no firsthand evidence on the immediate causes for the emergence of this order. Information has been culled from statements of members who became active later. According to them, an erstwhile Franciscan monk, Justus, whose civil name had been Bischoff, had taken a prominent part in its founding. Justus had spent years in the Orient, especially in Jerusalem, where he had struck up an acquaintance with Jewish Cabalists. He studied their disciplines and even obtained from them manuscripts which constituted the source for the Order's theosophic doctrines and ceremonial regulations. Although these details have not been corroborated, the traces of such a personality are very real, so that little if any doubt can be cast on his existence.[4] On another figure, Azariah by name, who is reputed to have given Justus the manuscripts, the evidence is rather doubtful. According to the testimony (which we shall examine presently) of Ephraim Joseph Hirschfeld, Azariah belonged to a cabalistic sect identified, according to another version, as a vestige of the Sabbatai Zevi movement. He entrusted all his affairs to his sons, while he himself traveled from place to place as an emissary of the sect. Nevertheless, even though the connection of the Asiatic brethren with the Sabbatian movement is conclusively proved by another source, as we shall soon see, the personality of Azariah lacks substance; information about him is too meager and full of contradictions.[5] It seems that his existence was invented by members of the Order to lend credence to the assertion that their tradition had

27

come from the Orient. The participation of a third person is beyond all doubt. He was Baron Thomas von Schoenfeld, an apostate Jew, who had made a name for himself as a prolific writer.[6] His participation is prominently featured in the historical description of the Order, and his share in its founding is known from another source.[7] Schoenfeld had much of the character of an adventurer, in both the intellectual and common connotations of the term. He turned up in Paris during the French Revolution and was executed during the Reign of Terror.[8] For the Order of the Asiatic Brethren, Schoenfeld fulfilled the function of copyist and translator of Jewish Cabalistic works. The Order's historian, Franz Josef Molitor, had it by tradition that Schoenfeld was a grandson of R. Jonathan Eybeschütz, whose collection of Sabbatian cabalistic works he had inherited.[9] We, however, are better acquainted with Schoenfeld's pedigree. He was a member of the Dobruschka family of Brünn and was in no way related, either by blood or marriage, to Eybeschütz.[10] Nevertheless, the assertion was not altogether fortuitous for Mosheh Dobruschka, alias Thomas von Schoenfeld, actually had been an active adherent of the Sabbatian movement.[11] As we shall see later, he incorporated liberal portions of Sabbatian doctrines in the teachings of the Order. It is doubtful whether Ecker und Eckhoffen was capable of distinguishing between the various Cabalistic systems of thought, and it is improbable that he was especially interested in the Order's possessing a specific Sabbatian character. Yet it is equally obvious that he wanted to tie the Order to a tradition derived, in some manner, from the Orient, as the name, "The Asiatic Brethren in Europe," clearly shows. The Order had to possess some novel trait to set it off from the other lodges and orders, and its novelty was the tracing of its descent to some Oriental source. Justus' connections with the East and Schoenfeld's provision of Cabalistic source material gave this contention some semblance of authenticity.

On the other hand, it is also doubtful whether Ecker had ever intended to make his order the catch-all for a mixed society of Jews and gentiles. In his above-mentioned book he had taken issue with the Rosicrucians for sinning against Jews by not accepting them as members unless they were extremely affluent.[12] His present, knightly order was presumably prepared to accept Jews—yet took no steps to pave the road for them to enter. True, the doctrines of the Ritter vom wahren Licht contained elements derived from Cabalistic sources. At this stage, however, the ideas were still clearly subject to Christian interpretation, and no syncretistic tendencies are discernible for merging the two religions.[13] Ecker had intended to present his program for the new order to an assembly of all the Freemasons which was to have gathered in Wilhelmsbad near Hanau in 1782. The assembly had been convened by the head of all the German Masons, Duke Frederick of Brunswick, for the purpose of reviving the movement by introducing improvements in the conduct of its business. In this endeavor, he received the cooperation of the Landgrave Carl von Hessen, who administered the province of Schleswig on behalf of the Danish monarchy.[14] Through Landgrave Carl, Ecker hoped to exert some influence in the forthcoming conference. He traveled to Schleswig at the beginning of 1782 and tried to gain an audience with the Landgrave.[15] What occurred between them is not known. Ecker did not, however, succeed in his quest, since a protest was filed against his appearance in Wilhelmsbad from a prominent quarter in the Berlin lodge. Had Ecker, even then, included in the opening of his constitution any paragraph providing Jews with the prospect of being accepted on an equal level with Christians, he could never have hoped to have his constitution ratified by the conference at large. The tenor of the Berlin protest, too, proves that the Jewish question had nowhere been placed on the agenda. Here the purity of Christianity, which the Masons were obliged strictly to uphold, was at issue. Ecker had been held to have contaminated Christian purity, not by attempting to open the gates of his proposed order to Jews, but by his Rosicrucian activities which were still held against him, and because he had been denounced as a magician consorting with occult powers.[16]

Possibly Ecker's failure to impose his patterns upon the existing lodges impelled him to build new organizational units of his own and, in so doing, he encountered Jewish candidates seeking to join his group. These were, after all, the years when the Edict of Toleration had been promulgated (in Bohemia, in October 1781, and in Austria, in January 1782). In the other German principalities as well, the eighties constituted the period when hopes ran high for a change in the political status of the Jewish community, as an ever greater number of Jews withdrew from the social and religious framework of their own people. The time seemed opportune for the removal of the barriers keeping Jews from joining gentile company and for the founding of a society composed of members of both faiths. The first paragraph of the general constitution of the Asiatic Brethren, which was completed in November 1784, announced the removal of these barriers:

> Any brother, irrespective of his religion, class, or system, may join the Order, provided he is an upright person in thought and deed. Since the good and welfare of mankind are the sole purpose of our approach, these cannot be dependent on any other circumstance, be it a man's religion, his birth, or the class into which he has been bred.[17]

The permission to enter presumably was intended for the rich Jews of Vienna and the enlightened Jewries of other cities who were attracted to Ecker's company for social reasons. It is even more astonishing that Ecker should also have found a Jewish associate who assisted him in promoting the spiritual activities which were to justify the existence of the group.

Having failed in Schleswig, Ecker returned to Austria and took up residence in Innsbruck, in the Tyrol. There he worked to spread the Order until his return to Vienna in 1784,[18] and there he became acquainted with Ephraim Josef Hirschel (later Hirschfeld) who was introduced to him as a rather unusual young Jew, well-educated but persecuted by his coreligionists on account of his ideas.[19] Hirschfeld had been living in Innsbruck since 1782. He was employed as a bookkeeper by the wealthy Jew, Gabriel Uffenheimer,[20] to whom the Tyrolian salt mines had been farmed out. Later, employee and employer quarreled, litigation ensued, and Hirschfeld was awarded a considerable sum of money by the court. While the proceedings were still in progress, he entered the local institution of higher learning and also accepted occasional, part-time employment as teacher and bookkeeper with the local aristocratic families. Through his work, he was brought into contact with the Baron who had him copy the writings of the Order, only to discover that the copyist himself had, in the meantime, become interested in their contents.

We are now familiar with Hirschfeld's origin and early life.[21] He had been born in Karlsruhe. His father was a cantor and Talmudic scholar, author of a work on rabbinic law (novellae on treatises of the *Babylonian Talmud*), learned in Cabalistic literature, and had produced a Yiddish translation of Rabbi Mosheh Alshekh's commentary on Genesis. The elder Hirschfeld was highly ambitious. He did not live at peace with the local rabbi, Nathaniel Weill, whose commentary he set out to attack in his own work. However, he received the written approbation of prominent rabbinic authorities in other cities, among them the renowned Rabbi Ezekiel Landau of Prague. Most extraordinary of all was the fact that he had prefaced his work with a dedication in German, addressed to the Margrave, Karl Friedrich of Baden—indicating that the father sought to attract the attention of people of high station. His son, Ephraim, reaped the benefit of the father's endeavors. Johann Georg Schlosser, Goethe's brother-in-law and a leading official in the Margrave's service, provided for the son's education, perhaps after the elder Hirschfeld had died. He enrolled him in the local gymnasium and later sent him to the University of Strasbourg to study medicine. Hirschfeld did not complete this course of studies; instead he acquired a grounding in languages, philosophy, and literature and became accomplished in the social graces, a rather unusual feat among his Jewish contemporaries. In addition to the habits acquired through education and training, Hirschfeld possessed unusual innate traits: on the one hand he tended to isolation and solitude, while on the other he excelled in the art of conversation, exuded charm and confidence, and stoutly defended his considered opinions. This combination of features drew attention to him as an original, though somewhat odd, person. After his sojourn in Strasbourg, Hirschfeld moved to Berlin, taking with him the recommendation of his benefactor, Schlosser, to Moses Mendelssohn. There he obtained employment as tutor and bookkeeper in the household of David Friedländer. According to the testimonial given to him by Mendelssohn when he left Berlin two years later, Hirschfeld had been a frequent visitor in the Mendelssohn home as well as in the homes of the city dignitaries.[22] According to Friedländer's brother-in-law, Isaac Daniel Itzig, Mendelssohn took an interest in Hirschfeld and tried to find an explanation for his strange conduct. (At times he would sit speechless, even in company, behavior which Mendelssohn ascribed to extreme hypochondria.) Mendelssohn befriended Hirschfeld just as he had befriended others who had entered his house and had subsequently developed into admirers and disciples. Hirschfeld, however, was an exception. Apparently he never had subscribed to Mendelssohn's rationalistic doctrines, even when he was closely associated with his mentor, and he later openly turned against them. At all events, he refused to throw in his lot with this circle of intellectuals, which apparently is the reason there is no record of his stay either in Berlin or Vienna among the written remains of that group. From Berlin, Hirschfeld went to Innsbruck where, as we have seen, he struck up an acquaintance with Ecker. There too he was admitted to the Order of the Asiatics[23] and its spiritual world. Hirschfeld frequently accompanied Ecker on his travels, and so made the acquaintance of other leaders of the Order.[24] In the spring of 1785, he joined Ecker in Vienna[25] and became attached to his home. They became firm friends and constituted, as one of the Vienna circle dubbed them, "a pair of originals."[26]

By the time Hirschfeld joined it, the Order already possessed a written, ratified constitution, and the Vienna group at least was governed by these laws. It is worthwhile to cast a glance over this group and see who (in addition to the founders we have met before) participated in its activities. There were outstanding dignitaries among the non-Jewish members. Molitor mentions the Duke of Lichtenstein, Count Westenburg, Count Thun, and, anonymously, the Austrian Minister of Justice (N.N.).[27]

Another source, relying on hearsay, lists the following: Max Joseph Freiherr von Linden, Otto Freiherr von Gemmingen, Freiherr von Stubitza, and others.[28] The documents in my possession mention several other members by name: J. B. P. Hartenfels, Franz Meltzer, Joseph von Juhász, Johann Gottlieb Walstein, Franz de Névoy, Fr. von Ost, Jacob Jg. Zuz. Three of these were army officers; two, court officials; one, a doctor of medicine; neither the status nor occupation of the one remaining is known.[29] As for these Christian members of the Order, Jews would have been only too proud to associate with their class on intimate social terms. Three wealthy Viennese Jews did belong to the Order: Arnstein, Eskeles, and Hönig,[30] and there is no reason for presuming that there were no others. The information concerning this Order comes to us purely incidentally. We have no roster of its members, nor do we know when each individual was initiated into membership and whether it was before or after the arrival of Hirschfeld. Nevertheless, the evidence is clear that Hirschfeld actively endeavored to attract Jews to the Order, and that the three honorable gentlemen were accepted through his intercession.[31] He maintained connections with wealthy bankers and engaged in financial transactions through the agency of Itzig in Berlin, Arnstein's brother-in-law, to the extent that his operations not only benefitted the coffers of the Order but filled his own pockets as well. He became financially independent as a result.[32] In spite of his continuing to live in Ecker's home, credence should be accorded his statement—made after the dissolution of their association—that he gave his hosts more than he took from them.

As time progressed Hirschfeld's functions in the Order of the Asiatics increased. True, the constitution had been completed before he arrived in Vienna and, according to Molitor, who derived his information directly from Hirschfeld, the other, basic writings of the Order were not compiled by him but by Baron Schoenfeld.[33] There were current needs, however, to attend to. Instructions had to be written down which would guide the members in their "work"; these consisted of reflective interpretations of the symbols, word and letter combinations, and so on. Consistent with the origin of the doctrine of the Asiatics as a whole, the material for this spiritual activity, too, had been culled from Cabalistic literature.[34] Very few members were at all familiar with these writings,[35] and the group had been forced to rely on Justus and Baron Schoenfeld. Hirschfeld claimed to have received his instruction in gaining understanding of this literature from the former, but it is possible that he had acquired the rudiments from his own father. Some time later, he wrote a book incorporating Cabalistic concepts.[36] It should not be assumed however that he really understood Cabalistic systems with any profundity. Yet he was a "discovery" as far as Ecker was concerned. Until then, Ecker had been utterly dependent on Schoenfeld, who had exploited his advantage by exacting whatever remuneration he wished. Now Schoenfeld was challenged by a competitor. Hirschfeld's abilities, however, fell short of the work he was required to perform, and so he conceived the idea of inviting his younger brother, Pascal—who was apparently better qualified,[37] since his education had centered mainly in studying the Jewish traditional sources—to join him. (Pascal was, however, his brother's inferior in personality traits and mental powers.[38]) As a result of the

33

presence of the two brothers, Schoenfeld was relegated to an insignificant position in the Order. Some time later he was expelled from the Vienna circle, though as we shall see, he did not sever his connections with the members altogether.

From 1785 to 1787, the two brothers served more or less as secretaries to the Order, and Ephraim Joseph was dignified by the title of *Oker Harim* (literally, "uprooter of Mountains"). The various offices, too, were designated by Hebrew terms, and the members were addressed by names culled from Hebraic sources. Heinrich von Ecker was called Abraham; his brother, Israel; Justus, *Ish Zaddik* (righteous person), and Baron von Schoenfeld, Isaac ben Joseph.[39] The use of the Hebrew language was no novelty, since this had been an accepted practice among Freemasons. The latter, however, generally restricted their choice to Biblical expressions, while the former drew upon the vocabulary of rabbinic literature, an indication that Jews who had received a traditional education exercized a considerable influence.[40] In their use of alien concepts, the Asiatics differed from the other Freemasons, whose reliance on Hebrew was intended only to surround Masonic activities with an exotic aura. Here it was intended to give prominence to the Jewish element incorporated in the Order. The full purpose of this custom is exposed by the fact that Hebrew names were assigned to Christian members only, while Jews were given names with Christian overtones. In their decision to admit Jews, the Asiatics relied upon the well-known paragraph of the English Masonic constitution, which limited the religious qualifications for membership to the universal principles common to all the sons of Noah.[41] In contradistinction to the English lodges, however, Jews and Christians were not accepted here without regard to their denominations. The two religions were not ignored. The intention was to extract principles from both faiths and to create from the combination a composite pattern of ideas which would serve as a basis on which the ceremonial procedures in which Christian and Jewish symbols both played their parts could be constructed.

In theory, the Order of the Asiatics had not been founded as a substitute for Freemasonry but to construct an upper level above the regular Masonic structure. The assumption was that the members had already become familiar with the three main levels of Masonic lore and that a new order had come into being which promised to open doors to additional mysteries. In this respect, the Asiatics were following the example of, among others, the Scottish rite, which also had been constructed over and above the three original degrees of the Masonic order. This is the implication of the sentence, quoted above, from the first paragraph of the constitution —that members would be accepted regardless of their religion, class, or "system"—the last term referring to the "system" of the Masonic lodge through which the candidate had previously passed. Yet, to follow this procedure in practice was quite difficult. Jews had not been permitted to become Freemasons; they should therefore have been ineligible for membership in the Order of the Asiatics.

It appears either that Ecker exerted considerable effort to pave the way for Jews to enter the Masonic brotherhood, or that he deluded Jewish dignitaries into believing that his efforts might meet with some success.[42] Yet anyone who might have given credence to his assurances was doomed to disappointment. The regular lodges were still barred to Jews. If the leaders of the Order of the Asiatics desired to follow the practice of admitting only former Masons, they would have to find some substitute to serve the needs of the Jews. A solution was found. Special "Melchizedek" lodges, so called to distinguish them from those named after John the Baptist, were founded. The writings of the Order of the Asiatics speak of the Melchizedek rite as well-known, the proof being that "Jews, Turks, Persians, Armenians, and Copts labor in it."[43] Yet, as we shall see later, this was an invention, a makeshift measure, but sufficient to show that some effort was being made to include Jews in the same order as gentiles. Jewish admission was made conditional, however, in practice if not in theory, on the candidate's relinquishing the Judaism that prevailed at that time.

The ideology of the Asiatic Brethren has been subjected to a critical analysis by Professor Gershom Scholem. His study has revealed that on its theoretical level this ideology was a conglomeration of principles drawn from Christian and Jewish sources.[44] Cabalistic and Sabbatian ideas were jumbled together with Christian theosophic doctrines. The same applied to symbols and festive and memorial days, which were fundamental to the activities of the various degrees of the Order. Along with Christian holidays, such as Christmas and John the Apostle's Day, Jewish festivals, such as the anniversaries of the birth and death of Moses, of the Exodus, and of the Giving of the Law, were celebrated.[45] The Christian Asiatic, however, did not have to suffer pangs of conscience. He could easily have regarded himself as completely faithful to the tenets of his religion—and even look upon himself as reverting to the same pristine form of Christianity which was preserved within Judaism. The Jew, on the other hand, could hardly remain oblivious to the fact that he was trespassing beyond the boundaries of his own traditions. The adoption of Christian symbols could on no account be reconciled with the doctrines of Judaism. And, if these acts were not a sufficiently serious breach of his faith, he was also required, as a member of the Order, to eat pork with milk as part of some solemn celebration.[46] Even the most ignorant of Jews was fully aware that he was thereby violating a law of his own religion. Such antinomian tendencies could only be found in Sabbatian conceptions, and this influence, as we have seen before, was clearly prevalent. The apostate and Sabbatian Moses Dobrushka-Schoenfeld served as the transmission line, carrying this influence to the Order of the Asiatics. Others too may have possessed a similar Sabbatian background, and their sectarian past paved the way for their participation in a Judeo-Christian society which had adopted their previous doctrines and observances.

The readiness of the Jewish members to transgress the boundaries of their religion might have been derived from another source. Hirschfeld had become estranged from Jewish observance even before he made the acquaintance of the Asiatic Brethren. His sojourn among the "enlightened" Berlin Jews and his earlier academic career at the gymnasium and university might very likely have led him away from his past. The other members of the Order were not known as past Sabbatians, but rather as adherents of the disintegrating tendencies of the Haskalah which, explicitly or tacitly, provided the justification for abandoning Jewish traditions. The histories of the Itzig and Arenstein families in Berlin and Vienna respectively furnish a clear example of this process of alienation, which impelled many to forsake Judaism altogether and left others behind, with their bearings lost and the security of their environment destroyed.[47] The lost souls of the latter group were easy targets for recruitment in orders of the Asiatic Brethren variety, since such an association offered them a new social haven, beyond the borders of

Judaism, but where they were not called upon to sever their former connections and to adopt Christianity. The religious syncretism of the Order, which might be interpreted as according a status to Judaism within Christianity, was less of a restraint and more of a stimulus and an attraction.

The Masonic orders were not local organizations. Their tentacles penetrated into numerous cities and countries. Following suit, the founders of the new order also sought to spread beyond the limits of Vienna. But Ecker failed in his attempt to establish his order as a superstructure for all German Freemasons, and was forced to divert his efforts to the founding of new societies in various localities. We have already met him between 1783 and 1785, traveling through Austrian and German cities, conducting his propaganda tour. As to the measure of his success, we have no reliable information; still, it seems to have been considerable. The center of the movement remained in Vienna until the end of 1786 or the beginning of 1787. There the "Sanhedrin" which governed the order had its seat. It was a body composed of seven members as well as several officeholders and salaried employees. The "Sanhedrin" delegated powers to the heads of the districts—four in number—for all of Europe and these heads conferred authorization on the individual cells in their respective regions.[48]

37

In theory, restrictive entrance requirements and a certain measure of supervision were supposed to be enforced by the "Sanhedrin." In practice, however, membership and new lodge authorizations were granted with the utmost generosity.[49] We know of the existence of Asiatic lodges in Prague, Innsbruck, Berlin, Frankfurt, and Hamburg. The *Encyclopedie der Freimaurerei*, published in 1822, mentions that the cities of Wetzlar and Marburg were teeming with devotees of the Order. A strong chapter must have existed in Prague, although we have almost no information on it.[50] In Innsbruck the society was composed of the local aristocracy.[51] As for Berlin, the sources yield only the name of Itzig,[52] but other relevant literature mentions Bischofswerder, Wöllner, and even the Crown Prince, who was later to become King Frederick William II of Prussia.[53] From Hirschfeld's 1787 visit to Frankfurt we learn of a lodge in that city; its members are not referred to by their real names, but by the pseudonyms conferred on them by their lodges.[54] Better known are the Hamburg brethren. Here lived Carl, Ecker's younger brother. He had been an active Mason even before the Order of the Asiatic Brethren came into existence. In his attitude toward Jews he showed himself ready to follow in his brother's footsteps. In 1783 he founded a lodge which admitted two Jewish members: Isaac Oppenheimer and Gottschalk Samson.[55] This society was short-lived, but two years later Carl von Ecker founded a new lodge, which was formally initiated in December 1785. His older brother, who lived in Vienna, happened to be in Hamburg on that occasion and he persuaded the group to join the Order of the Asiatics.[56] The 1786 membership roster [57] gives the names, ages, occupations, and class of twenty-four persons. No distinguished persons are included, for, unlike Vienna, Hamburg was not the residence of high nobility. Eight of the names, however, bore the prefix "von"; the others too seem to have been borne by men of substance, to judge by their occupations: bankers, merchants, physicians, and even a clergyman. Six can definitely be identified as Jews. Beside Samson, mentioned previously, they are Isaac Guggenheimer, Jacob Götz, Wolf Nathan Liepmann, Hirsch Wolf, and Marcus Jacob Schlesinger. Two were bankers; two merchants; one a court agent; one a physician. With the exception of the physician, Hirsch Wolf, these Jews were not among the culturally distinguished of the generation.[58] Their principal title to membership rested on their readiness to support the Order financially and their aspirations to rub shoulders with non-Jews.[59]

From data on the Hamburg and Vienna groups, we can project conclusions about the other cities where branches of the Order were established. Its swift spread is a clear indication of the internal disintegration of a specific stratum of Jewish society in Western Europe. We must also take notice of the fact that a certain section of non-Jewish society was ready to establish social and spiritual contact with Jews. Yet we should not exaggerate the dimensions of this section, even for the period of greatest social progress, the eighties and nineties of the eighteenth century. Only a few years after the Order of the Asiatics had been founded, its declared policy of including Jews and gentiles together in a single group framework was challenged.

The first public attack on the principle of equality in Freemasonry was launched in Hamburg in an eight-page brochure. According to its title, it purported to convey "unbiased and basic information on Jewish Masonic lodges and other secret societies in Hamburg." The author describes the admission of Jews into the local lodges as a startling innovation. Until that time even unauthorized lodges had categorically refused to accept Jews, since these lodges too assented to the basic Masonic doctrine that Jesus Christ was the cornerstone of their structure. Yet now certain lodges wished to enjoy the benefits of Jewish wealth, and whispered in Jewish ears that, in return for 100 reichsthaler, admission to the Masonic order could be obtained. According to the author, this hunt for souls was undertaken in the name of a certain prince, a Masonic *Grossordensmeister,* who had ordered that Jews be accepted from now on, "since sufferance and tolerance now prevailed universally." [60] Hardly any doubt remains that the prince in question was Carl von Hessen, who, as we shall soon see, became the *Grossmeister* of the Asiatics, and who could be described as tending to show tolerance to Jews. The founder of the lodge open to Jews must have been Ecker. Essentially the observations of the anonymous author agree with what is known to us from other quarters. He must have drawn his information from firsthand sources and was even aware that the initiation ceremony was concluded with a meal at which pork was served.[61]

The author was not as much interested to inform as to condemn. He scorned the Jews for having accepted the offer, as they usually did, but refusing to pay the price. His bitterest resentment was reserved for the founder of the lodge who had removed the restrictions against Jews entering the Masonic movement. He wanted to focus the attention of the city government on what had taken place in the hope of having an end put to this state of affairs.[62] That same year a reply was issued. The rebuttal did not deny a single allegation of the brochure. It rejected the slurs on Jewish behavior as being applicable only to the crude masses. In defending the existing practice, the rebuttal points to the custom of the English lodges which had never discriminated between Jew and gentile.[63] It is most reasonable to assume that the author of the reply was none other than Carl von Ecker himself.

This minor controversy which occurred in Hamburg in 1786 may be regarded as the opening shot in a crushing barrage which rained down upon the heads of the Order of the Asiatics a year later. We

39

have already noted that Heinrich von Ecker had come from Vienna
to Hamburg to attend the induction ceremony of his brother Carl's
lodge. The older brother's journey to northern Germany had a
clear, deliberate purpose: he was seeking the protection for his
Order of one of the princes who had some sympathy for Freemasonry and its mystic ramifications. Such persons were Prince Ferdinand of Brunswick and the Landgrave, Carl von Hessen, and Heinrich tried his luck with both.[64] He was in sore need of this
protection, since his personal standing and the existence of the entire Order in Vienna had been put in jeopardy. The heads of the
Freemasons (they belonged to the uppermost classes and had influence in government circles) had fought the Order of the Asiatics
from its very inception. By the end of 1785 they had succeeded in
persuading Kaiser Joseph II to promulgate a law which would have
placed all Masonic lodges under strict government supervision.[65]
Ecker sought to nip this threat in the bud by finding refuge in
royal patronage elsewhere, and in Schleswig he found a sympathetic
response on the part of the Landgrave, Carl von Hessen, with
whom he had exchanged words previously. All his life Carl had
longed to uncover the secrets hidden in Masonic doctrine, and he
believed Ecker's assertion that these were known to the members of
the Asiatic Order. He therefore consented to become the head of
the Order,[66] and invited Ecker, and through him, Hirschfeld, to
come and settle in Schleswig. Hirschfeld's brother, Pascal, remained
for the time being in Vienna.[67] Some time later, Prince Ferdinand
too responded, and Carl, the younger of the brothers, left Hamburg
to join the Prince's court in Brunswick.[68]

The removal of the center of the Order to Schleswig alerted the
Masons outside of Hamburg. At the time, Schleswig was under Danish tutelage and Carl von Hessen exercised his office as the deputy
of the Danish King. Freemasons in Copenhagen, afraid lest the
Order of the Asiatics acquire influence in their territory, resolved to
oppose it openly and expose its nature in public.[69] This was not difficult to do. The members of the Order had not been at all particular in whom they admitted. Their constitution was therefore not
properly guarded and was passed from hand to hand.[70] The Copenhagen Masons decided to publish the entire constitution together
with an introduction and critical notes, so as to show how far the
new Order had strayed from the authentic principles of Freema-

sonry. A person capable of handling the assignment was found, and the book, *Authentische Nachricht von den Ritter und Brüder— Eingeweihten aus Asien, Zur Beherzigung für Freymaurern,* was published anonymously in 1787. The author, however, son of a local Protestant clergyman, is known to have been Friedrich Münter, a Freemason, who afterward became famous as an Oriental scholar and the Bishop of Copenhagen.[71]

In his introduction, Münter associated the Order of the Asiatics with the occult current in Rosicrucianism which had achieved notoriety for its extortion of money from the gullible and for its frauds and swindles. Admittedly, the members of the Order of the Asiatics had held themselves out as opposed to the Rosicrucians, but the two were, in truth, of the same type. Their common feature was their pursuit of spurious, secret doctrines which confused minds and dulled senses. Münter spoke in the name of reason, of the sciences and philosophy of the enlightenment, which alone were the guarantees for the freedom, truth, and happiness of mankind. Hand in hand with these disciplines went rational theology, which stood in no need of any allegorical or mystical interpretation of the Holy Scriptures, which claimed authority "in spite of human intelligence."[72] Münter represented the position of the educated and enlightened Christian. What does occasion surprise is that this position, which had normally served as the starting point for a closer approach to Jews, now became his pretext for opposing the opening of the lodge doors to Jews.

Münter appended his notes to paragraph after paragraph of the constitution of the Order of the Asiatics. As for the paragraph which allowed Jews to be accepted in Melchizedek lodges from where they would become eligible for membership in the Order of the Asiatics, he attacked it from all sides. Jews were never, according to him, admitted into legitimate lodges conducted in accordance with the laws of the Grand Lodge of London. The exceptions were a few lodges in Holland, and they had acted illegally in this instance. The other lodges which had accepted Jews had never been granted authorization. He asserted that it was an established rule among all Freemasons, regardless of their rite, that only Christians were eligible, "and the entire constitution of the Order is predicated on this principle." As for the Melchizedek lodges, they were a pure invention of the Order of the Asiatics. Their story that such lodges

41

existed in Oriental countries and included "Jews, Turks, Persians, Armenians, and Copts" was a figment of the imagination, intended to legalize the entry of Jews into the Masonic lodges in the European countries.[73] Thoroughly familiar with Masonic affairs, Münter possessed in addition a keen sense for historical criticism. In this remark, he had undoubtedly hit upon the truth. Hirschfeld himself later conceded that the Melchizedek lodges existed only in the mind of Heinrich von Ecker.[74]

Münter's vigorous attack produced its effect. The Ecker brothers took the attack to be directed at them. Heinrich's name had been mentioned explicitly by Münter as one who had been an active member of the Order in Vienna and was now living in Schleswig.[75] Heretofore the brothers had always been mentioned in the same breath and each was made to suffer for the sins of the other. Both depended for their positions on the existence of the Order— Heinrich because he had been invited by Duke Carl of Schleswig as a result of the latter's belief in the truth of the Asiatic doctrines, and Carl because the group flourishing in Hamburg provided him with his keep. Now, however, the representatives of the Order had been portrayed as money grubbers and the Order itself as possessing a false and confused ideology. It was not surprising that both felt constrained to reply. Heinrich compiled a book of one hundred pages to which he appended his full name,[76] while Carl published his eighty-page reply anonymously.[77]

Possibly the brothers deliberately divided the functions between them. On the other hand, each might, on his own, have replied to those accusations which affected his personal circumstances. Heinrich, who had made his future dependent upon Duke Carl's belief in the spiritual benefit lying hidden in the ideology of the order, denied Münter's accusations on this aspect. He admitted the existence of the Order openly and even proudly. He delineated its history during the past generation and alluded to a prior genealogy from which the Order, as it now existed, had descended. All this argument was obviously intended to support the contention that the Order of the Asiatics indeed had access to the true interpretations of all Masonic symbolism. Such interpretations also entailed uncovering the very secrets of nature itself, and, although the Asiatics were not alchemists seeking to produce gold, they were nevertheless "far-seeing investigators of nature, possessing profound insights."

They sought to be no more than a group "engaged in the ultimate deciphering of all Masonic hieroglyphics, and as a group they occupied themselves with all the truths and cognitions of natural things following from that." [78] This modest claim advanced on behalf of the Order was calculated to pacify its adherents; as for Duke Carl, there was no limit to his credulity. For if it was true that the Asiatics possessed knowledge of the secrets of the world, then all other possible deficiencies were of no account in comparison. Heinrich von Ecker dealt only cursorily with Münter's other accusations. He referred in passing to the Jewish question. He denied, though not too vigorously, that the Asiatics had founded lodges of their own to provide themselves with members. But he flatly contradicted Münter's allegation that Jews had never been accepted in legitimate lodges. He himself cited the names of three Jews who had been admitted into the movement—one in London, one in Paris, and one in Gibraltar, "where many Jews visit the lodges." [79]

What was of minor importance to Heinrich was of major significance to his brother. Carl hardly touched on the question of the Asiatic Order. He contented himself with the assertion that there did indeed exist higher degrees than the basic three of the Masonic movement, and that those who reached these higher levels were vouchsafed revelations not disclosed even to the best among the Masons. It was therefore quite possible that the Order of the Asiatics did in fact contain these higher degrees. Nevertheless, preparation in the three Masonic levels was a precondition for ascending to the higher degrees.[80] Yet what were the prerequisites for the acceptance of members in the Masonic lodges themselves? Münter had asserted that such acceptance depended upon the candidate's adherence to the Christian faith, and so Jews were ipso facto excluded. This contention Carl von Ecker undertook to dispute, as the title of his work explicitly shows: *Werden und können Israeliten zu Freymaurern aufgenommen werden?* (Would and should Israelites be accepted as Freemasons?). This was the first time that the problem had been aired in public, and Ecker's book was the beginning of a whole series of publications which took up the question during the succeeding generations. Ecker's affirmative answer to this question was the fruit of the prevailing circumstances of his time and his locality.

Like Heinrich, Carl refuted Münter's contention that lodges

43

using the English rite had never accepted Jews. In England Jews had been and were still being granted membership. He mentioned the names of Jews known to him personally, which had appeared in the publications of the English lodges. For added support, he reprinted the authorization conferred by an English lodge on a Jew named David Hertz, in London, on July 24, 1787.[81] Those lodges which had accepted Jews conducted themselves in accordance with the original principle of Freemasonry, and here Carl von Ecker quoted the paragraphs of the constitutions discussed in Chapter II.[82] It was true that most of the lodges in Germany and some in France and Italy had deviated from this principle. It had been acknowledged by the German Freemasons that no lodge could legally function unless it had been authorized by the Grand Lodge of London. Yet they had adapted their constitutions to the conditions existing in their respective states, and these circumstances had been responsible for Jews being excluded from the lodges since, in Germany, discrimination against Jews was prevalent even among Freemasons, occasioned by religious fanaticism or hypocrisy or from fear of attacks by fanatics. The barring of Jews and the prejudice against them also stemmed from their inferior political status, for Jews had not been granted citizenship in the states where they lived.[83]

So far the defense rested on blaming the opponents of the Jews. Yet German Jews themselves were guilty to some extent. They lagged behind their brethren in England, France, and Italy. They did not follow the law of Moses, but observed absurd rabbinic customs. Carl found fault even with the enlightened Jews. These ostentatiously paraded their culture, yet found difficulty in liberating themselves from their original mentality. They forced themselves to discuss scientific topics, while their attention remained riveted on mortgage foreclosures and bad debts. Their very singsong intonation set them apart from the rest of civilized society.[84]

It is worthwhile to examine this argument in its various aspects. Here we have a description of an intense emotional revulsion in which elements of actual impressions are mixed with stereotyped imagination. Such portrayals emerge quite frequently in contemporaneous literature, which dealt extensively with the Jewish problem and the possibility of Jews being allowed to enter Christian society. Among those in favor of granting civil rights to Jews,[85] revulsion

44

was coupled with the rational reflection that a change could occur in the future. Carl von Ecker adopted this attitude, and so he was able to justify opening the doors of the lodges to Jews. At bottom human nature was the same. "Christians and non-Christians alike are suitable for this instruction [of the Freemasons] which includes, basically, what is known as the law of nature which is impressed on the heart of man by God." Christians, however, must take the first step. Since they have oppressed the Jews for so many generations, they are now obliged to restore human dignity and civil rights to Jews and to remove from the latter all the blemishes which had become attached to them as a result of their exclusion from society. A special responsibility devolves upon the Freemasons. "Why bar the way to Freemasonry against this people—the only way perhaps to enlightenment, the way through which they will more easily become reconciled with the rest of the human family and through which they will mend their habits and refine their ways of thinking?" [86] Hamburg Jews, who belonged to the lodge headed by Ecker, could then see themselves as marching steadily forward, as a result of their Masonic membership, toward integration in the general, human society. And so they certainly did regard themselves at the time.

45

Carl von Ecker pointed to the anomalous situation. Precisely those lodges which acknowledged no other Masonic authority than that derived from the Grand Lodge of London were the ones to deny the principles of that very Grand Lodge in matters affecting Jews.[87] It is no less paradoxical to see the representatives of the Order of the Asiatics, so utterly removed from the rationalism of English Freemasonry, justify the admission of Jews by reference to that rite. In actuality, principles, tendencies, beliefs, and ulterior motives, all together in utter disorder, influenced Masonic attitudes toward Jews, so it should not be surprising to find in the history of the Asiatic lodges twisting and vacillating and a lack of consistency.

The representatives of the Order apparently stood the test successfully. They had publicly defended the right of Jews to be admitted to their society and to all Masonic lodges. The Jewish participant in the leadership of the organization, Ephraim Joseph Hirschfeld, maintained his position in Schleswig, and we find him there fulfilling an important part in the functioning of the Order.

Sent in 1787 by Duke Carl, he had undertaken an extensive tour on behalf of the Order. He traveled to Frankfurt and from there, by way of Nuremberg and Regensburg, to Prague and Vienna.[88] After his return, he settled in Schleswig, but still maintained contact with Hamburg.[89] The center of the movement was now located in northern Germany: in Schleswig under the patronage of Carl von Hessen, and in Brunswick under the patronage of Duke Ferdinand. Senior officials in Carl's administration were active in the Order, and Hirschfeld made friends even on this level of society. There, as in Vienna, his function was to provide the Order with exercises in meditation culled from Cabalistic printed works and manuscripts. Although he had drawn upon others and had even accepted assistance from his brother when he was in Vienna, in Schleswig he relied, at least during the earlier years, upon his own resources. To this end, he fortified himself during his Frankfurt sojourn with the necessary textbooks.[90] It is doubtful whether anyone else in Schleswig was capable of reading a Hebrew book or of expounding the texts of the Order which had been compiled by the founders in Vienna and were based on Cabalistic writings. The members needed to understand the doctrines of their Order, and so they, and Duke Carl, their leader, were forced to depend on Hirschfeld. His position now seemed secure because he was indispensable.

Nevertheless, Hirschfeld did not enjoy peace and quiet in his new home. He was obviously more isolated in Schleswig than he had been in Vienna. Here he was an alien, a foreigner, probably the only Jew in the group. Although the Ecker brothers had defended the principle of equality in their Order, the Schleswig members were reluctant to accept its validity. Some were of the opinion that, although Jewish members already in the Order should not be expelled, new applicants should not be admitted in large numbers. According to Hirschfeld's own account, the Schleswig "Sanhedrin" rejected a Jewish candidate on the grounds of his religion, and Hirschfeld undertook the defense of the principle and the struggle to have it implemented in practice.[91]

This information is corroborated by another source which recounts an incident occurring in Hamburg. Carl von Ecker sought to obtain Masonic authorization for his Order from Ferdinand of Brunswick, and the latter made the granting of his authorization dependent upon the expulsion of Jewish members from the group.

46

Duke Carl, who wanted to save the Jewish members, proposed that they be organized in a separate lodge named Melchizedek, such membership being intended to confer the right on Jews to visit Christian lodges. Carl thereby acknowledged the distinction instituted between two types of lodges by the Order of the Asiatics, but without raising the status of Jews to equality with Christians. The Jewish members of the Order, whose number had risen to twenty, rejected the proposal and left the Order.[92]

Duke Carl tried to placate the Jews,[93] but not at the expense of his connections with Christianity. Though he longed to learn the meanings of the secrets by having recourse to Jewish sources, he believed that such revelations would lead him to truths that were basically Christian.[94] Heinrich von Ecker, too, adapted himself to the Schleswig atmosphere and made sure that he was seen reading Scripture with all due Christian fervor.[95]

Given these circumstances, it is not surprising that Hirschfeld began to feel that he was a victim of discrimination. Although rumors spread upon occasion that he had been [96] or had appeared to be converted [97] to Christianity, the truth is that he refrained from taking this step. Even in his religious position he remained an exception, as we shall see later. Not everyone considered this a fault, and several persons in Schleswig were attracted to his unique personality. Nevertheless, here as in every court society, social standing was determined by the mere fact of a man's belonging to a particular class or religion. Carl von Ecker's friendship for the Jew availed him nothing. The honors conferred on Ecker, the noble, were denied to Hirschfeld, the Jew.[98] Social discrimination strained their relations and in the end led to an open breach between the two old friends.

Details and minutiae of the quarrel and the resulting litigation do not fall within the scope of this discussion. In brief, Hirschfeld sued Ecker for the payment of debts owing to him, and Ecker, in turn, accused Hirschfeld of threatening his life in the presence of Duke Carl.[99] As the trial progressed, it became evident that Ecker was exerting an increasingly strong influence on the Duke and the officials conducting the proceedings. Distraint was levied on Hirschfeld's personal effects and the manuscript in his possession, and he was placed under house arrest.[100] The Order of the Asiatics, too, turned its back on the very person who had once been its central

47

spiritual pillar. It was resolved to expel Hirschfeld from the Order, and a circular was sent to all branches explaining why this disciplinary action had been taken.[101] The legal proceedings and the act of expulsion clearly reveal anti-Jewish overtones and warrant our attention as evidence that the social status acquired by Jews, even in a marginal group such as the Order of the Asiatics, was of a doubtful nature.

In the course of the trial both parties gave accounts of the history of their association and cooperative efforts. Ecker did not fail to relate how he had promoted Hirschfeld, even in Innsbruck, despite his Jewishness.[102] To refute Hirschfeld's contention that he had given him financial assistance in Vienna and Innsbruck, and not vice versa, Ecker invited high-level acquaintances to submit their testimony in writing. Many of these letters reek with contempt for the Jew, Hirschfeld—and undoubtedly echo Ecker's call for aid in his suit as a wronged noble against a Jewish extortioner. One of the Innsbruck writers stated quite bluntly that in his locality no Jew would have the audacity to institute legal proceedings against a nobleman of the social eminence of Ecker und Eckhoffen.[103]

A similar tone is sounded in the notification of the Order of Hirschfeld's expulsion. He was accused, among other things, of having imposed a Jewish, Cabala-derived pattern on the rites of the Order. The authors of the circular acknowledged the value of Cabala as a source for Masonic meditation, but argued that the object of these intellectual exercises should have been to lead the Christian far beyond the limits attainable by a Jew.[104] Nor was this all. I do not have the complete text of the circular, but the reaction to it—other than on the part of Hirschfeld—shows clearly that its arguments could have proved injurious to all the Jewish members of the Order.

What is most interesting about Hirschfeld as a person and the stand he took is, that, although he was most sensitive to, and would defend himself most vigorously against, any affront to his honor, he did not regard himself as being attacked as a Jew. Nor apparently did he feel that his Jewishness had played any part in the deterioration of his position. Once his doom had overtaken him and he was imprisoned, he turned wherever he could to prove that he was innocent and had not committed any crime. Yet nowhere is there any indication that he had been made to suffer because he was a Jew.

48

This might have been sheer simulation, yet it is possible that his fervent desire to regard himself above any Jewish-Christian conflict may have inhibited him psychologically from identifying his lot with that of his people. This neutral attitude may have crystallized within Hirschfeld over the course of years. In his reply to the circular's accusation he denied that the Cabala was dependent on any positive religion, and argued that anyone, be he Catholic, Moslem, or Jew, who occupied himself with it would thereby pass beyond the confines of his specific religious tradition and reach "the one and only, true, pure, and over-all religion." It is also true in this instance that he was here giving Carl von Hessen, to whom he had addressed his reply, the grounds to believe that the Christian would eventually find, in the authentic wisdom of the Cabala, the truths of Christianity heretofore concealed from the ordinary member of that religion.[105] In his distress, Hirschfeld went so far as to deny his own conception, which had been based on the belief that there was a single, mystic wisdom common to all religions.[106]

Hirschfeld's oblivious attitude to the attacks upon him as a Jew was not shared by all the Jewish members of the Order. We know of the reaction of one of the more important members, the wealthy Berlin banker, Itzig, previously mentioned as being active. He was one of those to whom Hirschfeld had appealed to extricate him from his present predicament.[107] By using his influence with the royal court, Itzig could have obtained a Prussian government position for Hirschfeld who would then have enjoyed diplomatic immunity. Instead of this wild plan, Itzig tried a more direct approach. He addressed a long letter to Carl von Hessen to intercede on behalf of the distressed Hirschfeld.[108] He praised Hirschfeld's character and cited Moses Mendelssohn's encouragement of him as a young man in Berlin. Itzig also indicated that he was prepared to defray any costs involved in settling Hirschfeld's affair with Ecker, if financial considerations were in fact involved.[109]

Itzig's plea did not refer to the personal instance of Hirschfeld alone. He also submitted his own claims to the Duke in respect to the anti-Jewish accusations which had risen above surface in the publications of the Order dealing with the Hirschfeld affair. Itzig protested most vehemently against the insults hurled against "the entire Jewish people, and especially the Jewish brethren" of the Order. "How can a few individuals have the effrontery to cast aspersions for the second time upon a people with whom they have no acquaintance and which has no acquaintance with them?" Such an attempt had in fact been made once before in the worthless pamphlet *Werden und können Israeliten zu Freymaurern aufgenommen werden?* Itzig's remarks prove that the negative portrayal of Jewish character by Carl von Ecker at the time in his brochure had not gone unnoticed, at least by the Jewish members of the Order. It also proves that the circular contained some of the very allegations disseminated by the pamphlet, and that both had issued from a common source—the hands of the Ecker brothers.[110] The whole affair throws a lurid light upon the true nature of the tolerance of the Eckers and their like. This was a product of cold, intellectual calculation to be destroyed by the first, emotional outburst fanned by personal considerations.

We do not know whether Itzig's protest made any impression on the Duke. Help reached Hirschfeld from an unexpected quarter. His antagonist, Heinrich von Ecker, suddenly died in August 1791, before the trial had ended.[111] Even before that, help had been extended to Hirschfeld in the field of communication by the publication of a book entitled *Der Asiate in seiner Blösse oder gründlicher Beweis dass die Ritter und Brüder Eingeweihten aus Asien aechte Rosenkreuzer sind* (The Asiatic in his nakedness, or a thoroughgoing demonstration that the initiated Knights and Brethren from Asia are genuine Rosicrucians). This served as the last stage of the controversy over the acceptance of Jews into Masonic lodges, at least at this period of the history of the problem.

The booklet was anonymous both in respect of its author and the place of publication.[112] The author proceeds to attack the Order and especially the Ecker brothers on the basis of new material which had not been available to the author of the *Authentische Nachrichten*. He adduces numerous proofs for the assertion that the Asiatics merely constitute a manifestation of the former Rosicrucians. He reverts to the question whether Jews are fit for membership, not in the Freemasons this time, but in the Asiatic brotherhood. He argues that they had been deceived, since they had been induced to swear allegiance to Jesus the Redeemer and his laws. Now the author had failed to detect the syncretistic intent of the Order, and so he hoped that some Jew would come forward, divest himself of the false oath he had been unwittingly tricked into swearing, and expose the Order's secrets in public.[113] It is almost certain that he had good reason to believe that this would happen. Taking a definite stand on the Hirschfeld-Ecker controversy, he argued that all the wisdom of the Asiatic Order had been derived from Marcus ben Binah, alias Hirschfeld, whom in the end the very Asiatics themselves had persecuted and imprisoned. He called upon the Christian Freemasons to rally to the rescue of the victim, but at the same time indicated another means to secure his release. Pascal, Hirschfeld's brother, was still alive. Let him threaten to disclose all the secrets of the Order unless his brother was freed.[114]

Ecker's death put an end to Hirschfeld's confinement. He proceeded to make peace with the Duke, and later effected a reconciliation with Carl von Ecker as well. The Duke granted him an annuity in lieu of the debt owed him by the deceased Ecker, and still took an interest in Cabalistic material supplied by Hirschfeld, as well as in his advice on the times, favorable and unfavorable, for engaging in its study. But Hirschfeld never was restored to his former standing in the Order, the Duke himself stipulating that he was to keep away.[115] In addition to the previous resentment against him, Hirschfeld was now suspected of having been the author of the exposé, *Der Asiate,* which had subjected the Order to such vicious attack. To clear himself of the suspicion, he undertook to write a pamphlet which would demolish all the arguments of *Der Asiate.* Work on this reply became bogged down, and Hirschfeld was called upon to explain his inaction.[116] The truth is that he was probably not the author, but had only supplied the author with the material in his brother's possession to prepare his defense. No wonder his stay in Schleswig had become uncomfortable![117] But he had become burdened with debt—probably because of the expense of the litigation—and was unable to leave. He relied on his tested means: an urgent call for help went out to his former groups in Berlin and Vienna, and they hastened to his rescue.

In February 1792 there appeared in Schleswig a person referred to as I. Ben Jos. He was introduced by Hirschfeld as a leading member of the order. Having heard of, but never having seen him, the Schleswig brethren found it difficult to believe that he existed. This leading brother paid 550 thaler to discharge Hirschfeld's debts, and now all barriers to departure were gone. Hirschfeld wanted to take advantage of the presence of his guest to gain pres-

51

tige. Unfortunately the Landgrave Carl was not home at the time. So Hirschfeld introduced him to all the other important members, and then took him to Brunswick, hoping to introduce him to Duke Ferdinand. There they dined at the table of Carl von Ecker. During the meal the guest was identified as a Jew. Though he neither denied nor admitted the fact, all hope for an audience with the Duke vanished. Thereupon, Hirschfeld and the leading brother left northern Germany, and we find them in Strasbourg in May or thereabout. There they parted company. Hirschfeld returned to Germany, arriving in Karlsruhe, his birthplace, in the middle of June. There he waited for the promised return of the leading brother.[118]

Who was this obscure person? Molitor's account gives the solution by relating that Hirschfeld had accompanied Thomas von Schoenfeld to Strasbourg (where they made the acquaintance of the famous spiritualist St. Martin, author of *Des erreurs et de la vérité*).[119] From another source we learn that Schoenfeld arrived in Strasbourg in March 1793, and that from then onwards he appeared under the name of Junius Frey.[120] The data agree, and the facts leave no room for doubt. What can reasonably be deduced from them is that Hirschfeld's appeal to the veteran members of the group led them to summon the aid of the arch-adventurer Thomas von Schoenfeld. He came to Schleswig from the city of "P.," that is, Prague, by way of Vienna, Berlin, and Hamburg.[121] Certainly he did not draw the money to discharge Hirschfeld's debts from his own pocket. The money had been raised among the rich brethren in Vienna and Berlin, who had involved themselves in the issue and rallied to Hirschfeld's aid. Schoenfeld took the opportunity to cross into France—or else this was his original destination, and his mission to Schleswig was later incorporated into his itinerary. It is a fact that his brother and sister joined him in Paris when he arrived there in the middle of June.[122] Hirschfeld waited for him in Karlsruhe.[123] Declaring later that he had seen his bitter end in a dream Hirschfeld claimed that Schoenfeld might have been engaged in a mission on behalf of the Austrian government.[124] This suspicion may have been well founded; yet it is equally possible that this was a post facto supposition. One thing is clear: the leading brother had abandoned his spiritual, for the much higher stakes of the great political adventure that had seized Paris. He died on the guillotine on April 5, 1793.[125]

Hirschfeld's rescue was the last activity, as far as we know, of the Jewish group within the Order of the Asiatics. There are grounds to assume that Jews continued to leave the Order,[126] and that the Order itself went into decline. Soon after Hirschfeld's departure from Schleswig, the Order lost one of its patrons with the death of Duke Friedrich of Brunswick (July 1792). Carl von Hessen lived on. He did not reject the doctrines of the Order [127] but turned to other groups and ideologies for explanations of the Masonic secrets.[128] He maintained some contact with his spiritual mentor, Hirschfeld. As for the latter, he settled in Offenbach—near Frankfurt—the center of the Frankist movement.[129] From time to time he tried to interest people in his spiritual, conceptual system,[130] and in the next chapter we shall meet these two remnants of the Order of the Asiatic Brethren in a new context.

53

IV   The Frankfurt Judenloge

The Order of the Asiatic Brethren was a broad attempt to erect some type of Masonic framework within the borders of which both Jews and gentiles would be included. But it was not the only attempt. In 1790, even before the Order had finally ceased to exist, two Christians, Hirschfeld and Catter,[1] had founded the Toleranzloge in Berlin with the avowed object of admitting both gentiles and Jews. These two men were by no means original thinkers. Their conceptions were a diluted solution of humanistic principles: belief in truth, brotherhood, and beauty, mixed with the vestiges of certain Christian doctrines: the fall of man and the necessity of his moral regeneration.[2] They even retained some of the Christian symbols current in Masonic usage; Jews took their oath on the Gospel of Saint John, not "on a Hebrew Old Testament." Nevertheless, the founders proclaimed that "Freemasonry is obliged to bring Jews and Christians closer together and to eliminate outworn prejudices. It is their duty to make Jews, if one may say so, more human and to raise them to higher levels of culture." It was admitted, however, that only such Jews were worthy of membership as had already approached more closely to Christianity and whose open adherence to that religion was only obstructed by family circumstances. In the eyes of the founders, men like the Itzig brothers, Professor Herz, and Levi, the banker, were considered to fit into such a category.[3] It may be presumed that these Jews, and especially Isaac Daniel Itzig, had a hand in establishing the lodge. Its founding possibly may have been from the very beginning a reaction to their disappointment at the anti-Jewish mood then pervading the Asiatic Order.[4] At all events, Itzig became busily engaged in searching for a patron for the new lodge. The founders had approached the Grand Lodge of Germany to grant them an approved constitution. Their request was refused. Instead, Itzig was able to procure a letter of approval from King Frederick William—whose trusted banker he was— stating that the King consented "to tolerate the lodge in question and to protect it as long as it harbored no tendencies toward *illuminatismus* [an order which had gained notoriety for its social and political extremism] and toward 'Enlightenment.'" This royal patronage was not the equivalent of actual recognition, but at least it allowed the lodge to function for more than ten years and to earn the praise of the cultured as an organization with an exemplary humanistic goal.[5]

A second attempt occurred that very year (1791–92)—this time in Hamburg. The initiative was taken openly by a Jew named Israel. No details can be elicited from any other source, and the information on the lodge itself is meager.[6] Israel, who had been initiated as a Mason in London, now wanted to bestow the benefit on his Jewish brethren of an education "by social contact with the Christians." His lodge was called Toleranz und Einigkeit, and among its members echoes of slogans of the French Revolution could be heard. He found Jews who wanted to belong to his lodge (we do not know whether they were former members of the Asiatic Order or not) and even obtained the support of gentile dignitaries.[7] Yet he could not gain recognition from a Mother Lodge. In Hamburg, Berlin, and London his applications were refused. The excuse given by the London lodge for its rejection was rather ironic: authorization should not be granted to a Jewish lodge, since religious questions were beyond the scope of Freemasonry.

Both the Berlin and Hamburg lodges represented a direct attempt to absorb Jews into the Masonic fraternity. There were other lodges, not founded with this specific purpose in mind, which accepted Jews de facto. These lodges paid no special heed to the accepted Masonic rules and were branded as unauthorized. Having until then suffered complete exclusion from the surrounding society, Jews could look upon their admission, even to these marginal associations, as a significant social advance. Yet if one aspired to acceptance as an equal in the surrounding society, he could not fail to consider his admission to a *Winkelloge* as a mockery rather than a fulfillment.

A case history throws light on the prevailing state of affairs. Sigismund Geisenheimer, later to found the Frankfurt lodge (to be discussed soon), described in a letter (a copy in his handwriting is still extant[8]) to Dr. Ludwig Baruch (Börne) how he first made his way into the Freemasons. He was a native of Bingen, and was subsequently employed by the House of Rothschild in Frankfurt as head clerk.[9] He had read about the Freemasons, and it occurred to him that the lodges might serve as the most useful instrument for unit-

55

ing Jews and Christians, or at least bringing them closer to one an
other. He was by nature a very practical man, as he demonstrated
later by his founding of the Jewish lodge, and earlier by founding
the Philanthropin Jewish school, which earned him even greater re
nown. In this instance, too, Geisenheimer immediately took steps to
carry his idea into practice. First he sought to become a Freemason
himself. To this end, he traveled to Berlin and enlisted the aid o
Itzig. The latter recommended him to a certain group—we may
venture the guess that it was the Toleranzloge—and he was initi
ated with all due ceremony. Armed with his membership certificate
Geisenheimer now approached a regular Masonic lodge, but he was
very politely refused admission. Slowly the realization dawned or
him that the first lodge had received no real sanction and that its
membership certificate was utterly worthless, meaning nothing to
genuine Freemasons. He considered himself cheated, and the insul
smarted for many years. It may be assumed that the hurt impelled
him to press all the more energetically in his struggle to pave the
way for Jewish entry into the legitimate Masonic lodges.

With the spread of the French Revolution, new prospects opened
up for Jews even, apparently, within the framework of the Masonic
movement. In France itself all restrictions against Jews seem to have
been lifted completely.[10] As the conquering French armies advanced
into the various European countries, the soldiers, and the civilians
who followed them, opened Masonic lodges; and these Frenchmen
behaved in their new environment as they had at home.[11] The
changed situation is reflected in the lives of the founders of the
Frankfurt lodge. Before they opened this lodge, all twelve of them
(eleven were Jews) had been registered as members in other
lodges:[12] four (among them Geisenheimer) had been members o
Les Amis Indivisibles, and one of Anacreon, both lodges located ir
Paris; four, of two London lodges, Hyram and Emulation; one, o
the French, Trois Palmes, in Darmstadt; and one, of the Trinité ir
Frankfurt itself. We know that Geisenheimer gained admission to
the Paris lodge during one of his business trips to that city;[13] the
other members probably succeeded in entering lodges outside their
home towns in the same way.

Certainly membership in a distant lodge was no more than a sub
stitute for the true fulfillment of their desires; they still aspired to
acceptance in the lodges of their own localities. But the Frankfurt

lodges were not open to Jews, even when they presented themselves with the certificates of authorized out-of-town lodges; otherwise they would never have undertaken to found a lodge of their own. We accept as reliable the remarks of Dr. Jacob Weil, one of the veteran members, in the speech he delivered in 1832 on the occasion of the semi-jubilee of the Frankfurt lodge: "Our workshop came about by the founders' knocking on other gates in their birthplace. These were not opened because the monopolists of the light looked upon the believers in the Old Testament as doomed to everlasting darkness." [14] The founders of the new lodge could not, therefore, entertain hope of obtaining recognition from any local Masonic body. A district lodge known as the Zur Einigkeit had existed in Frankfurt since 1789, and it has been empowered by the Mother Lodge in London to open new lodges in the vicinity. [15] But the members of the new lodge had to seek authorization from afar and they communicated, through the medium of Hypolite Cerfbeer, [16] with the Grand Lodge of Paris. The authorization was formally granted on June 17, 1807. The solemn installation ceremony took place on June 12, 1808, and the lodge thereupon assumed the name of Loge de St. John de L'aurore Naissante (in German, Loge zur aufgehenden Morgenröthe). Representatives of lodges from Paris, Toulouse, The Hague, Mayence, Metz, and Bonn—and even from a French lodge in Frankfurt itself [17]—attended the ceremonies.

The description of the installation and the texts of the speeches —most in French with a few in German—delivered on that occasion were printed. From these records we can ascertain how the guests and hosts evaluated the event in which they had played a part. Most of the speeches were encomiums of Freemasonry—the soil destined for the cultivation of brotherly love, for the promotion of virtue, and so on. Here and there, however, the remarks are directed to the present and its background, as for instance the observations of the delegates from the French Amis Réunis of Mayence and from one of the Paris lodges.

The first speaker described the occasion as a day of victory for reason, in that members of different groupings, whom prejudice and religious fanaticism had driven apart, were now united. The second praised "the great nation, which had previously possessed a fruitful land, but is now scattered over the various continents of the earth," yet had nevertheless succeeded in preserving its unity, its freedom, its mode of worship. Membership in the Freemasons, however, from now on obliged the sons of this nation "to double and redouble their efforts, so as to broaden more and more the dimensions of their moral perfection [*les relations de la morale perfectionnée*] by means of a deep feeling of brotherhood. . . . Now all men are equal." [18]

A special significance was ascribed to the event by a Christian member, Franz J. Molitor, who had joined the lodge a few months after its inception.[19] In Molitor the lodge had acquired a personality of intellectual stature, one able to view matters in their philosophical perspective. His remarks seem to vacillate between mourning over the decline of the old world and rejoicing at the dawn of the new. The old world consisted of a unified existential totality: state, religion, and mysticism (Masonry). The advantage of the new world lay in the abolition of the notion that there existed "a natural, absolute division between men. All classes are beginning to look upon each other as brothers, and on the differences forced upon them by circumstances as having no substance. And so the illumination of the Enlightenment penetrates to all classes of society, and estates that diverge in the State return united in the world of the spirit." In the forging of this unity, Molitor assigned an important role to the Freemasons. In the political events of his time—the Napoleonic heyday—he discerned the renewal of the face of the earth.[20]

The initiation of the lodge could have been a source of gratification to the Jewish members. Whether their rejoicing was complete is rather doubtful. As has been shown, the Christians present at the affair were either the few unconventional individuals who had joined the lodge or else were representatives from abroad. As for the Frankfurt long-standing lodges, the Loge zur Einigkeit and the Socrates zur Standhaftigkeit, they had certainly been invited, but had sent no delegates, stating explicitly that they did not recognize the new lodge as legitimate.[21]

Permission to visit other lodges was denied to the members of L'aurore Naissante, even if they presented themselves as members of a different lodge. Geisenheimer and Baruch had obtained membership in a Mayence lodge, which was subsequently invited to attend a celebration of the Socrates lodge in Frankfurt. The invitation was accepted. Among the others, the two Jews were also appointed to represent the Mayence lodge on that occasion. The Frankfurt hosts, however, refused to admit the delegation to their meeting hall on the grounds that two of the representatives belonged to the unacceptable L'aurore Naissante. The delegates protested to the Grand Orient in Paris, and a great many letters were exchanged between Frankfurt and Paris.[22] Nor was this an isolated instance. Jewish members of lodges authorized by the French Grand Orient were confronted with refusals on the part of German lodges. Complaints reached Paris from the Grand Lodge of Baden and from others under French patronage. The entire matter was brought up for discussion in the Grand Orient, which rendered as its considered and authoritative ruling that lodges should not occupy themselves with political or religious questions. A candidate's application for admission should be considered on its merits, without reference to the person's religion.[23] In the deliberations preceding the decision, the question was put whether a Jew could be raised to the fourth, Scottish degree, which possessed a definitely Christian character. The opinion was expressed that a Jew could not, and would not want to, be accepted into that degree—but the Grand Lodge members concurred that this deficiency should exert no influence in respect of the first three degrees.[24] A proclamation issued on June 19, 1811, brought the views of the Grand Orient to the attention of the lodges, but avoided all mention of the problem of the fourth degree. It merely stated the principle that a man's adherence to a particular religion was not to affect his rights to membership in the Masonic movement.

Although the course of events which led to the formation of the new lodge is self-explanatory, its significance becomes even more profound when viewed against the background of the historical events affecting the Jewish community at large. 1807, which witnessed the founding of the "Jewish lodge," was just one year after the old order in Frankfurt had been abolished, after an independent, royal city had become transformed into a minor principality under the tutelage of Napoleon. This change marked the time for the Jews of that city to begin their struggle for the same rights that Jews in France and the other regions overrun by the Napoleonic armies had begun to enjoy. Hampered, hindered, and delayed by the hesitancy of Prince Dalberg and the obduracy of the city council, the struggle continued till 1811.

The years 1806 and 1807 also saw the convening of Jewish dignitaries and of the "Sanhedrin" in Paris. Frankfurt Jewry participated by sending a letter of encouragement and by dispatching a delegation of two members,[25] one of whom, Isaac Hildesheim (who later changed his name to Justus Hiller), was a founder of the new lodge. Some of the Jewish community viewed the latest events as harbingers of a radical change in their political and social status. Among these no doubt were the members of the new lodge. The proceedings of the group, like all other Masonic activities, were conducted with secrecy. At their very first meeting the members had pledged each other to silence.[26] The lodge had never entertained any declared political or social objective; nevertheless, its founding was a sign of the times, and it was so interpreted by the more conservative members of the Jewish community. According to information emanating from Geisenheimer himself, he was placed under the ban by the rabbi of Frankfurt, Zvi Hirsch Horowitz, who lifted it only when he became convinced of the sincerity of Geisenheimer's motives.[27] Geisenheimer might have exaggerated in recounting the difficulties he had to surmount—no actual ban may have been pronounced against him.[28] His account does, however, contain an audible echo of the opposition of the conservative elements to this bold innovation.

The period was one of radical change. What had seemed most improbable before, now became an accomplished fact. Despite opposition from within and from without, the lodge became consolidated within a very short time. I have a copy of the membership list for 1811 [29] and the roster of lodges with whom the L'aurore Naissante had succeeded in establishing contact, either through mutual recognition or through the exchange of information. From these lists, we can gauge the measure of success achieved by the lodge on all fronts. In that year the lodge numbered eighty members, the overwhelming majority of whom resided in or near Frankfurt. Their proximity to the lodge permitted active participation in all its affairs. A significant part was played by those who had settled in Frankfurt in the last generation, like Geisenheimer himself.[30] The old, established families were also well represented: the Adlers, Speyers, Reisses, and Sichels. Even the richest and most powerful Frankfurt families were included: the Ellisons, Hanaus, Goldschmidts, and Rothschilds.[31]

Solomon Meir (who afterward moved to Vienna), the second of the five Rothschild brothers, became a member if only for a short time.[32] Several members were over forty-five years old at the time, but the majority were between twenty-five and thirty-five. It may confidently be asserted that the lodge possessed a particular attraction for a specific type among the younger generation. As for Geisenheimer, we have already stated that his motives in joining the Freemasons were to create some framework within which Jews and Christians could approach closer to one another, and perhaps even become united. Naturally not all the members entertained his far-reaching intentions. Such aspirations were quite typical, however, of intellectuals and energetic men of affairs who were eager to hasten the process which had begun to transform the Jewish community in the last generation or two.[33] Of these, there were two or three in this lodge: Geisenheimer, Michael Hess,[34] principal of the Philanthropin school, and Justus Hildesheim (Hiller), who had raised his voice in the counsels of the Paris "Sanhedrin" [35] and who had been appointed Orator to the Lodge. In the address he delivered on the occasion of the founding of the lodge he too emphasized the common foundation of all religions, which differed from one another as did the diverse languages with which all expressed the same thoughts.[36] Another, who joined as early as in 1808, was Dr. Ludwig Baruch (later Börne); but he withdrew in 1811 for some time,[37] and so his name does not appear on the roster of that year. Most of the members were engaged in commerce. Having received a practical education, they were well versed in worldly affairs. Without being committed to any world-shattering ideals, they sought new areas of social contact beyond, if possible, the barriers of the isolated Jewish community.

In its social compositon and in its spiritual goals the lodge differed from the other marginal associations which had, in the previous generation, sought to include both Jews and gentiles. It is almost obvious that, in choosing between limiting their degrees to the first three and instituting the higher ones, or between humanistic aspirations and mystic or quasi-mystic doctrines, the lodge decided in favor of the former in each instance. During the very first stage of its existence, it was proposed that the Scottish rite with its high degrees be instituted, but this idea was summarily rejected.[38] The members experienced no special craving either for unraveling

61

secrets or for attaining spiritual elevation. Their goals were far more modest: to discover some social environment offering possibilities for associating with Christians, through the cultivation of brotherhood and friendship based on the belief in the brotherhood of man entailed in monotheism. The new lodge fulfilled this function. Precisely because it was from its inception a reaction to the exclusion of Jews from other lodges, it strove to assume a nondenominational character. Within a short period of time it succeeded, during the French hegemony, in achieving its aims. Of the eighty members of the lodge in 1811, twenty-five were Christians.[39] The latter were accorded a distinct priority in the managing of the lodge's affairs; it was headed from 1809 to 1812 by a Christian, Josef Severus, and five other Christian members occupied high offices in the nineteen-member executive committee.

The desire to accord the lodge a nondenominational character is especially noticeable in the election of honorary members, men living elsewhere whom the lodge chose—presumably with their consent—to dignify with such an appointment. Of the fifty who received this recognition, only five can positively be identified as Jews. All the rest were Christians, and we shall presently take account of their national and social origins. The Morgenröthe could justifiably be proud of its connections with other lodges. Seventeen maintained reciprocal relations (*affiliés*) with it, that is, these lodges were prepared to conduct joint activities with it or to allow each other's members to attend meetings as visitors. All seventeen were located either in Paris or in west German capitals which had fallen under French control (such as Mayence, Cologne, and Mannheim). Twenty-seven other lodges corresponded with the Morgenröthe, some from as far away as Leipzig, Dresden, Nuremberg, Hannover, Bremen, Amsterdam, and even Berlin (Du Bellier).[40] Whether the lodge was recognized as Jewish or not, it succeeded in attracting gentile members and in gaining access to gentile lodges.

Impressive as this success may have been, it was only an outflanking maneuver rather than a direct victory. Only one of the twenty-five Christian members was a native of Frankfurt. The honorary members, who lived in other areas, either possessed French names or were French soldiers or officials residing in Germany. In those years a circle of admirers of France and of Napoleon in particular, had emerged in Germany. They believed that the future of their country was bound up with the success of the new Emperor. Prince Dalberg, the governor of Frankfurt from 1806 to 1813, is an outstanding example of this circle.[41] They adopted new, French attitudes and were prepared to conduct themselves accordingly in their social relations. This accounts for the ability of the Frankfurt lodge to gain the favor of gentiles of the highest rank.

The new outlook did not by any means penetrate to the general citizenry. Its population was still locked within its traditional organizations and tied to conservative ideas. The two older lodges in Frankfurt also still persisted in their stubborn refusal to recognize the Jewish lodge. They now even invented some device specifically aimed at forbidding the acceptance of Jews. In 1811 new ceremonial procedures were introduced in the Eclectic Covenant, which was headed by the two Frankfurt lodges. At the initiation ceremonies this question was now addressed to the candidate for membership: "Do you acknowledge that religion which was the first to open the heart of man to the desire [*Wohlwollen*] for human brotherhood and which we call, after its sublime founder, the Christian [faith]?" [42] Until now Jews had been excluded de facto; now they were barred de jure.

That year the citizens of Frankfurt had been compelled to consent to the granting of civil rights to Jews. They were powerless to resist the force of circumstances, the French conquest. Yet they made no effort to conceal their chagrin at the Jewish success, and they translated their feelings into action in areas beyond state control. One expression of this resentment was the device of that year excluding Jews from the Masonic lodges. The members of the older lodges even tried to reverse the process of events. They petitioned Prince Dalberg to grant them the exclusive right to maintain lodges in the city. "Only so will it be possible to remove French influence and to send the Jews back to the synagogue." [43]

How short-lived the Jewish success was became manifest with the political changes that followed in the wake of Napoleon's defeat. All the circles that had emerged under the rule of the Emperor and on which the members of the Jewish lodge had pinned their hopes vanished in an instant. Even though lodges were obliged to keep their affairs free of political involvement, the reliance of the Jewish lodge on the authority of the Grand Lodge of Paris now appeared

63

as a blemish. No sooner had Napoleon suffered his first reverses on the battlefield than the members hastened to eradicate the words "under the patronage of the Orient of France." [44] Once the French retreated from the conquered territories it was decided formally to sever relations with Paris. Even in the internal affairs of the lodge attitudes became adjusted to the new conditions. If in previous years the members had indulged in lavishing praise in speech and song upon human brotherhood, and even at times in mentioning Napoleon as the uniter of peoples,[45] they now transferred their highest approbation to the conquerors of Napoleon, the liberators of the German fatherland.[46] Expressions of patriotic pride in the German War of Liberation stole into the songs of the Jewish Masons. Attachment to the Grand Orient was no longer desirable. It is not surprising that the members cast about for some connection, however tenuous, with German patronage. This was not easy. They had nothing to hope for as far as the other Frankfurt lodges were concerned. But light seemed to emanate from another quarter. Since 1812 the lodge had appointed as its head Franz Josef Molitor, a close personal acquaintance of Ephraim Joseph Hirschfeld. The latter still maintained his connections with Carl von Hessen of Schleswig, who had been accepted as the head of all German Freemasons. Hirschfeld arranged for the two to meet, and Molitor set out for Schleswig, his mission being to obtain a new constitution and authorization for the lodge.[47]

Whether Carl von Hessen knew that the lodge represented by Molitor was for the most part composed of Jews later became a subject for debate.[48] At all events, Molitor returned from his journey much more richly rewarded than his fellow members could have dared to expect. First of all, he brought with him the constitution for a lodge of the first three degrees to be named after Saint John. Secondly he was given a document authorizing the formation of a lodge to be conducted according to the Scottish rite, to which the lodge of Saint John would be subordinate. In theory, the lodge now had been raised to a degree higher than that on which it was maintained during its French affiliation.

For the Jews, however, there was an obvious disadvantage. The Scottish rite was distinctly Christian in character, and, though the fact had not been stated explicitly, it was understood that only those who acknowledged Christianity could find their place in it.

And even the lodge of the first three degrees leaned toward Christianity. During the French affiliation, candidates for admission took their oath, after the French custom, on the constitution of the Freemasons; [49] now they were forced to swear allegiance on the Gospel of Saint John, in accordance with the practice obtaining in the German lodges. In addition, it was laid down that the two highest offices, the Master of the lodge and the Orator were to be reserved for Christians.[50] The Jewish members felt trapped. They were subjected to severe restrictions in their own home. Some members were not prepared to submit to the directive that they swear on the Gospel of Saint John. When Molitor submitted the constitution to the lodge, they gave notice of their intention to challenge many of its paragraphs. Their appeal was brought to the notice of the Prince. Very possibly it was only then that he realized that he had granted authorization to a lodge which, in the composition of its members, was basically Jewish. He was, however, prepared to compromise. The restrictions in regard to the Master remained in force, but he would allow a change in the administering of the oath: Chapter 14 of Genesis could be substituted for the Gospel of Saint John.[51]

It is not difficult to guess at the cause of this choice. In that chapter of Genesis, the name of Melchizedek appears. As we have seen before, this was the name given to the lodges founded by the Asiatic Brethren, and these lodges differed from those bearing the name of Saint John in that they were open to Jew and gentile alike. Carl von Hessen himself had applied this distinction during his connections with the Asiatic Order. He had allowed a Hamburg lodge composed of Jews to function on the condition that the members be known as Melchizedek Masons.[52] In choosing the chapter mentioning Melchizedek as a substitute for the Gospel, he was hinting at that very condition.

The new proposal did not placate the Jewish members. They saw themselves falling from the frying pan into the fire. If the oath on the Gospel was an outrage of their religious conscience, the new one branded them as Jews. They had founded their lodge to create some framework that would stand above religious difference, and now the distinctions had been set forth in all their stark clarity in the very rites of the lodge. An attempt was made to remove this obstacle. A delegation of three members was sent to negotiate with

65

Prince Carl. Molitor was the leader, and one of the three, Frank by name, was apparently Jewish. Yet this delegation succeeded only in obtaining concessions that were in effect a further compromise. Carl agreed that Jewish candidates should take their oath on a Bible with the Old and New Testaments bound together. The Frankfurt lodge was duly authorized to accept Jews and to raise them to the third degree. By contrast, the Scottish rite was to be restricted, and it was expressly stipulated that here only Christians could enter. The Jews were assured, however, that parallel degrees would be instituted for them. In addition, the document of authorization stated that the assent of the Prince was granted with the hope that, through the acceptance of Jews in the lodge, "it would be possible to show them the path to the light"—the path, naturally, to the acceptance of Christianity.[53] Clearly the Prince and the Christian members of the lodge, among them Molitor himself, did not unreservedly acknowledge that Jews were fully fit for Masonic activities. They also apparently clung to the opinion that for the leading positions in the Frankfurt lodge only Christians could be eligible.

The conduct of Carl von Hessen in the affair is hardly surprising. Although he had been an ardent member of the Asiatic Order and had sought to insert Cabalistic elements into the Masonic pattern of symbolism, he never had yielded on the preferred position of Christianity as compared with Judaism. Whether the nature of the request addressed to him had been clear from the first, or whether it only later became apparent that he was dealing with a Jewish lodge, he could not now come to terms with the situation except by way of concession and compromise. Molitor's attitude on the other hand lacked consistency. He had originally joined the Jewish lodge and subscribed to its principles—the complete equality of Jew and gentile—on the assumption that within the lodge all religious differences would be ignored. In the address delivered at the opening ceremonies in 1808, he had upheld humanistic principles. In the later period, however, Molitor came to view Masonry as a many-storied construction, the upper floors of which could only be reached by an acceptance of the symbols of the Christian religion. His position, then, had changed. In the end, he developed a philosophical-historical system consisting of a synthesis of the Jewish Cabala and the beliefs and ideas of the Catholic Church.[54] Molitor's retreat from a simple, humanistic standpoint occurred between 1808 and

1815. He himself had stated that he had begun to lean in the direction of Christianity even before his trip to Schleswig. His meeting with the Landgrave Carl ("only through him did I become a Christian"[55]) completed his change of heart. Here is the explanation for his attitude toward the new Masonic constitution, which no longer maintained the complete equality of the adherents of the Jewish faith with the rest of the Freemasons.

Hirschfeld's function and position in the entire episode are somewhat mysterious, though by no means inexplicable. As has been stated, he was the intermediary between Molitor and Prince Carl von Hessen, and he did not cease his behind-the-scenes manipulations even afterward. He reported to Prince Carl on what was transpiring in the lodge and attempted to induce the Jewish brethren to accept what, they felt, conflicted with their religious principles. We know of this from a letter written by Hirschfeld on April 6, 1816, addressed to one of the non-Jewish members,[56] and the information is corroborated by Molitor's testimony concerning certain details of Hirschfeld's biography.[57] According to this letter, Hirschfeld made an attempt to introduce the rites of the Asiatic Order in the Frankfurt lodge. We can therefore accept as reliable the information emanating from a hostile source that, while negotiations with Carl von Hessen were still in progress, Hirschfeld himself initiated several members in the Asiatic rite,[58] and that his failure filled him with grief.[59] We are familiar with Hirschfeld's *weltanschauung* from his letters (in print and in manuscript).[60] This was a Jewish-Christian syncretism based on the Cabalistic system of ideas, a conception which had formed the foundation for the Asiatic Order from its very beginning. Hirschfeld adhered loyally to this view, and when he came into contact with the Jewish lodge in Frankfurt he thought that he had discovered fertile soil where he could implant his doctrines. It is not surprising that he was deeply disappointed when the members of the lodge rejected his ideas and publicly disowned him.

This disavowal of Hirschfeld came as the result of a pamphlet published in 1816 attacking the Jewish lodge while the negotiations were going on. The anonymous author, known to have been Dr. Johann Christian Ehrmann of Frankfurt, was thoroughly acquainted with the lodge and its difficulties. As far as he was concerned, the very fact that it was founded as an affiliate of the Grand Orient of

67

Paris during the French conquest rendered it suspect, and he insinuated that the lodge had repaid, as it were, the French police for the courtesy extended to it. He jeered at the panic that had seized the Jews when Napoleon was finally overthrown, and he described their frantic efforts to find a German patron for themselves through Hirschfeld's intercession. Fully grasping the syncretistic nature of Hirschfeld's conception, he accused the latter of plotting by this Jewish admixture to contaminate both Freemasonry and Christianity.[61] The entire argument was pervaded by a hatred of Jews and Judaism in general, and was openly inflammatory in nature, after the manner prevalent in anti-Jewish publications in Frankfurt and the rest of Germany in that year.[62] Ehrmann's specific contribution to anti-Semitic literature was to cast suspicion on the Jews as penetrating into the Masonic movement so as to convert it into an instrument for world domination.[63] The title of the brochure loudly proclaimed its purpose: *Das Judenthum in der Maurerey; eine Warnung an alle deutschen Logen* (Jews in Freemasonry, a warning to all the German lodges).

The members of the Morgenröthe could not afford to ignore this attack. In reply they published an excerpt of the minutes of the lodge meeting held on August 13, 1816,[64] which expressed their vigorous protest against the allegations of this agitator. Concerning the aims of their lodge, they declared that it had confined itself to the three basic degrees, and had operated in conformity with the principles of the Masonic constitution, the purpose of which was to "foster true culture and humanity among men." The lodge had never occupied itself with speculations or alchemistic pursuits, rabbinic or otherwise. No individual by the name of Hirschfeld was a member.

This declaration avoided any reference to previous hesitations about introducing the Scottish rite, and it denied all knowledge of Hirschfeld as if he had never had any connection with the lodge. True, the entire episode now belonged to the past. By the time the reply to Ehrmann was made public, all connections with Carl von Hessen had been cut off, and there was no longer any need for Hirschfeld to act as intermediary. The delegation headed by Molitor had returned in the middle of June,[65] and immediately afterward elections were held for the "Grand Master of the Chair." Despite the stipulation that this office be reserved for Christians, a Jew, Carl Leopold Goldschmidt, was elected to fill it.[66] In reaction to this choice Molitor brought a notice from the Prince withdrawing his authorization and ordering the lodge to disband.[67] The members refused to obey, and sought to gain time by endeavoring to establish direct contact with the Prince. In reality they despaired of continuing to function under his auspices, and were looking about for help from other quarters. Goldschmidt succeeded in communicating with the Mother Lodge of London. On May 22, 1817, he was able to report to his colleagues the good news that he had in his possession a letter of authorization signed by August Frederick, Duke of Sussex, which empowered the Frankfurt brethren to operate as a Masonic lodge without any restriction.[68]

This recognition seemed a signal victory. The conflicts with Carl von Hessen had placed the very existence of the lodge in jeopardy. Now, by virtue of its connection with London, it could safely continue to function as fully authorized. Yet its being once more compelled to seek support from abroad only served to emphasize the weakness of its position. What the lodge really wanted to achieve, ultimately, was the recognition of the local lodges in Frankfurt and nearby states, and the admission of its brethren as welcome guests, perhaps even as full-fledged members. Yet the Zur Einigkeit formally disputed the validity of the London authorization. This lodge, as we have seen, was granted the power by the Mother Lodge of London to grant authorization to other lodges in the Frankfurt region. The members argued that by acceding to the request of the Morgenröthe, the Mother Lodge had broken its signed agreement and committed an illegal act. To this allegation, the Mother Lodge replied that the Einigkeit itself had exceeded its authority by instituting, in contravention of the principles of the Mother Lodge, the statute of exclusion against Jews. Nor did the controversy end there. Relations between the two became progressively more strained until they were finally sundered. The Frankfurt Zur Einigkeit, together with the Socrates lodge which was bound to it by the Eclectic Covenant, proclaimed itself an independent Mother Lodge in 1823, and was recognized as such by the other German Mother Lodges.[69] A circular letter renouncing connections with London in consequence of the authorization granted the Morgenröthe bristled with anti-Jewish animosity that had finally succeeded in breaking through to the ranks of the Freemasons themselves.[70] The Christianity of Ma-

69

sonry was no longer advanced as the pretext for denying access to Jews. Now Judaism was branded as the disqualification. It is common knowledge, the circular stated, "that the essence of Judaism cannot be reconciled with Freemasonry," and it protested against "Jewish interference in Freemasonry"—a wording both venomous and insulting.

The strained relations between London and the Zur Einigkeit on account of the Jewish lodge did not ingratiate the Jewish lodge with its non-Jewish counterparts. Even lodges that had no formal cause for complaint against the Grand Lodge of London resented its interference and refused to recognize its authorization. German lodges near and far refused to have anything to do with the Frankfurt Morgenröthe, and protests and warnings not only emanated from the district lodge of Frankfurt but were issued in the name of the three Grand Lodges of Berlin.[71]

Condemned to utter isolation, the Frankfurt lodge became almost totally Jewish. Once the Prince withdrew his patronage, Molitor and his associates left and formed a lodge of their own.[72] A few Christians still remained behind.[73] These served as a front, symbolizing the nondenominational character of the lodge when the occasion arose. In 1820 the lodge entertained an important guest, Mirza Abdul Khan, the Persian ambassador. The reception committee consisted of three members: a Catholic, a Protestant, and a Jew. The Grand Master of the Chair delivered an eloquent address on the function of Freemasonry, namely "to unite in a brotherly, purely humanistic covenant that which differences of tribe, nation, and mode of worship could divide but not split asunder."[74] But such events and declarations could not rescue the lodge from isolation. Members who tried, by virtue of their belonging to this recognized lodge, to join in the activities of other lodges in their city or elsewhere, were met with a firm refusal. The Morgenröthe members were entitled to invoke the protection of the Mother Lodge in London, which could have repaid in kind the refusal to admit members enjoying its patronage. Such an attempt was made, and in 1820 the Mother Lodge sent a warning to the five Hamburg lodges: if they persisted in denying admission to members of the Frankfurt lodge, the same treatment would be meted out to their members in England.[75] These pressure tactics, however, achieved no tangible results.

The members of the Jewish lodge found some consolation in

their own activities. Their strong cohesion conferred benefits upon them, even in areas beyond the scope of Masonic activities, and their dependence on their own lodge served as a basis for organized mutual aid. Already in 1819, they had founded their Sustentation-Fond (mutual aid fund) which was open to paid-up members upon the additional payment of an entrance fee of 100 guilders. The purpose of the fund was to assist members in time of need, and to help support their widows and orphans when they died.[76] In the preamble to the constitution, the reason for restricting membership in the Fond to lodge brethren was given: Masons have a special duty to help one another.

Force of circumstances or free choice limited the lodge to intramural activities. It had abandoned for the time being any attempt to breach the walls of alienation surrounding it. And if it did so by design, this was with the full recognition of the existing reality. The exclusion of Jews permeated all public life in Germany. Struggling against the status quo offered no prospects of success. The student societies, known as *burschenschaften,* after many debates and much hesitation decided upon the exclusion of Jews from their ranks.[77] All types of organizations, from learned societies to sports clubs and newspaper-reading circles, enacted their statutes of restriction.[78] As for the Freemasons, the question of Christian principle was never absent from their deliberations and found its way into all their literary organs.[79] Here the problem revolved round the very definition of the aims and essence of the entire Order. Yet even in that epoch, there was no complete dearth of weighty opinion which sought to base Freemasonry on elements independent of any positive religion. Obviously the members of the Frankfurt lodge derived encouragement from such openly expressed views,[80] just as they drew support from the declaration of the London Mother Lodge that the exclusion of members from lodges on account of religion was an "un-Masonic act." In 1827 the Frankfurt lodge issued a circular—the work of the intellectuals among the members: Michael Hess, Jacob Weil, Michael Creizenach, and Ludwig Börne—containing an exposition of the principles followed by the lodge in conducting its Masonic activities.[81] The circular protested vehemently against the "mysticism" that was penetrating Masonry, where mysticism was equated with Christian content. Yet again no perceptible results were achieved. Nor did any positive results emerge in consequence of the views of

71

Christian Freemasons who tried to draw a distinction between their adherence to the Masonic movement and their loyalties to their own religion. For all practical purposes the principle of Christian exclusiveness was securely entrenched in the German Freemason movement during those years.

During Revolution and Reaction

A great many events affecting freemasonry and the Jews occurred in Frankfurt and the evidence left behind makes it possible to describe what took place in considerable detail. Yet there is no lack of data on what transpired in other cities as well, and we are able to present a comprehensive summary of Masonic action on the Jewish problem in those localities. This summary will show that what happened in Frankfurt was not the result of random, individual, action but the expression of a historical trend which involved both Jewish and non-Jewish society at the time.

In 1790 a Mason named Johann Joachim Christoph Bode reported: "The question whether a Jew was acceptable as a Freemason" was taken up publicly.[1] Bode was referring in this remark to the Asiatic Order controversy described in Chapter III. But "public" did not mean the people at large but the Masonic public; it included at that time, the period of the French Revolution, a recognizable section of cultured society. In this community Masonic literature, which consisted of circular letters, printed excerpts from their minutes, and so on, was disseminated. Appearing in that literature once, a question would become an integral part of the Masonic tradition. If until now lodges had been able to decide ad hoc whether to accept a certain Jew as member, they would henceforth be compelled to consider the entire issue as one of principle.

Indeed, during the French Revolution and Napoleonic hegemony, the lodges became increasingly preoccupied with this particular problem. The cities of Magdeburg,[2] Brunswick,[3] Mayence,[4] Cassel,[5] Göttingen, Eschwege, Berlin, Hamburg,[6] Leipzig,[7] Hildesheim, Heiligenstadt, Nordhausen, Einbeck, Ulm,[8] and others are mentioned as localities where Jews were nominated for membership. Whether they were accepted or rejected, the evidence is definite that in all these places Jews were eager to join local Masonic lodges. All the decisions—except the constitution of the membership which is not known to us—were dependent upon the stand taken by the Mother Lodge to which the particular lodge was affiliated. The "French" lodges founded by the Grand Orient of Paris, such as the des Arts et de l'Amitié in Cassel [9] (1809) and the Les Amis Réunis in

Mayence,[10] accepted Jews either of their own volition or under the pressure of the liberal Mother Lodge. A tolerant attitude toward Jews was also adopted by the Grand Lodge of Hamburg. It had long followed the English rite and, during the French hegemony— from 1806 onward—conducted the lodges under its jurisdiction in the same manner.[11]

Such obstacles and barriers as were erected were the work of Berlin, where three Grand Lodges functioned at that time. One, the Royal York, followed the English rite; the others, Die Grosse Landesloge von Deutschland and the Grosse National Mutterloge zu den drei Weltkugeln, adopted patterns of their own creation. All enjoyed the patronage of the King of Prussia, for which privilege they were obliged to submit to the constant surveillance of the government in regard to both the composition of their membership and their current activities.[12] These three Mother Lodges held undisputed sway over the Freemasons of Prussia, since the existence of any individual lodge was conditional upon its acceptance of the authority of one of the Berlin Mother Lodges. Even when individual affiliates existed beyond the borders of Prussia, they were bound by the principles governing the Mother Lodge.

Paradoxically, it was in Berlin, the very center where Jews and Christians first began, in the day of Moses Mendelssohn, to come closer to one another socially, that the most determined opposition to the admission of Jews became crystallized. The hardening began in the eighties, as we have seen. From then on, the attitude persisted unchanged, and even became intensified during the French Revolution and conquest, when the number of attempts made by Jews to enter Berlin-affiliated lodges sharply increased. In 1806, the National Mutterloge was still somewhat hesitant concerning the reply to be given to its Magdeburg affiliate which had applied for permission to accept a Jew as a member. Finally, the decision was rendered that no Jew be accepted even if he were to convert. The Jewish problem reached such proportions in those years that the three Mother Lodges saw fit, in 1808, to engage in joint consultations. Together they arrived at the ruling that "no Jew may be admitted to the Order, nor may any Jew, admitted elsewhere, become affiliated with it." As for Jewish Masons from other localities being allowed to attend as visitors, here the Mother Lodges were not altogether consistent. The constitution of 1799 had prohibited even such visits. The 1806 ruling communicated to Magdeburg now granted permission, but it was stipulated that a careful investigation first be made of the visitor's personal fitness. The conference of the three Mother Lodges left this question open.[13] No agreement apparently could be reached on how far the restriction could be extended.

In their attitude toward Jews, the Prussian lodges were at variance with the trends prevailing at that time. The very same year that the three Berlin lodges reasserted their obdurate opposition, a proposal was submitted to the King of Prussia for the amelioration of the condition of the Jews; four years later this proposal was enacted as the first edict of emancipation.[14] Nevertheless, the two tendencies were by no means contradictory; to some extent they were complementary. The granting of citizenship to Jews became a political necessity once it was realized that a social order based on rigid distinction of estates could no longer maintain itself. The structure of the modern state was based on the direct dependence of the citizenry upon the central authority, without any intermediate classes or corporations intervening. Yet it never occurred to the conservatives that they would have to abandon their exclusive cohesion in their own society and groups. On the contrary, the course of events indicates here, just as in Frankfurt, that the tendency to break down barriers on the political and legal plane, produced the reaction of withdrawal behind firmer barriers on the intimate, social plane.

75

There was no lack of excuses for keeping Jews out of the lodges. We have no source material of the time directly reporting the discussions, yet where the lodges were directly involved the problem must have excited earnest and lively attention.[15] Those in favor of admitting Jews relied in their argument on the original Masonic conception, that no distinction was to be made between one man and another on account of his origin or religious affiliation; this idea fitted neatly into the revolutionary slogans which were spreading abroad because of the appeal of their inherent validity and the political pressure behind them.[16] The opposing opinions must be reconstructed from the few extant literary remains available.

The same Johann Joachim Christoph Bode,[17] who attested to the public proportions the problem had assumed, also took sides in it. He denied harboring any hostility against the Jews "as a nation." He also testified from personal experience to the existence of individuals who, in their moral character, were worthy to keep company with Masonic brethren. His first concern was that Jewish Masons might suffer persecution at the hands of their own community, who would by no means remain indifferent to the defection of their coreligionists. Indeed, according to Bode, adherence to the Jewish religion and membership in the Masonic fraternity were in blatant contradiction. Only if the movement were to amend its ritual could Jews join with clear conscience. Such a change was inconceivable. Any Jew, therefore, who became a Freemason would be guilty of disrespect for the practices of his own religion, and this would constitute an indication of his levity toward a matter of grave importance. In a society such as the Masons, which strove to incorporate within itself the elite among men, this frivolity would offer sufficient grounds to disqualify an applicant from membership.[18]

Similarly, another participant in the debate, a member of the Balduin zur Linde of Leipzig, declared that "a Jew as such is incapable, on account of his religious principles, of becoming a Freemason." Another argued that "the Masonic covenant of brotherhood was founded by Christians for Christians; the Jew who becomes a Freemason will cease being a Jew, since he will no longer be able to observe the Mosaic and Talmudic codes; his own religion would forbid him to join the Freemasons." [19] The members of the Heiligenstadt lodge maintained that the Jews in their town were morally inferior because of their adherence to the Jewish religion, and there was no hope of Jews' being accepted in the Masonic fraternity unless they were first baptized. Members of the Einbeck lodge disqualified Jews because they possessed undesirable traits which they were powerless to change.[20]

It is not difficult to break these arguments down into their constitutive elements. First of all, Judaism here is presented in its traditional guise, its outward aspect being the observance of the practical precepts which hindered the mixing of the Jew in gentile society. The argument was not fallacious; at most it lagged behind in its awareness of the progress of the historical process. For precisely in that generation, a new Jew became distinguishable, one who found meaning in his Judaism without strictly adhering to its traditional observances. To anyone not watching the course of events closely, abandoning the patterns of accepted Jewish living without accepting the tenets of Christianity would not have appeared as a transition to a new pattern of Judaism, but rather as the casting off of all religion.

Yet these arguments also contained elements of that negative appraisal of Jews and Judaism which had been handed down from previous generations. Judaism was presented as a religion of rigid, petrified forms, and the Jew as a creature devoid of ethical or brotherly feeling toward any person not of his kind or his community. This stereotype, molded by popular, religious, and literary traditions of long standing, had been reinforced by the Jew's appearance, which seemed to set him apart from his fellow men.

Such stereotypes are not easily destroyed. The resistance encountered by Jews entering European society through the wide breaches in the ghetto walls, is striking testimony to the power of endurance of an image ingrained in the consciousness of a group. All these contentions were constantly brought up wherever the discussion turned to the possibility of allowing a Jew to penetrate into an area previously closed to him. The ensuing controversy was merely another variation of the general debate raging on the issues of emancipation and citizenship for Jews. In Freemasonry, however, the stereotype was guarded by a more strongly fortified position. There was more to lose. While in the area of civil rights the destruction of the stereotype could only have resulted in formal rights being conferred on Jews, in Freemasonry it would have allowed them to join the company of an intimate group, of a brotherhood of the elect.

77

This state of affairs and its accompanying overtones changed with the withdrawal of the French and the breakthrough of the spirit of nationalism into German political and social life. Even in the political field—in the granting of civil rights to the Jews—a retrogression set in, and this was even more pronounced in the field of social integration. The exclusion of Jews could now find support in the general, prevailing mood which regarded Germanism and Christianity as synonymous. Anyone seeking to distinguish between the two seemed to contradict the obvious.[21] Nor did this new outlook fail to affect the Masons. Here and there lodges were obliged to rule on actual cases. And the Frankfurt lodge was not the only one to disaffiliate from the Mother Lodge of Paris. In Cassel the Freemasons banded together in the state-wide organization of Kur-

Hessen under the patronage of the Royal York of Berlin. Jews who had gained admission during the French hegemony were summarily expelled. The members of the Des Arts et de l'Amitié applied to the new Mother Lodge for permission to function as a special Jewish lodge, but the request apparently was not granted.[22] Yet some Jews still dared to present themselves as candidates for admission to the Masonic order. Those who had volunteered for active duty in the armies which had crushed Napoleon were boldest in demanding their rights.[23] So in Hannover, in 1816, Ensign M. A. Meyer von Landbataillon applied to the lodge Zum schwarzen Bären. His case was referred to the district lodge in that city, from where the question was transferred to the Mother Lodge in Hamburg. The district lodges were in a quandary because they knew of no precedent, no Jew ever having been accepted in any of the affiliates. However, the Mother Lodge, which followed the English rite, expressed the opinion that, according to the Masonic constitution, no man's religion, whatever it might be, could bar him from being admitted to the Freemasons.[24] Apparently Ensign Meyer attained his goal; and we hear also of another lodge, the Brunswick, having two Jewish members.[25]

78

As in earlier times, the lodges also had to render decisions on the applications of Jewish Masons carrying membership certificates awarded to them abroad. Such members had the right to apply for membership in the local lodges or at least to seek permission to attend meetings as visitors. Long left in abeyance, this question was now revived by the force of events. After the establishment of the Jewish lodge in Frankfurt, and especially once it had received authorization from the London Mother Lodge in 1816, its members began to appear at lodges in other cities, and the lodge itself demanded recognition as a legitimate and authorized lodge. The other lodges tended to act restrictively, even in respect to allowing visits, as the Royal York proves. Among the Berlin lodges, it had previously been the most lenient. Its new constitution, adopted in 1815, however, contained a clause barring visits by Jews.[26] Nor will it surprise us to learn that the previous year the same lodge had turned down the request of the Cassel lodge for recognition as a special Jewish lodge.[27] In 1825 the Mutterloge published a summary, as it were, of its doctrines and directives. There the goals of Masonry were defined as the reconciliation of human beings with one another through the agency of religion, religion being identical with Christianity, whose different denominations were admonished to be tolerant to one another and not to be jealous of, or compete with, each other. Contrariwise, a Jew—a non-Christian in the terminology of that text—could find no place in the lodge, for immediately upon entry he would be confronted by the New Testament lying before him—to be used in swearing the Masonic oath—and as he advanced to higher degrees, he would find himself enveloped in a world of Christian symbols. Obviously aware that certain lodges did accept Jews, the authors of the summary undertook to guide the older Masons in explaining this fact to the new, inexperienced members. Such lodges as accepted Jews were of a different type, *toleranzlogen;* they treated Masonry lightly and only adhered to externals. Good and beneficial institutions where Jews, Moslems, and pagans could participate were quite conceivable, but such could never be Masonic lodges.[28]

At all events, we have concrete evidence that the Jewish problem, which absorbed the attention of German public opinion to the point of irritation in the year following the Congress of Vienna, also robbed the Freemasons of their rest. "The issue, whether a Freemason must necessarily only be one who accepts Christianity is now widely being debated especially in Germany, in a spirit of aversion [*Abneigung*] to Jews, and often with great bitterness," wrote Georg von Wedekind in 1818.[29] The point at issue, according to him, was the definition of the essence of Freemasonry; the bitterness, however, was aroused by anti-Jewish hatred.

In its open hostility to Jews and in its disqualification of them on the grounds that the inferior nature of Judaism was incompatible with the sublime essence of Freemasonry, Dr. Ehrmann's brochure (about which we learned in connection with the Frankfurt incident) was perhaps exceptional. He depicted Jews as the embodiment of the power of evil, which sought to penetrate, to corrupt, and to make Christian Freemasonry subservient to its own nefarious purposes. Yet an undertone of animosity and contempt was also discernible in the arguments of others seeking to deny Jews the right to join the Masonic fraternity. In an anonymous article appearing in the *Zeitschrift für Freimaurerei* in 1822, the Jews are depicted as a dissident element ("a state within a state") which refuses to acknowledge equal obligation toward strangers. "A Jew can never

79

love a Christian as intensely as he loves the members of his own faith; he will never do or feel for the former what he would do or feel for the latter . . . How can Christians and Jews in the lodges love and trust each other in brotherhood?" [30] Even Wedekind who had not reached completely unfavorable conclusions, argued that the ordinary Jew "is not commanded to act ethically except toward Jews; toward others he is only enjoined to act in accordance with the rules of political expediency." Nevertheless, the verdict on the Jews was not derived by direct, logical deduction from the current anti-Semitic literature, since it was now obvious that a new type of Jew had emerged who did not fit into what had commonly been conceived as the pattern of the eternal Jew. Neither the Jewish peddler nor the Talmud-permeated rabbi, whose inferiority and freakishness had made them the butt of prejudice, had ever applied for admission into the Masonic order, but the enlightened Jew, who had discarded these distinguishing features, acquired the same culture, and evinced the same conduct as other human beings. In any event, the acceptance of a candidate depended upon the appraisal of his individual character by those who had to vote on him. This consideration led Wedekind to conclude that no one deemed fit in respect of his personal worth should be denied membership on account of his Jewishness. Could admission be refused to Maimonides, Spinoza, and Mendelssohn, if they were to knock at the gates of the lodge? [31]

The author of the anonymous article mentioned earlier recoiled from such far-reaching conclusions. True, before his very eyes stood the new type of Jew whose aspirations toward Masonic ideals were above reproach; he had, of necessity, to make some concessions. He therefore agreed that such Jews should be allowed to form lodges of their own and in that way acquire the human perfection which Masonry was capable of evoking in its faithful adherents. Against the admission of Jews into Christian lodges, he adduced every conceivable argument. Jews who were thrust into Christian lodges were compelled to make infractions in their religion, and so were deficient in the virtue of loyalty. Although not identical with the Church, Freemasonry was interspersed with Christian symbols and concepts, and the two institutions were intimately connected. Jews were ipso facto excluded from Christian Masonry; the better and nobler among them realized that here was no place for them. All of Mendelssohn's Christian friends had been Freemasons, yet he had never made any attempt to gain admission to their Order. Those who tried to force themselves where they were not welcome were thereby rendered suspect of harboring impure motives and were despised, as well, by their Jewish brethren. Moreover, even if the gates of the lodges were opened only to such as were worthy, others would break in by force of their money and influence. The lodges would then become filled with unworthy individuals, "and we already find, without this, a sufficient number of doubtful persons in our lodges." [32]

In its obvious inconsistency, the article reflects the mood prevailing among the rank and file, who persisted in the practice of barring Jews and seized upon every pretext to justify their actions. Nevertheless, even in that period the voices of the proponents of the removal of all barriers were not reduced to silence. C. Lenning's *Encyclopädie der Freimaurerei* of 1824 gathered under the entry "Jew," the main points of the pro-Jewish opinions of the time.[33] The encyclopedia tended to follow in the footsteps of Karl Christian Friedrich Krause, who sought to find in Freemasonry a covenant comprehending all mankind (*menschenbund*).[34] It was the function of the lodge to inculcate friendship and brotherhood precisely among such persons who, if not for the Masonic union, would forever remain apart, separated from one another. The re-establishment of friendship and brotherhood is premised upon the cultivation of human virtue as such, included in which is the relation of each individual creature to his Creator. Such a capacity is possessed in equal measure by all men, including Jews. Krause was still infected with the prejudice against the old type of Judaism. "The laws and statutes of the Jews contradict pure humanism in certain respects." Yet he laid down that "many Jews already exist who in their heart and soul have abandoned the antihumanistic laws and statutes." Such Jews were fit for admission as Freemasons.[35]

Views favorable to Jews, but not necessarily based on the abstract reasoning of Krause, found support in many lodges. This explains the fact, for which there is much evidence, that debate on this issue refused to die down. Nevertheless, no tangible results ensued. Even where the majority tended to be sympathetic, they refrained from forcing their views upon the minority. They were afraid that the implementation of a majority decision would lead those who considered Christianity as such a sine qua non for Masonry to leave the lodges.

81

VI Achievements in the Age of Liberalism

Jewish hopes of being accepted as equals in the lodges soared in the early thirties during the rise of Liberalism, as is shown by the change which affected the Frankfurt Masons. A new lodge, the Zum Frankfurter Adler, was added to the previously organized Morgenröthe. Established in 1832 with the consent of the Grand Orient of Paris, it too was Jewish in the composition of its membership. We have no direct evidence on the circumstances leading to its formation, but it is possible to reconstruct the background from the available data.

The Morgenröthe brethren were extremely discriminating in accepting new members. To belong to the lodge was considered a distinct privilege, since it not only opened the gates to that lodge itself but to others abroad as well. The Morgenröthe in turn derived prestige from the men of renown who belonged to it, among them Ludwig Börne, the author; Gabriel Riesser, the publicist; Moritz Oppenheim, the artist; and many others. The honor and prestige of belonging to the lodge depended on its remaining a small, select group. Furthermore, hope had not yet been abandoned that recognition eventually would be obtained from the rest of the German lodges. Such hope could only be entertained, however, as long as the high quality of membership was maintained without being weakened by the addition of individuals unworthy of the Masonic insignia.

Large numbers of candidates undoubtedly sought admission. Nor were these confined to local residents; many applied from other localities as well. In 1828, the Morgenröthe counted 129 members, among them 48 from other localities. Membership increased to 213 in 1844, although the number of brethren from other cities increased only by 14, bringing that total to 62. In the meantime the Frankfurter Adler had come into existence; only eight years after its inception it had 166 members, of whom more than half, about 84, were from beyond the city limits.[1] Indubitably the Frankfurter Adler had been transformed into a reception center for candidates aspiring to Masonic membership but unable to gain entry to the veteran lodge.

The Adler succeeded in acquiring some Christian members, though their number never exceeded six or seven. Also several Christian dignitaries agreed to accept honorary membership in the lodge. Nevertheless, it remained essentially Jewish in respect to its composition and its attitudes. Obviously the Morgenröthe considered the other lodge a rival, and it is doubtful whether it ever looked with favor upon the Adler.[2] Possibly personal reasons, unknown to us, may have played their part in arousing tension between the two. Yet the older must certainly have feared the younger lodge, since the latter's lower standards could prejudice the standing of the Morgenröthe in the eyes of Christian Masons. Echoes of the strained relations became audible even in the press. Just six years after the founding of the Frankfurter Adler, we find Eduard Reiss sternly castigating the Morgenröthe from the columns of the *Allgemeine Zeitung des Judenthums* for its lack of sympathy for the "younger sister." [3]

Although for the time being the lodges were unable to maintain cordial relations with one another, they worked in the same direction in their confrontation with the outside world. Both regarded their dependence on a foreign Mother Lodge as a temporary, makeshift solution. The protection thus acquired indeed accorded them the status of a recognized lodge, but also branded them as rootless in their own land. This fact had social as well as political implications. For some time the governments had been keeping close watch on what was transpiring in the Masonic lodges especially during the thirties when revolutionary upheavals, ascribed in great part to the activities of secret societies, had shaken princes and kings with terror. Even in areas where no direct supervision was exercised over the composition of the membership, as it was in Prussia, the governments required some assurance that the lodges were free of subversive political activity. The subordination of the individual lodges to national centers, that is, Mother Lodges, furnished some such security. There are grounds for believing that this arrangement was what prevented direct government intervention in internal Masonic affairs.[4] In this respect the Jewish lodges were open to criticism. Even though we do not hear of their actually being harassed, fear of such harassment could not have failed to occupy the attention of the leaders of the Jewish lodges. At any rate, they openly aspired to the acquisition of the patronage of a German Grand Lodge.

The closest target for the realization of their hopes was the Mother Lodge of the Eclectic Covenant of Frankfurt. In spite of its categorical rejection of their attempts in the recent past, signs of change appeared in the thirties, and there was reason to hope that what had once appeared impossible might become a reality. These were the days of the rise of Liberalism. The spirit of liberty and the desire to remove ancient barriers also made themselves felt among the Freemasons. Here and there doors had been opened to Morgen-röthe members; Gabriel Riesser considered it important enough to announce from Hamburg in 1833 that he had been granted permission to attend meetings of lodges following the English rite. The personal bonds that had been forged between Jewish and non-Jewish members from the earliest days of the Morgenröthe were kept intact, and new attachments with others were formed as well. Christian members came from Frankfurt and other cities to attend the celebration of the semi-jubilee of the lodge in 1833.[5] In the previous year, the Frankfurter Adler had sent invitations to Christian lodges to attend its inauguration ceremony. The central executive of the Eclectic Covenant refused the invitation on the grounds of decisions reached long before. One of the lodges, however, the Einigkeit, had only submitted to the decision as a matter of discipline. Actually, it had expressed the opinion that the hand of friendship should have been extended that group, "which, together with us, strives for similar elevated goals." [6] That same year the Einigkeit proposed that the two Jewish lodges be granted full recognition as authorized lodges.[7] Thereupon a struggle on the "Jewish problem" ensued in the Eclectic Covenant, one which disturbed the tranquillity of the Frankfurt lodges for the next fifteen years.

At the time the question was thrown open for discussion members of the older generation still headed the Eclectic Covenant. They refused to budge from the long accepted practices, no matter what the problem. In addition, with regard to Judaism they accepted the old stereotype evaluation which had gained support even among eminently liberal individuals. "The members of the Jewish community constitute a separatist political and religious sect maintained in the spirit of Mosaism, and they do not establish family ties with any other sector of human society. Very many, although certainly not all, of them still await the appearance of a terrestrial Messiah who has been promised to them alone, insofar as they are God's chosen people," [8] the head of the Eclectic Covenant at that time asserted. This judgment corresponded with the formulation of the liberal Protestant theologian H. A. G. Paulus, Gabriel Riesser's famous antagonist.[9] Yet the day of the old guard was over. In the Eclectic Covenant they were now confronted by the fighters of the new generation. The conflict blew up in the main over the acceptance of Molitor's lodge (Loge Carl zum aufgehenden Licht) which had preserved its existence as a separate lodge, ever since it had broken off from the Morgenröthe, yet was not content to continue in isolation. The members of the Eclectic Covenant were opposed to admitting it, since its rites tended to mysticism and theosophy.[10] The newer generation of Masons, however, were inclined to be tolerant toward that lodge, provided that it undertook to accept the constitution of the Eclectic Covenant. So, too, the newer generation was willing to open the doors to Jewish lodges seeking to escape from their isolation. Tolerance gained the upper hand in the struggle. In 1835 negotiations with Molitor's lodge were initiated, and in 1840 it was admitted to the Covenant. In similar vein discussions were begun on the question of the Jewish lodges as well.

At that time Dr. Georg Kloss, a Frankfurt physician, headed the Eclectic Covenant. In his youth he had been associated with, and influenced by, Molitor. Later, he arrived at his own, independent position on Masonry, as a result of his study of the history of the movement.[11] Kloss concluded that Masonry in essence was only concerned with the cultivation of the humanistic in man, which included contemplation and religious experience, but which stood above the conflicts of doctrine and the frameworks of churches and sects. Kloss wanted to convince the Eclectic Covenant to adopt this broadminded position and to achieve this goal in his own days. He was supported by Philipp Jacob Cretzschmar, the head of the Socrates lodge of Frankfurt. Both had been entrusted with the assignment of examining the history of the Eclectic Covenant in order to determine whether its principles and constitution obliged it to exclude Jews from its ranks, as had been the accepted practice heretofore. The results of their research into this problem were summarized and published by Cretzschmar in a book printed in 1838.

There he advanced a historical reason for the emergence of the principle of exclusion. It had been instituted, according to him, as a protest against the authorization granted to the Jewish lodge by the French Grand Orient, and also as a barrier against an excessive influx of Jews of the first generation liberated from the shackles of the ghetto. Since, even then the Masons had wanted to avoid excluding Jews in explicit terms, they had introduced certain specifically Christian symbols so as to achieve their ends by circuitous means. Yet it had never entered the minds of those who had introduced these practices thereby to lend a Christian character to Masonry. Only the generation of the Reaction had identified Freemasonry with Christianity, and this in order to have some reason for keeping Jews out of the movement by disqualifying them on principle. In so doing, however, the members of that generation had compromised the very basis of Freemasonry which only required man's attachment to a Supreme Being as the means for acquiring human perfection. The Church or community through which man established his attachment to his Creator made no difference whatever. Jew, Christian, and Moslem were equally fit to build their own selves through the educational and stimulating activities of the Masons.[12]

Cretzschmar's premises entailed the conclusion that all reservations against admitting Jews should be abolished. Yet neither Kloss nor Cretzschmar dared go so far in practice. Nor did the Jews expect that a basic change in their position would occur all at once. On September 26, 1837, the Morgenröthe submitted its request to the Grand Lodge of the Eclectic Covenant that permission be granted members of the unaffiliated lodges to attend meetings as visiting brethren. A week later a similar letter of request was received from the Frankfurter Adler. There was no talk as yet of Jews being accepted as full-fledged members of the lodges of the Covenant, or of the Jewish lodges becoming affiliated with the Eclectic Covenant.

We have the expressions of opinion, in manuscript, of the Grand Lodge headed by Kloss and Cretzschmar. From these we can learn how circumspect they were in matters which carried practical consequences. The expressions of opinion were identical with the universalist views voiced in Cretzschmar's work. These speak even more openly of the real reasons which in the past had impelled the Christian lodges to bar Jews and to deny recognition to the Frankfurt

Morgenröthe. A vast gulf separated Christian citizens from the Jewish ghetto of the time, and a deep mutual hatred kept the two apart. Jews were uncultured and alien in their civil and religious behavior. All this, however, had changed. And, as we shall see, the expressions of opinion attributed much of the change to the Morgenröthe. Indeed, the older lodge was accorded manifestly greater approbation than its "younger sister," the Frankfurter Adler, which had not yet undergone a sufficiently long period of trial to receive the stamp of complete approval. The statement therefore recommended that the application of the Morgenröthe be taken up immediately, while the Adler's request be deferred to some future date. In reality, however, even unqualified approbation of the Morgenröthe was not sufficient to remove all obstacles. Those in favor of the withdrawal of all barriers knew that they had of necessity to reckon with the views of all the ramified affiliates of the Eclectic Covenant, with the opinions of the rest of the German lodges—some inclining in the one, others in the opposite direction—with the rulers of the various states, and with public opinion at large beyond the borders of the Masonic fraternity.[13]

To enlist support for its views on the unaffiliated lodges, the Mother Lodge now polled the opinions of daughter lodges in the various cities (such as Frankfurt, Nuremberg, Darmstadt, Giessen, Mayence, and Offenbach). It even gave assurance that, in the event of the majority's approving the admission of Jews to the lodges, the views of the majority would not be forced upon the dissenting minority. Of the nine lodges that replied, only two declared themselves against the admission of Jews; the other seven were in favor of granting permission, yet some of them requested that the privilege be confined to the members of the Morgenröthe only, to the exclusion of the Frankfurter Adler. From now on, the admission of Jews became dependent upon the attitude of each individual lodge. Most, though not all, opened their doors.[14]

In Frankfurt, Molitor's lodge had joined the Eclectic Covenant a year after permission to visit had been granted the Jewish lodge. Yet his own lodge still persisted in denying such permission and in using manifestly Christian symbols such as the Trinity—the Father, Son, and Holy Ghost.[15] According to Molitor's explicit assertion, no man could ever attain the excellence aspired to by the Masons through his own efforts, unless he was aided by Christian divine grace.[16] The inevitable conclusion of such a view was the exclusion of Jews. Opposed to this definite Christian attitude, Kloss's humanistic view gave no advantage to the Christian over the adherent of any other religion in his ability to attain perfection. Kloss endeavored to persuade the Eclectic Covenant to acknowledge this principle. He was dissatisfied with the compromise which only granted visiting rights to Jews. Time was apparently on the side of the humanists, and Kloss believed, in 1843, that the day of decision had dawned. That year a request was received by the Mother Lodge from an affiliated lodge in Erlangen asking permission to admit two Jews as members, one a lawyer, the other a physician, both of whom "had remained loyal to their Jewish faith out of conviction, despite not a few blandishments." [17] Kloss sought to have the Grand Lodge accept the principle that all restraints against the acceptance of Jews be removed in all the lodges of the Eclectic Covenant. At this time, however, representatives of Molitor's Christian lodge occupied seats in the Grand Lodge and, as a result of their influence, no vote was taken. A decision was deferred sine die.[18] As a result of this conflict, relations between the two sides became acrimonious, and a year later Molitor's Lodge was expelled from the Eclectic Covenant, since their manifestly Christian doctrines and symbols contradicted the principle of Masonic neutrality to any positive religion.[19]

The members of the Frankfurt lodge derived a grim satisfaction from the inability of the Christian lodges to agree among themselves, and of course ascribed this disharmony to their equivocating and their ignoring the principle laid down by their predecessors, namely, that Freemasons stood above all questions of belonging to any particular religion.[20] Yet the Jewish aspirations did not advance, and Jacob Weil summed up his Morgenröthe report of that year with the remark that the lodge remained utterly isolated in its immediate environment. Yet he comforted himself "with the exalted feeling that we represent and promote, together with our sister, the Frankfurter Adler, that principle which has no little significance in the struggle between light and darkness, between the old, authentic Freemasonry and the new mystic trends." [21] It seemed to the Jew, there as in other instances, that in waging his struggle on his own behalf, he had become the vanguard in the fight for the vital need of the day.

The controversy over the nature of Freemasonry, and the conclusion it entailed for Jews, was not the concern of Frankfurt alone. Almost all the German lodges were involved in some degree or other. Reactions were also forthcoming from lodges beyond the borders of that country. Repeated attempts were made by the Grand Lodges in England, Holland, France, and the United States to bring pressure to bear upon the German lodges, and the Berlin Mother Lodges in particular, to relent. We shall hear more of this later in connection with the history of the struggle within the Prussian lodges. In one point, however, the endeavors of the Freemasons outside Germany were connected with what was transpiring in Frankfurt. It will be remembered that the Frankfurter Adler had become affiliated with the Grand Orient of Paris. In 1846, when Paris too decided to exert pressure on Berlin to change its attitude, the Frankfurter Adler was suspected of having incited its Mother Lodge to interfere in the internal affairs of the German lodges. During the first decade of its existence, the Frankfurter Adler had refrained from raising its voice in public. In 1843, however, it began issuing an annual circular, and from then on it engaged more actively and vigorously in the struggle than the older Morgenröthe. In a circular letter disseminated among the lodges in 1846, the Adler launched an attack on the obstinate and antiquated exclusiveness of the Freemasons. The Leipzig Freimaurer Zeitung took violent exception to the acrimonious language and requested the Jewish Masons to exercise forbearance. The periodical added the warning that Jews should at all events refrain from seeking the assistance of outside lodges. A sharp rejoinder was hurled back by the Frankfurt Jewish lodge, which categorically denied that it had taken any part in impelling the Paris members to take action, even though, as an affiliate, it was fully entitled to seek the protection of the Mother Lodge. "Even if we are forced to belong to an alien Mother, *all our sympathies are deeply rooted in the soil of our beloved fatherland*" (emphasis in original). Yet how could they put an end to this humiliating situation where brother Masons were excluded from participation on account of their religion or origin? How long were they to wait? As for patience, who more than they had exercised this virtue to the very limit of human endurance? "One need only be a German Jew and Freemason to become a master of patience." Never before had Jewish Freemasons permitted

89

themselves the use of such language. The author of the Frankfurt rejoinder himself observed that hitherto they had been accustomed to giving soft answers ("we believed that we had to wrap every word in cotton wool and to dip it in milk and honey"), but lately their patience had snapped.[22]

It seems that protracted frustration was not the only reason for the change of tone. In the public arena as well tongues had become sharper. Demands for emancipation had grown ever more insistent at the end of the forties, and no little success had been gained so far. The Freemasons began to feel that they would soon be lagging behind other areas of life. Were the Masonic lodges to wait until they were put to shame by the liberalism of choral and gymnastics societies?[23] Despairing of becoming an affiliate of the Eclectic Covenant in its own city, the Frankfurter Adler had found a patron in the Hamburg lodge in 1847. It no longer had to rely upon French protection. The lodge was formally inaugurated on April 9, 1848, and even members of the Frankfurt Eclectic Covenant participated in the celebration. Events of the time were the determining factor. What discussing and urging had been unable to achieve was brought about by the revolutionary disturbances which spread to, and penetrated within, the lives of the closed societies. That same year, the Eclectic Covenant rescinded the paragraph barring the acceptance of Jews into the lodges. Henceforth no candidate would be asked whether he acknowledged Christian dogmas, but instead whether he assented to the principles obliging one to love God and man.[24] The Eclectic Covenant granted formal recognition to the Morgenröthe. This lodge, and presumably also the Frankfurter Adler, were invited by Christian lodges to hold joint banquets and ceremonies. The Jewish lodge played host to prominent guests from high Christian society who gathered together in Frankfurt during the year of the revolution.[25] Echoes of these activities give evidence of the deep satisfaction experienced by the members of the lodge at having finally reached their objective. They now found themselves in the company of those whom they longed to emulate, and by whom they had aspired to be recognized.

As was to be expected, once the gates of the other lodges had swung open, the importance of the Jewish lodge declined. Its historian, to whom all documents pertaining to its affairs were open, complained of the alarming indifference that had settled on the

90

brethren soon after the years of the revolution. The lodge continued to exist. It still played some specific part in Jewish social life of
Frankfurt in the nineteenth and even the twentieth century. It remained loyal to the London Mother Lodge until after the Franco-
Prussian War of 1870. In 1866 Frankfurt was annexed by Prussia.
In that country the Freemasons were tolerated only on the condition of their activities being subject to state supervision. The government exerted pressure on the Morgenröthe to sever its connections with London. For several years the lodge was able to
withstand the pressure. In 1871, however, the year of the German
victory over France, they finally yielded. Their connection with
London was broken, and the lodge joined the Eclectic Covenant of
Frankfurt.[26] The change hardly affected the internal operation of
the lodge itself, nor did it possess any significance from the point of
view of Jewish history, either local or general. What is important is
the history of the forty year's struggle (1807–1848), and we must arrive at a final summing up of its nature and significance.

The historical significance of the struggle, as well as the scope of
the function fulfilled by Freemasonry in the social entrenchment of
Jews in their respective localities, can only be evaluated by broadening our description to include the relations between the Jewish
Freemasons and Jewry as a whole in Germany.

Indeed, the history of the Frankfurt Lodge has an interest of its
own. This lodge in its heyday was comprised of an intimate group
of the elite of the Frankfurt Jewish community. As we have seen,
several better and lesser known individuals of other cities had also
been admitted to membership. To those mentioned previously we
can add the names of Gotthold Salomon, preacher in the Reform
Temple of Hamburg; Berthold Auerbach, the author; and Jacob
Dernburg, the jurist. The nucleus of the group, however, consisted
of local residents. Among these were intellectuals of the caliber of
Jacob Weil, Michael Hess, Michael Creizenach, and the historian
Marcus Jost. Most, however, were men of affairs—merchants, bankers, and professionals, the latter mainly physicians. Many lodge
members had achieved distinction in public life, especially in the
Jewish community.

Some indication of the connection between the activities of the
lodge and transformations in the community appears in Jost's delin-

eation of its history.[27] Evidence that the members of the lodge were identical with the leaders of the Jewish community is provided by the biographical sketch of Sigismund Geisenheimer by Heinrich Bier, a teacher at the Philanthropin, himself a member of the lodge since 1848. According to him, for a very long time the wardens of the community were chosen almost exclusively from the lodge members.[28] This assertion is authenticated by a comparison of the names of the heads of the community appearing in the Frankfurt *Staats-Calender* with the names of the members published from time to time in the special Masonic lists. Already in 1808, the wardens of the Frankfurt community had been appointed by Prince Dalberg, and he took care to maintain the balance between the conservatives and those who inclined toward innovations. With the conferring of citizenship upon Jews in 1811, new faces appeared in the community executive.[29] We meet the same names again in the roster of the Masonic lodge, and must assume that these belonged to the innovators. From 1817 to 1832 all the wardens of the Jewish community belonged to the Freemasons, and even in the next decade they constituted the overwhelming majority of the directorate.[30]

92

Heinrich Bier dealt in detail with the influence exerted by this personal identification upon the entire community. "The solemn ceremonial, the festive seriousness, and the measured order characteristic of the Freemasons joined with the necessity of allowing free speech and the keeping of exact records" constantly impressed the members. Traits and habits which had become attached to the leaders as a result of their lodge activities were carried over to the framework of communal institutions, to the benefit of those institutions and the raising of their standards. Moreover, Bier ascribed the initiative in the introduction of the Reform movement into the community to the wardens who were at the same time Freemasons. "They soon recognized the necessity for reform in life and worship and, being convinced in their own minds, they endeavored to implement [these reforms] with decisive energy." [31]

Nor was Bier the sole witness to this sequence of events. Corroborative evidence is furnished by the Frankfurt Christian Masons. From the statement of opinion of 1837 prepared by the heads of the Eclectic Covenant and mentioned above, the following excerpt may be quoted: "The men [members of the Morgenröthe] . . . are known to all of us . . . they constitute the kernel of the good, learned, and enlightened among the Jewish community. . . . The projects begun and completed by it are now clearly shown to have been not only for the benefit of the lodge and those belonging to it, but for the good of the nation as a whole. These Israelite brethren are no longer the Jews of 1789, they are Masons . . . who are devoted in all respects to the true veneration of God, to knowledge, to the virtues which adorn civil and family life . . . we are forced to admit that their participation in Masonry has made all their culture stride forward with giant steps." The statement of opinion relies in the main upon the observations of Cretzschmar who gave credit to the Morgenröthe members, "for their intentions to bring Judaism closer to Christianity by the founding of schools and houses of worship." [32]

There was more than a grain of truth in this testimony. After all, Sigmund Geisenheimer, the founder of the lodge, was also the founder of Philanthropin, an exemplary school of the Reform movement. Those wardens of the community who had charge of the educational aspect of the school were lodge members, as were a significant number of its teachers—Hess, Creizenach, and Jost, mentioned above, and, in the years that followed, Leopold Beer, Herman Zirndorfer, Jacob Auerbach, and Theodore Creizenach (the son). The Philanthropin also established a house of worship which served the adult community no less than the pupils of the school.[33]

Finally, the members of the lodge served as a source of influence on the entire Jewish community, propelling it along lines similar to those taken by the humanistically inclined Masons in pursuing their religious goals. As we have seen, the Jewish lodges had previously asserted that Masonry coincided with the original religion of mankind which, according to this theory, lay at the base of all the historical religions. This faith was perfectly tailored to the needs of the Jewish Reform movement which, too, sought to base the Jewish religion on principles equally valid for all men. We should not be surprised to learn that henceforth the group gathered together in the Frankfurt Jewish lodge had given its encouragement to the penetration of the Reform movement into the local community.

The influence of the Freemasons on the character of the Frankfurt Jewish community accounts for at least a partial explanation of an astonishing phenomenon in events in that city during the first half of the nineteenth century. That community, which had always been proud of its own particular ancient Jewish tradition, divested itself of all Jewish tradition with astounding rapidity. When Samson Raphael Hirsch repaired to Frankfurt in 1851, it was in answer to a call issued by a small minority which was anxious to organize itself in strict adherence to Jewish tradition. Most of the community, by contrast, as well as the official institutions followed the trend of the Reform movement. This situation differed from what prevailed in corresponding communities, such as Hamburg and Prague for instance. There groups of "enlightened" Jews and of those who strove for Reform, did exist, but only on the margin, from where they endeavored to turn the flanks of the Jewish community. Not so in Frankfurt. Here the Orthodox very quickly became the minority and had to struggle desperately against the Reformist behavior of the majority. A contemporary named Bonaventura Meyer, who could hardly be accused of partiality since he was a Jesuit monk, who evinced interest in the lives of communities, deplored the decay of the old Judaism (for his own reasons) and set down, in 1842, his appraisal of the relative strengths of the conservatives and reformers.[34] He estimated that in Bohemia more than half of the community had strayed from the paths of their fathers. In Hamburg, a third of the community had become Reformed, while in Frankfurt, not more than 200 of the 3,000 local families had remained Orthodox.

When we learn that the intimate society of the Freemasons had been constituted by sons of the most prominent Frankfurt families, and that the lodge members had become the leaders of the community, we can account for this phenomenon. Samson Raphael Hirsch and his faithful followers laid the blame for the undermining of the traditional foundations upon the deliberate and willful action of the communal leadership; nor can there be any doubt of the validity of the facts on which his allegation rested.[35] What he regarded as destruction, however, was hailed by Jewish Masons as reconstruction.

I do not insinuate that the Freemasons sat down together in their lodges and plotted to reform the community. Lodges were not conspirational cells—as their enemies alleged in ascribing to them all the acts which led to the overthrow of the old order in Europe, from the French Revolution to the destruction of the temporal power of the Catholic Church. The nineteenth-century Freemasons were peaceful individuals, who cherished human dignity and civil tranquillity more than anything else. The Jewish lodge too was most anxious to appear as cultured and civilized. Not for nothing did it earn approbation for its conduct on the part of the Eclectic Covenant. It is equally certain that the brethren did not, at lodge meetings, engage in discussions of the affairs of the Jewish community. First, even though the composition of the lodge was for the most part Jewish, several Christians were members during all the stages of its existence. Furthermore, among the Jews themselves there were converts to Christianity, like Ludwig Börne, who was readmitted to membership in 1818, the year of his conversion. The lodge took pride in him later on, as one who achieved great distinction.[36] And the Jews themselves undoubtedly desired to pursue their Masonic activities in an atmosphere of neutrality free from the intrusion of the affairs of the community or congregation into their proceedings.

Nevertheless, the evidence must be accepted as valid that the Masons as a group did exert a marked influence on the destiny of the local Jewish community. Once the group had banded together in the intimate contact of lodge life, members undoubtedly worked together outside the lodge with a certain unity of purpose. This is the sociology of a sub-group, whose members depend on one another, assist each other, and demonstrate their ability to work together beyond the confines of their formal association. If this was true of all other activities, it applied even more strongly to the abandonment of the old traditional mold of communal life. The very joining of the lodge was in great measure an expression of withdrawal from the traditional patterns of Jewish life. It is difficult to conceive how a religiously observant Jew could adapt himself to Masonic ceremonies, take their oath, partake of their meals, and so on. In another sense, participation in Masonic ceremonies inculcated the idea that it was sufficient for a person to accept the abstract faith common to all human creatures. Masonic ceremonies afforded an opportunity for experiences of masculine companionship—so the Masons repeatedly testified of themselves, and such remarks should not be dismissed as empty metaphors. In this manner their faith became reinforced that they were following the way of truth. No wonder they were anxious to incorporate some of their Masonic "truths" in the framework of the Jewish community! [37]

VII   The Struggle for Masonic Emancipation in Prussia

Not only in Frankfurt did the lot of the Jews change for the better. In other cities individuals of liberal outlook, in whose eyes the discrimination against Jews was questionable or even illogical, kept entering the lodges. Opinions changed, as did the subject under discussion. Many still regarded the individual Jew as the embodiment of the accepted stereotype, yet few could refuse to admit that exceptional individuals had succeeded in ridding themselves of the obnoxious characteristics normally ascribed to Jews. The modern Jew, whose language, education, and manners were molded by the dominant culture, stood out conspicuously, and he could on no account be measured by standards different from those applied to others. The appearance of the modern Jew was accompanied by a new attitude. He was fully conscious of his similarity to his environment, and he fervently believed that the only difference between him and his contemporaries was the allegiance to different religions. Now since religious affiliations were no longer as important as before, his exclusion from the general society constituted no more than senseless discrimination.

Awareness of this meaningless discrimination spurred Gabriel Riesser in his struggle to secure political rights for the Jews,[1] and the same spirit animated Jewish Freemasons in their efforts to eliminate discrimination from their order. We can follow the progress of this struggle step by step. The first was taken by twelve persons in the city of Wesel in the Rhineland,[2] long under Prussian rule. Of the twelve, eleven were members of other existing lodges: seven of Dutch lodges; one of the French lodge in Osnabrück at the time of the occupation; and two of the "Jewish" lodges in Frankfurt, Zur aufgehenden Morgenröthe and Zum Frankfurter Adler.[3] In the city of Wesel a lodge was operative by the name of Die Loge zum goldenen Schwert, affiliated with the Grosse National-Mutterloge zu den drei Weltkugeln in Berlin. It is not surprising to learn that Jewish Freemasons, including those who belonged to other approved lodges, were not permitted to participate in the activities of the local lodge. The members of the Dutch lodges were especially offended by this attitude, since they had never been accustomed to such discrimination in their own country.

The Wesel brethren refused to acquiesce in this situation. Yet what could a small band of Jews accomplish in the face of this wall of opposition? Slowly, however, it became evident that the opposition to the participation of Jews was by no means unanimous. Members of the Wesel lodge indicated to the Jews that they would not have barred them from entering their society, were it not for the authority of the constitution of the Mother Lodge in Berlin.[4] Clearly a change could only be brought about by a shift of opinion among the broad masses of Masons. The first symptom that such a transformation had begun appeared in 1835. In a circular, distributed by the Apollo lodge in Leipzig, the view was put forward that Jews should be allowed to attend lodge ceremonies as visitors. The Leipzig Masons had no doubt that lodges were permitted to accept Jews as members. Once a recognized lodge had granted membership to Jews, they were entitled to participate as visitors in the activities of every other lodge. Religious affiliation could make no difference. All depended upon whether the persons were "freemen of genuine good name," who were prepared and fit to advance the purposes of Freemasonry. That there were such men in the Jewish community, who on account of their moral and intellectual attainments fulfilled these requirements, even the most fanatical opponent of the admission of Jews to Freemasonry could not deny.[5] A year later, on June 24, 1836, a circular was sent out on behalf of the five Hamburg lodges. They declared that the goals of Masonry and Christianity were identical; yet they drew the conclusion that the Masonic order should include all persons of ethical aspirations, irrespective of class or creed.[6] To the ears of the Wesel brethren, these statements appeared the answer to what they were seeking.[7] From now on they could hope to find support even in the public domain, and they decided to take their struggle to this arena. They submitted a request to the three Mother Lodges in Berlin to remove the restrictions against Jews. If, however, these lodges were prevented by government authority from permitting the acceptance of Jews, the petitioners would submit to this decision ("since we respect and obey the law even if it oppresses us"). Nevertheless, the right to attend all lodge meetings belonged to them as members of recognized lodges,

97

and this right they were not prepared to forego. Not only was the formal request dispatched to its destination, but copies were printed and an accompanying letter drafted in both Dutch and German versions. Each lodge in Holland and Germany received a copy of the original request and an accompanying letter in its own language.

The request is an extremely interesting document, revealing the inner feelings of the Jewish Masons. They presented their case forcefully. "We do not appear before you as petitioners begging for favor and mercy, but as relying on the rights which the sanctity of the covenant [*Die Weihe des Bundes*] confers on us." The granting of visiting rights to Christians exclusively was arbitrary, and contrary to the basic principles of Freemasonry. "Freemasonry calls itself a world-wide covenant; its aim is directed toward spreading the greatest possible unity among mankind—to uproot preconceived ideas, hatred, and strife and to implant love in their place." [8] There were localities where Freemasonry was true to its principles. In England and Holland Jews were accepted; and in Germany there were Masons who demanded that Jews be accepted. Yet the officials who wielded the power of controlling and guiding the lodges maintained Christian exclusiveness. Christianity was interpreted as formal allegiance to the Church, the act of baptism being the decisive factor, not the belief in Christian principles.[9] The accompanying letter added that Jews themselves would be admitted to the lodges were they prepared to join the Church merely as a matter of paying lip service. The exclusiveness of the lodges therefore appeared as pressure to secure conversion at any price.[10] As against this formal conception of man's religious affiliation, the Jewish members revealed their outlook on the nature of religion, and so testified to the character of their own faith. "Freemasonry strives for truth. But truth reposes in the human spirit and not in the external forms with which human consideration has found fit to adorn religion. Forms have changed with the circumstances of the times, but the inner spirit has always remained the same." [11] This was the great principle of rationalism—and of Reform Judaism. In the name of this principle the differences between the Jewish and other religions were minimized, and the significance of observing Jewish religious commandments and ritual denied.

The appeal of the Wesel brethren evoked wide response. The Zum Silbernen Einhorn lodge in Nienburg announced itself completely in accord with the ideas expressed in the circular. They had conducted themselves in such a way, and had just accepted the Mason Heine as a visitor to their lodge. They were incapable of influencing the Mother Lodges in question, however, since they were not affiliated with Berlin but with the Grand Lodge in Hannover.[12] A somewhat similar reply was received from the Ferdinande Caroline lodge of Hamburg. This and other lodges in that city operated on the same principles as the English rite, and accordingly no restrictions prevented Jews from paying visits. The Hamburg lodges were even prepared to take in Jews who had been accepted by other lodges, and had done so recently in the case of a member of Frankfurt's Zur aufgehenden Morgenröthe, who would soon be raised to the second degree. These activities were carried out according to the accepted rules of the English rite, and needed no ratification by members. On the other hand, the respondents admitted that they refrained from proposing for membership Jews who were not already Masons for fear of hurting the applicant's feelings "by the result of a vote which, regrettably, is often determined by prejudice." The Hamburg Masons reminded the Wesel brethren of the fact that the Mother Lodges in Berlin were completely committed to Christian principles.[13] They concluded by drawing attention to their own circular sent out the previous year, where they had stated their view that even those identifying Freemasonry with Christianity were obliged to act broadmindedly toward members of another faith. Nevertheless, they openly admitted that they were neither prepared nor able to influence the Berliners to implement this principle.

Full support for the demands of the Wesel brethren was given by the Agrippina lodge of Cologne, affiliated with the Royal York in Berlin. Its members had long regarded the clause limiting lodge membership to Christians as contradictory to basic Masonic principles, and the address of the Wesel brethren afforded them the opportunity to express their views to the Mother Lodge in Berlin. "We can only regret the fact that Jews, and especially the enlightened among them, to whom the Masons belong, are not, while fulfilling the same duties, accorded the same rights as the other subjects of the country." [14] It was doubly wrong to carry over this discrimination to social life in general and lodge life in particular. The members of the Agrippina proposed "that the discriminatory clause be eliminated from the Freemasons' constitution, and that the lodges not only permit Jewish Masons to enter their halls, but also freely accept Jews as members." In their extreme liberalism, the Cologne Masons were exceptional, as we shall see later. The Wesel brethren could have derived no little satisfaction from the replies reaching them.[15] Any tangible results, however, would depend upon the attitude adopted by the Mother Lodges in Berlin.

An unequivocal stand was taken by the Landesloge, which did not answer the printed letter of request. Two members of the Wesel brethren again approached that lodge in March 1837, and received a clear and cutting reply soon after. "Our union is totally and utterly Christian, and we are obliged, by virtue of our indisputable laws, to take care to preserve the institution in the form that we respect, without any change. . . . This stems neither from fanaticism nor from lack of a humanistic attitude in this matter. We would want every person to find, in the faith of his fathers, the peace of soul which grants him bliss in this world and the next. We respect man as man everywhere. Admission to us, however, can only, in accordance with our laws, be allowed to adherents of the Christian faith." [16] As far as the Landesloge was concerned, the discussion was closed.[17] No less negative, for all practical purposes, was the stand taken by the National-Mutterloge with which the Wesel lodge was affiliated, although this Mother Lodge had difficulty in finding a clear and consistent principle on which to base its attitude. At first it avoided giving any reply, on the pretext that the letter of request had only been a printed copy and had not been signed by the complainants. Only on February 11, 1838, after formal rectification had been made by submitting the letter with the signatures of the writers, did it give its reply.[18] Here signs of confusion and evasion are clearly evident. Whilst the Landesloge testified to its being a completely Christian institution into which no Jew could be admitted, the Mutterloge based its opposition on the Jew's religion, which made it impossible for him to participate fully in Masonic ceremonies. The Mutterloge used the old argument that a Jew who was prepared to make concessions at the expense of his religion thereby disqualified himself from Freemasonry on account of this defect in his character.[19] Nevertheless, the Mutterloge did not dare to deny the designation of Mason to Jews accepted by other lodges, and even declared itself prepared to fulfill all the duties of Masonic brotherhood toward them,[20] other than that of admitting them to the activities of the lodges themselves. The Mother Lodge even found it necessary to protest against any allegation of anti-Jewish feeling or prejudice. In a special circular it directed its affiliates how to conduct their affairs, to refuse to allow anyone entrance to the lodges unless his attachment to Christianity was beyond doubt, but at the same time not to hurt visitors' feelings and to avoid giving any impression of anti-Jewish bias.[21] The Berliners were afraid that any controversy between those who approved and those who disapproved of the attendance of Jews might provoke a storm. The authors of the circular reminded lodge members that they were forbidden to air matters affecting Freemasonry in public without the express permission of the Masonic authorities. Clearly the Mother Lodge was interested in suppressing the controversy, but whether it succeeded is doubtful. We know of one reply to its circular, that of the daughter lodge of Luxembourg. In that city, which lies beyond the German frontier but has a predominantly German population, there functioned, in addition to an affiliate of the Mutterloge, a Dutch lodge with the French name Les Enfants de la Concorde Fortifiée,[22] which had several Jewish members. The two lodges maintained cordial relations with each other and members of one would often visit the other. The only exceptions were the Jewish members of the Dutch lodge who were denied this right. A directive of the Mutterloge forbade the "Prussian" lodge to grant them entry. The "Prussian" brethren reluctantly submitted to this ruling, hoping for its abolition with the rise of the spirit of toleration. The letter sent out by the Berlin Mother Lodge, however, shattered all hope, and the Luxembourgers decided to enter a protest. In their own circular of 1838, they presented their arguments in detail against the general refusal to accept Jews and the particular statement of the Mother Lodge. The Berlin Masons' recommendation that Jews be kept out of the lodges but that this be accomplished with all due delicacy might constitute a lesson in diplomacy but it hardly conformed to the forthright character of the Masons. These openly critical remarks were not only disseminated among the Masons but published in the *Zeitschrift für Maurerei* as well.

The Royal York, too, refrained from replying at first, its formal excuse being that the petitioners had not signed the request. Moreover, they were accustomed to answer lodges and not individuals. Individuals were obliged to submit their complaints to their own lodges.[23] Nevertheless, there were several members of the Royal

101

York—seventeen to be exact—on whom the arguments of the Wesel brethren had left an impression, and they expressed the opinion "that the accusation of injustice leveled at our Grand Lodge has some justification." These Masons proposed that the Grand Lodge decide "that non-Christian brethren as well, who have been accepted by a lodge we recognize . . . be permitted to participate in our proceedings." The leaders of the Grand Lodge held this proposal a matter of such grave importance that they considered it wrong to make a decision before receiving the replies of the affiliated lodges. These were now polled; thirteen replied in the affirmative, eight in the negative. Apparently then, the majority were in favor of an affirmative decision. The Master of the Grand Lodge, however, belonged to the opposition. He and those who shared his views exerted all their power to prevent the proposal becoming law. The replies of the lodges were no more than expressions of opinion; only their representatives, all of whom were resident in Berlin, could vote a proposal into law. The initiative to abolish the restrictions had first come from among these representatives, but the vehemence of the opposition made them recoil from demanding the practical enforcement of their proposal. They were content to compromise. First, it was proposed that any decision be deferred to the date of the revision of the constitution, which had been set for 1845. Finally it was decided that the amendment be adopted in principle immediately, while the practical enforcement alone be postponed to the previously mentioned date.[24]

Despite the distinct, liberal awakening, even in Berlin the conservatives still held the upper hand. The most progressive elements among the Masons were concentrated in the Royal York lodge, but it was unable to act on its own authority. It was connected with the other two Grand Lodges, and the prohibition against admitting Jews had been agreed upon among all three.[25] Apparently, the conservative lodges worked behind the scenes to prevent the Royal York creating a breach. The fear of opening schisms between the three Mother Lodges was certainly a factor in the reluctance of the Royal York to carry out in practice what had been decided in principle.

The bond between the three Lodges was strengthened rather than weakened during the years following the discussion of the

Wesel brethren's request. In 1840, the Prince of Prussia—brother to King Frederick William IV—the future Wilhelm I of Prussia (1860), later Kaiser Wilhelm of Germany (1871), became the patron of all Prussian Freemasons. From then on, he was given the title of Protector, an office without precedent in the history of the Prussian lodges. Whether this reflected the will of the Masons, or the initiative of the Royal Palace and Prussian government, is unknown.[26] Clearly, however, an extreme conservative element was now introduced into Masonic life in that country.

We can trace the activities of the Prince of Prussia in connection with the status of Jews in Freemasonry. His first action involved him in the consequences of the Wesel brethren incident. The affair was not closed by the decisions of the three Berlin Mother Lodges. It will be recalled that these brethren had also addressed themselves to the Dutch lodges to which a majority of them belonged. The letter they had addressed to the Dutch lodges was much stronger in tone than the German version. Dutch Masons were reminded that the barring of Jews from visiting Prussian lodges had already furnished a subject for discussion at the Grand Lodge in The Hague in 1828 and 1834, and that the intervention following those discussions had brought no results.[27] The doors of the Prussian lodges were still closed to Jews, even to those who were able to show Dutch membership certificates. The signatories to the letter insisted that their Dutch brethren demand satisfaction for this insult which was, in effect, directed against all Dutch Masons, and seek redress for them.

A broad reaction among the Dutch brethren was evoked by the Wesel brethren's request. Even before they had received the letters, the La Bien Aimée lodge of Amsterdam had forwarded a strong protest to the Zum goldenen Schwert in Wesel for having prevented M. Jac. Meyer from participating in its activities, even though he was a member of the Amsterdam lodge. In reply, the Wesel lodge stated that it was compelled to conduct its affairs in accordance with the constitution of the Mother Lodge in Berlin, and that it was prepared to abandon this practice if the decision to change the constitution would come from above.[28] It became clear to the Dutch brethren that the protest should properly be addressed to Berlin; hence it must come from the corresponding body in Holland, the Grand Lodge in The Hague. Those responsible for the protest now directed their efforts toward their Mother Lodge. Most active in this effort was the Loge Orde en Vlyt in the city of Gorinchem. It gathered all the documents which had accumulated as a result of the Wesel brethren's struggle, and a memorandum was compiled to form the basis of the demands upon the Mother Lodges in Berlin.[29]

Opinion in the Dutch lodges was unanimous on the need to protest against the attitude of the Prussians toward the Jewish brethren; yet views differed on how forceful a protest should, at first, be made. In Holland, too, the Royal Palace was connected with the Masons. In contrast to the Prussian Protector, Prince Frederick was the elected head of all Dutch Masons. Apparently the Prince counseled moderation, and he refrained from signing, on behalf of the Dutch lodges, the letter of protest forwarded to the Grand Lodges in Berlin in 1840. The recipients of the protest cast doubt on the authenticity of the document in their hands, and the Royal Protector took it upon himself to clarify the nature of the protest with the Dutch prince. The two met on July 20, during the visit of the Dutch prince to Prussia. It became clear to the Protector that, although the Dutch prince himself inclined toward moderation, he was admittedly neither prepared nor able to prevent his Masons as a body from insisting on the fulfillment of their demand that Jewish Masons be accorded the same status as Christians.[30] The Berlin lodges could no longer evade answering the Dutch Masons. The replies of the Landesloge and Mutterloge have been preserved, and they reflect the views and opinions we have already encountered.[31] The first declared that from its very inception it had been constituted as a Christian institution and hence was categorically forbidden to allow any non-Christian to participate in its activities. What is new here is the fact that the name of the Protector was specifically mentioned as one of the participants in the consultation preceding the decision. The Mutterloge, this time too, sought excuses to justify its position. The respondents on its behalf compared the exclusion of Jews from Christian lodges with the exclusion of Masons of lower degrees from the meetings of Masons of higher degrees, and this could not therefore be understood as an insult. In order to remove the sting, they added, as on previous occasions, that Mohammedans and members of other non-Christian religions also would not be admitted to their lodges. The entire purpose was to calm the anger of the Dutch Masonic leaders, who were requested to warn their Jewish members not to seek admission to German lodges. In this way unpleasantness would be avoided both for the Jews themselves and for the persons to whom the requests would be addressed.

The calm that the Berliners hoped to achieve did not materialize. The replies failed to placate the Dutch Masons. They demanded that the restrictions which hurt their Jewish brethren be removed. Prince Frederick himself signed the protest on March 28, 1841, and, when this second letter did not achieve any results, warned the Prussian Protector that he could no longer pacify his Dutch brethren.[32]

The refusal of the Berlin lodges to relax their resistance stood in contradistinction to the developing trends in social and political spheres. Even among the Freemasons, a beginning had been made in implementing the principle of universality. The Apollo lodge in Leipzig carried out the declaration adopted in principle in 1835,[33] and a year later, on June 4, 1836, admitted its first Jew—Sulzer by name—to membership; several others were admitted soon afterward. In 1838, a decision favorable to Jews was adopted by the Grand Lodge of all Saxony.[34] Hamburg had long before allowed Jews to visit its meetings,[35] and in 1841, the Ferdinande Caroline allowed a member of the Frankfurt Morgenröthe[36] to join their lodge. The Stuttgart lodge had begun admitting Jews at the beginning of the forties. They put certain specific questions to these candidates, however, to ascertain whether the applicant was not prejudiced in favor of Jews as against other members of the human race.[37]

The liberalism of these lodges only set the harshness of Berlin into sharper focus. The importance of this city derived not only from its central and decisive position but from the fact that in Prussia only lodges under the aegis of one of the Grand Lodges were allowed to function. In 1840, the three Grand Lodges encompassed one hundred and thirty-seven daughter lodges with more than 20,-000 members in Prussia alone. Another twenty-seven lodges outside Prussia were affiliated with, and subject to the jurisdiction of, the Berlin Grand Lodges.[38] Inhabitants of large Jewish communities like Berlin, Breslau, and Königsberg were completely barred from Masonic lodges. In Hamburg, as we have seen, there were five lodges which adopted the English rite, while others were controlled by the Grand Lodges of Berlin. Those who considered the exclusion of Jews from voluntary societies an implication of Jewish inferiority had good reason to be concerned.

In 1841 a group of twenty-three Masons, all previously admitted to membership in other cities, gathered in Berlin and decided to storm the Masonic stronghold at its weakest point.[39] It seemed that such a point was the founding of the protectorate. The group, headed by two brothers, Dr. Fr. J. Behrend and Joseph Behrend, imagined that if they could win over the Prince to their side, his influence would be decisive in turning the scales in all, or at least some, of the Grand Lodges. These Berlin Jewish brethren had a better grasp of affairs than the Wesel group. They knew that the Landesloge was completely committed to the principle of Christianity, and they did not delude themselves that they could change its attitude. The Mutterloge, by contrast, had adopted a compromise previously, by admitting that other lodges possessed the right to grant Jews Masonic initiation. To close its doors to those whom it acknowledged as Masons was a glaring contradiction. Most seriously challenged was the opposition of the third Grand Lodge, the Royal York. We have seen that the Royal York had already decided, in 1838, to abolish the restriction against Jewish visitors, but that the implementation of this decision had been deferred till the date of the revision of the constitution which was to have taken place in 1845.[40]

The Jewish Masons addressed the royal patron to assure themselves of his support, or at least to avoid any obstruction from that respected quarter. They repeated the main arguments entitling them to be accepted as visitors, pointing to the Prussian lodges as the sole exception in this matter, as contrasted with lodges outside as well as inside Germany. The writers affixed their signatures with the expression of hope and trust "in the great sense of justice and righteousness, which is deeply ingrained in Your Royal Highness as it is in all the noble members of the Royal Family and which constitutes the happiness and welfare of our Fatherland."[41] The Prince's reply was delayed for over a year,[42] and, when it finally did arrive, caused bitter disappointment. The Prince regretted his inability to help the Jewish brethren attain their desire. With the conferring of his patronage, he had become duty-bound to observe the basic laws of the lodges, and to protect them against all innovations which might deflect them from serving their purpose. Any attempt on his part to influence the lodges could only give rise to quarrels and strife.[43]

The letter was worded diplomatically. It could have been interpreted as indicating the personal identification of the Prince with the principle of Christian exclusiveness, and equally as his having to yield to the force of circumstances. It is possible, however, that even the Protector himself, at first, doubted whether the time had not come to accede to the many requests coming from within and without Masonry and make some concessions to the Jewish Masons. On the other hand, he took the position that the decision must be unanimous and acceptable to all three Grand Lodges—a condition that would automatically foil any idea of change. The formal contact between the three Grand Lodges was maintained through the Grossmeister-Verein, a society consisting of the Masters of the three Grand Lodges which met periodically for joint consultation. The Protector convened this group on January 31, 1842, a week after he had received the letter from Dr. Behrend.[44] The request of the Berlin Jewish brethren and the urgent intercession of Prince Frederick on behalf of the Dutch Freemasons were the joint items on the agenda. The majority of those participating in the consultation expressed the opinion that no bar should be placed before Jewish participation in the work of the lodges. This group, however, lacked any authority to make decisions, and the Protector informed them that he would bring the question before the three Grand Lodges for their consideration. He emphasized that the organizations were free to decide, each according to its own views, yet expressed the hope that these decisions would not conflict with each other.

There was no question what the decision of the Landesloge would be. Its members had never retreated from the position that their lodge was a completely Christian institution.[45] The Mutterloge took up the matter on March 3, 1842.[46] Of the twenty-seven members, the larger number voted to permit visits by Jews, but since a constitutional change required a two-thirds majority, which was not obtained, the prohibition remained in force. There was no need for any decision to be taken by the Royal York, since its members had one and for all voted in 1838 that the restrictions against

admitting Jews as visitors would not be included in the revised constitution of 1845. The Protector took no notice of this fact. In his
letter he states that the restrictions were enforced by all the Prussian
lodges. This plunged the members of the Royal York into confusion
and conflict. Their decision of 1838 obliged them to eliminate the
restrictive paragraph from their constitution as from 1845. Yet they
could only fulfill their pledge by disobeying the directive of the person to whose patronage they were subject. When the time for their
action drew near, the Protector explicitly informed them that the
implementation of the resolution of 1838 would not be in accord
with his wishes ("weil er sonst als Protektor sämtlicher Logen in
den Preussischen Staaten in eine schiefe Stellung gesetzt werden
würde"). The members of the Royal York understood this intima-
tion as a threat that the Protector would resign, that is, withdraw
the royal patronage they had hitherto enjoyed. The Royal York
yielded, and their minutes report that they had been compelled to
submit by considerations of a very high nature ("sie hält sich ver-
pflichtet höhern Rücksichten nachzugeben").[47] The restrictive paragraph, which they had decided to remove, was reintroduced into
the revised constitution of the Royal York in 1845.

Information of what was happening in the Grand Lodges leaked
out to the press. On June 12, 1843, the *Frankfurter Ober-Postamts
Zeitung* reported that the Jewish question had been decided by the
patron, the Prince of Prussia, to the detriment of the Jews, and that
in future even Jewish converts would not be admitted.[48] A vehement denial of these statements appeared in the issue of June 30,
declaring that "His Royal Highness had, out of true humanitarian-
ism refrained from rendering any personal judgment, and had categorically left the decision in the hands of the councils of the lodges
and their heads." There is no truth whatever in these denials. That
the walls barring Jews were not breached at that time must be
blamed on the House of Hohenzollern.[49]

By his decision that the doors of the lodges in his country would
not be opened to Jews, the Prince placed the Prussian lodges in an
embarrassing position vis-à-vis the lodges in other countries, and
also in other German states. The Protector, however, argued that
the Prussian lodges should mainly concern themselves with the preservation of their own unity. As for the outside lodges, some means

to come to an arrangement would be found.[50] This forecast proved
to be correct.

Even though the protest of the Dutch Masons grew more vigorous,
it did not lead to the severing of their ties with Berlin, or to any reprisals against members of Prussian lodges in Holland. Apparently
the members of the Dutch lodges had become wearied by their exer-
tions. On the other hand, a new front against Berlin was opened
soon after Dr. Behrend's request had been refused by the Prince of
Prussia. In July 1843 a letter addressed by the Grand Lodge in New
York reached the Berlin Mutterloge. It complained against the
treatment meted out to registered Masons of the American lodge,
who were refused admission by German lodges because of their Jewishness.[51] The New Yorkers were apparently unfamiliar with the
complexities of the situation in Germany, and they addressed their
protest to the Hamburg Grand Lodge as well. Its leaders promptly
replied that they exercised no bar against Jews; on the contrary,
they had fought for the Masonic rights of Jews.[52] The Mutterloge
in Berlin, for its part, replied by politely describing the local state
of affairs.[53] Even though the protest included, in principle, the
threat of breaking relations, the New York lodge was satisfied by
the replies it received and did not press the matter any further.[54]

The action of the French Masons assumed weightier proportions.
In that country, the Behrend brothers' group had become known
through the publication of the details of the affair in *L'Orient,* a
Masonic periodical with a large circulation. Protests arose on many
sides against the infraction of a principle of Freemasonry.[55] Especially provoked were the lodges in northern and eastern cities,
Bourg, Lyon, Lille, Avize, and Metz being mentioned by name.
These lodges maintained contact with their sister lodges across the
Rhine, and possessed firsthand knowledge of the discrimination
against Jews practiced by the Prussian lodges.[56] One of the personalities prominent in this action can be positively identified, even
though his name has been distorted. He was brother Kirsch, "orateur de la Loge de Luxembourg et prêtre Israelite," none other
than Samuel Hirsch, the philosopher, whose participation in the
struggle of the Jewish Masons in Germany and whose contribution
to Masonic thought will be dealt with later.[57] Hirsch had lived in
Luxembourg, which had been under Dutch rule. There he served
as rabbi and also played since 1843 an important role in the local

109

lodge. Invited to address the Metz Masonic lodge, he delivered a protest oration. This lodge, like the rest of the French lodges mentioned above, had previously delivered its protest to the Grand Orient in Paris, and has asked that the latter intervene on behalf of the Jewish brethren in Prussia. From Metz too came the proposal that the Grand Orient take the initiative in organizing a union of all the Grand Lodges in the world, and so exert combined pressure on the Prussian lodges. The Grand Lodge, which could hardly ignore the request of its daughter lodges, placed the responsibility on its standing committee to prepare a report and to draft a resolution for action. The report was tabled on April 3, 1846, and was published in the bulletin of the Grand Lodge of the same year.

The report unreservedly identified itself with the protest of the daughter lodges. Its author, Charresin, regarded the Masonic lodges as "the eternal religion of mankind," where members of the religions of Moses and Jesus could meet without any barrier. The action of the Prussian Freemasons was considered contrary to the principles of the Order, and was deserving of every protest and censure. Yet protest and censure were the only actions the author of the report was prepared to recommend to the Grand Orient. Reprisals, the measure-for-measure closing of the doors of the French lodges to Prussian Masons or the complete severing of connections with the Prussian lodges, were ruled out on account of the very principle of tolerance which underlay Masonry. To this argument on principle, considerations of expediency and effectiveness were added. The author of the report was fully aware that many of the Prussian Masons were in full agreement with the protesting Frenchmen but were victims of the force of circumstances, as the predicament of the Royal York and the vote in the Mutterloge had proved. Hence, it seemed that it was better to wait for the change to be effected by the power of Masonic truth asserting itself from within rather than to try to force the change on those who, for the time being, refused to recognize its necessity. The view of the compiler of the report was upheld by the standing committee and by the Grand Orient itself. The Prussian lodges listened to the reading of the censure and the protest, and then passed on to the regular order of business.

Some minor action was taken by the Grand Lodge of London.

There, too, bitterness had long been felt at the infraction of the universal principle of Freemasonry. This lodge had demonstrated its positive attitude toward Jews by taking the Frankfurt lodge Zur aufgehenden Morgenröthe, which served at that time as the main door for the admission of Jews to the Masonic order in Germany, under its auspices. London also maintained direct contact with Berlin. The Royal York conducted itself in accordance with the English rite. It was represented by a delegate at the Grand Lodge of London, and vice versa. But the harmony between the two lodges was disrupted in consequence of an incident. The Prince of Prussia, Protector of the Prussian lodges, visited London in 1844.[58] The London Lodge requested that the high-ranking guest be accorded due honor. During the course of the discussion, however, the question was raised whether he deserved such honor at the very time that the lodges under his aegis practiced discrimination against Jews. Opposition was withdrawn when the Royal York delegate remarked that the attitude of the Berlin lodges toward Jews was soon to change. Doubtless he was referring to the elimination of the clause from the constitution of his lodge, which was expected to take effect in 1845. However, the date passed by and the expected change failed to materialize. Instead, new protests on the prohibition against Jews' visiting the Prussian lodges reached the Grand Lodge of London.[59] It thereupon abolished the exchange of delegates with the Prussian lodge, although reciprocal visits between members of the English and Prussian lodges were not forbidden.[60]

Protests by Masons outside Germany against the actions of the Prussian lodges were issued mainly as a matter of principle. In Germany, however, the exclusions actually disturbed lodge life itself. In Hamburg, Mecklenburg, and Lübeck, and certainly in other localities, Prussian lodges existed side by side with the affiliated lodges of Hamburg and visits by members of one lodge to another became an almost daily occurrence.[61] Once the Hamburg lodges had begun, in the forties, to accept Jewish members, their exclusion from the Prussian lodges became a constant reminder of the basic differences between the two types of lodges. The administrative heads of the liberal lodges wished to prevent the obtrusion of these differences; every Jew admitted to membership was informed that he was now

111

entitled to visit all lodges, but that, through some misunderstanding of the rights of Jews on the part of the Prussian lodges, it were better for him to stay away from them.

At first this arrangement was accepted as a modus vivendi. As the number of Jewish members increased, however, and the hoped-for solution did not materialize, the anomaly became all the more pronounced. There were several Christian Masons, too, who saw in the continuing discrimination against Jews an insult to themselves and their principles. A radical group brought pressure to bear on the administration of the Hamburg Grand Lodge to end its policy of appeasement and to insist on the practical enforcement of the rights of its Jewish members. They decided to bring the matter to a head by direct action. Dr. Lazarus, a lawyer by profession and a Jewish member of one of the lodges, appeared at a lodge meeting in Hamburg and sought admission, on the ground that he was an authorized member of a lodge recognized by the host. When he was refused permission to enter because he was Jewish, all the Christian members accompanying him demonstratively rose and left in protest.

112

This event obliged the Hamburg Lodge to take action. The Christian participants demanded in effect that the Hamburg Grand Lodge rally to the defence of the insulted Jew, and prohibit members of Prussian lodges from visiting the Hamburg fraternities until the Prussian lodges would permit the entry of all recognized Masons, without any religious discrimination. The organizers of the protest, however, suffered a bitter disappointment. The Grand Lodge discussed and debated the matter, but accorded the proposal only meager support. Instead of siding with the victim of the discrimination, they accused him of perpetrating a premeditated scandal. Dormant anti-Jewish feelings were aroused, and veteran Masons gave vent to slanderous remarks on the impudence of the Jew's intruding where he was not wanted. The Grand Lodge of Hamburg was satisfied to protest to the Landesloge in Berlin about what had happened, and to demand that the situation be corrected in the future. In Berlin the matter was taken up at a meeting of the delegates of the three Grand Lodges headed by the royal patron. They tended to compromise by silence, by adopting the rule, observed occasionally in the past, that no questions be put to any visitor concerning his religion. If he did not openly declare himself Jewish the issue was to be ignored. The meeting had taken place on February 12, 1847. However, the letter the Landesloge sent in reply two days later disregarded the decision and reiterated its affirmation of the rule that non-Christians were not permitted to enter Prussian lodges. It is apparent that in the internal struggle among the Berlin Masons—a struggle, which had to be carried on behind the scenes because of the Protector—the conservatives held the upper hand. The reply placed the blame for the Hamburg scandal on those who had sought by force to bring a guest into the Prussian lodge which, by its very principles, was barred from permitting his entry. The letter nevertheless expressed the hope that the Grand Lodge of Hamburg would not act with greater severity toward the Prussian lodges than had London and Paris. Their Jewish members had not been admitted, yet they had not closed their doors to Christian members of the Prussian lodges. Furthermore, the Berlin lodges declared that, even if Hamburg were to bar their members, they would willingly continue to grant entry to every Christian visitor.

The authors of the reply correctly gauged the limits to which the Hamburg lodges would go in their defence of the Jewish Masons. The Grand Lodge of Hamburg declared that it did not seek to punish lodge members for the deeds of their leaders, hence it would not forbid reciprocal attendance. On the other hand, it decided to sever all official contact: mutual representation, the exchange of information, and so on, between itself and Berlin. For all practical purposes, Berlin had emerged from the scuffle with Hamburg, too, completely unscathed.

The events traced in this chapter indicate the difficulty of putting liberal ideas into practice under the then existing circumstances. Just as in public life, so too in the lodge halls high-sounding slogans had echoed. Yet concrete action was very limited, and mostly only marginal. The continued preservation of Christian exclusiveness was undoubtedly resented by the majority of lodge members, even in conservative Berlin and certainly in the other cities such as Hamburg, Frankfurt, Leipzig, Stuttgart, and Bayreuth.[62] The endeavor to remove the restrictive barrier against Jews received support from lodges in other countries; yet this support was only moral and had no coercive force backing it. The liberals would not even resort to the means of reprisal at their disposal against the intransigent. All the attacks of the liberal movement broke against the walls of conservatism, its Masonic stronghold being the Landesloge in Berlin, which was reinforced by the Royal House of Hohenzollern. Against the stubborn resistance of the conservatives those who aspired to change were helpless. The idea of placing the Jewish question before a general conference of Freemasons (which was to have convened at Strasbourg) was put forward, but was abandoned in the end as having no prospect of achieving concrete results.[63] Obviously, opponents to the admission of Jews were to be found even in localities outside the jurisdiction of the Berlin Landesloge. These were everywhere evident in voting against the removal of restrictive barriers and probably in voting down individual Jewish candidates for membership even where in principle Jews were permitted to join. In such polls the conflicting outlook on social problems found legitimate expression. On the other hand, the action of the Landesloge in Berlin, prompted by those who wielded power, was to use the authority of the state to prevent the free and spontaneous interplay of social forces.

Ideological Standpoints

Throughout the 1830s and 1840s Masonic thinkers felt impelled to publish their considered opinions on the events that were taking place in the lodges, the events just described. We have already noted the various positions the Masons had taken up on the resolutions proposed in their various societies. Here, however, the attitudes they adopted during the debates were frequently influenced by the individual circumstances affecting their particular lodge. At the same time, the arguments were also presented in systematic form and were incorporated in articles and books. Just as the status of Jewry in society and state had become a primary concern of the community at large, so their status in the Masonic lodges now occupied the center of attention of those fraternities.

Most of the publications dealing with the Jewish problem during the middle of the thirties manifested liberal tendencies. The humanistic outlook on Masonry was presented with greater or lesser consistency. I have earlier referred to the work by Philipp Jacob Cretzschmar.[1] Its purpose was to argue in support of the 1838 proposal for an improvement in the attitude of the Eclectic Covenant toward Jews. Its reasoning was based on a broad historical and ideological analysis which attempted to set Masonry upon foundations far removed from the conflicts between the positive religions. Two years earlier, Theodor Merzdorf had published *Die Symbole, die Gesetze, die Geschichte, der Zweck der Masonei schliessen keine Religion von derselben aus* (The symbols, the laws, the history, the aim of Masonry do not exclude any religion from it), the title explicitly stating the purpose of the book. He aimed to restore Masonry to its pristine purity. Denying any justification for the existence of the higher degrees which involved Christian symbols, he demanded the expurgation of the Christological elements which had crept in, in practice, to some of the lower degrees as well. No Jew or Moslem could be required to take the Masonic oath on the Gospel of John. Indeed, Merzdorf contended that this oath was by no means a long-established Masonic practice. In France the initiates would repeat their oath over the Book of the Constitutions, in England over the Bible—but there it was readily acknowledged that members of other religions had the right to use any other book they regarded as holy. Only in Merzdorf's own lodge, the Apollo of Leipzig, "was a closed Bible placed before us, and our hand given [*Handschlag*], as in all English lodges, on the whole Bible. Not that we take upon ourselves to believe in all its contents, but only in the pure Divinity in which everyone can believe without damaging his own positive religion." This obviously represented a compromising and weakening attitude toward Christian dogma as such. And Merzdorf similarly assumed that the Jews seeking entry to the Masonic lodges also allowed themselves the privilege of a free interpretation of their own religion. He indicated, at least, that the Jews accepted into his own lodge belonged to this type. They were educated, yet "not indifferent to their own faith, even though they had abandoned certain prejudices and modes of worship." The formal observances of the average Jew did not play as important a part in their lives as did the spirit. They did not look upon other religions with disdain, nor did they regard their own as the only true way in which to worship God. Now that both Jew and gentile had shed the peculiar characteristics of their individual religions, they could unite in respect of the residual minimum. "Hence Masonry regards all men as brothers, and excludes no man who believes in God, in ethics, and in the eternity of the soul." [2]

116

Merzdorf honestly regarded himself a Christian; nor did the other Masons who had subscribed to this view on the Jewish problem ever explicitly deny their Christianity. Their decisions had not been dictated by their attitude toward Jews but were a result of their own conception of Christianity and the status accorded to that religion within the Masonic brotherhood. Whoever was satisfied with little, whoever could declare "that the Masonic religion is the quintessence of all other religions . . . and is no more than ethical conduct and the belief in a Supreme Being," could easily reach the conclusion that, in respect of Freemasonry, there was no difference between Christian and Jew. So wrote L. von Orth of Stuttgart in 1838. In his thinking on the subject, Orth could discover no reason for the exclusion of Jews from the German lodges other than the prejudices prevailing against them. "They want no truck with Jews. They do not wish to be in their company. But so as not to exclude them by name, the laws lay down that only Christians be admitted or allowed to visit." [3]

Nevertheless, anti-Jewish motives and tendencies occasionally intruded quite openly even in the remarks of writers sympathetic to Jews. Such was Rudolph Richard Fischer, editor of the *Neueste Zeitschrift für Freimaurerei*,[4] in "lay" life the archdeacon of the Leipzig Church of St. Nicholas. A doubly competent authority, therefore, on the question of the Christian or neutral character of Freemasonry, he repeatedly expressed his views on the Jewish problem and the conclusions these views entailed.[5] He drew distinctions between religion and theology, between Christianity and the Church. Theology, he claimed, was reserved for theologians, and Church doctrine for houses of worship. In the Masonic lodges one article of faith alone united the participants, namely, belief in God. All Masonic symbols, including the Bible, were intended only to proclaim this belief.[6] Freemasonry, then, was a universal human institution, and Jews could undoubtedly find their place there no less than Christians. Fischer therefore unhesitatingly supported the demand to eliminate the paragraph limiting Jewish participation. He denied the allegation that there were no Jews fit for membership. "Among Jews as well, men are to be found in all places who can rival any Christian in respect of intellectual, moral, and aesthetic enlightenment." That these enlightened Jews had divested themselves of the accepted practices of Judaism did not disqualify them in Fischer's eyes. As a liberal theologian capable of distinguishing between the essential and incidental in his own religion, he could show understanding toward such Jews as had exercized the same sense of discrimination in their own religion. "If a Jew comes to recognize that this or that commandment, this or that custom of his religion cannot be reconciled with the demands of his intelligence . . . it is not possible to require of him that he waive his own free thought and calmly bear the chains." He testified to having known such Jews. It was not just the plain, ordinary Jew who joined him at meals without choosing between one food and another, but "even the most prominent and respected members of the Jewish clergy, together with many others of their coreligionists, partook of Christian meals without the slightest qualms." [7]

Nevertheless, Fischer agreed that caution should be exercised in admitting Jews to Masonic lodges and that the numbers should be limited. He justified this qualification by referring to Jewish traits and social behavior, even within the boundaries of the lodges. His

117

remarks offer an interesting insight into the obstacles hindering the adjustment of the two sides to one another. In 1838 no real contacts with Jews in lodges had as yet been made, and Fischer only found himself constrained to warn that the same care be observed in voting on a Jewish, as on any other candidate. Six years later he was able to render a clearer verdict. By then, he had found Jews to be calculating individuals who only minded their own interests. His main accusation was that they refused to mix with other lodge members, that they cohered in their own groups, strove to increase their own numbers, and united to achieve their own particular ends. He cited an actual incident to support his contention. Christians had noted with alarm that the Jews entering their lodge had been arrogating one office after another to themselves. To demonstrate their dissatisfaction, the Christians rejected a Jewish candidate on the grounds of his religion alone, whereupon the Jewish members retaliated by leaving the lodge.[8]

Fischer represented the liberal Christian outlook. The adaptation of the Jews to the pattern of their environment met with its approval, and it expressed the hope that all Jewish particularistic features would rapidly disappear from both their public and private life. "Is it at all worthy of us Christians to be obstinate or blind, and not to see that even in Judaism, especially German Judaism, a healthy spirit has been awakened to life, straining to march forward with the times, while trampling down the molds of superstition?" So wrote Christian Grapengiesser, Master of the Ferdinande Caroline lodge of Hamburg, one of the first to permit Jews to cross its threshold. These remarks were uttered in 1845, a year after the first Synod of Reform Rabbis had convened in Brunswick. Grapengiesser had drawn upon Reform rabbinical writings and the minutes of the conference to prove that a strong urge was impelling Jews "to conform to our German and Christian patterns of life and to abandon the old prejudices."[9] In the religion of reason and with the spread of enlightenment, both of which were conceived as purified versions of Christianity, Masons could hope to find common ground with Jews. One writer grafted the religious partnership with Jews on the concept of Noachism[10] which, as we have seen, had struck some roots in Masonic history.[11] In most instances, however, these Masons were favorably inclined to the absorption of Jews into the lodges because their own belief in the Christian tradition had so

weakened that what remained would not be in conflict with the
remnants of faith of the enlightened Jew.

The liberal awakening of the thirties and forties and the emergence of the new type of Jew, whose features had been shaped by
the liberal ideal, severely jolted the old preconceived ideas which
had been so deeply ingrained in the consciousness of the German
public. Even those who for the time being were opposed to the political and social integration of Jews had left the door open, for the
most part, for exceptional cases or at least in anticipation of future
favorable developments. The obdurate upholders of restrictions
against Jews were constrained to look about for reasons which
would not appear absurd to their contemporaries. We have discerned such signs of adaptation in the Berlin Masons' choice of language. They did not dare to brand Jews as unworthy to keep company with them, but classed them as belonging to the category of
"non-Christians." [12] In this way the impression was to be created
that the restriction was not aimed at Jews as such; indeed, Moslems
and Hindus were often mentioned in the same breath.[13] The expression "non-Christians" implied that Jews were not excluded from
Freemasonry because of any undesirable traits, but because of the
inherent nature of Freemasonry, which confined it to believing
Christians alone. So now we find that, in addition to the conven-
tional anti-Jewish arguments, which had not disappeared entirely,
there were frequent and deliberate attempts to base the exclusion of
Jews on the manifestly Christian character of Freemasonry.

We have previously made the acquaintance of the representative of
the Christian approach, Franz Josef Molitor, as he developed
later.[14] In the name of this positive Christianity, he and his henchmen fought against the Eclectic Covenant's repudiation of its Christian responsibility. From that same circle must have come the author of the anonymous tract *Der Freimaurerbund seinem
philosophischen religiösen und geschichtlichen Standpunkte nach;
nebst Hinblick auf das Verhältniss der Israeliten zu demselben*
(The Freemason Covenant, from a philosophic, religious, and historical aspect; also a view of the relationship of the Jews to it),
which appeared in Darmstadt in 1843.[15] Like Molitor, its author
represents a nonconfessional but nevertheless positive Christianity
possessing certain incontrovertible dogmas. "Man is tainted with sin

[*sündhaft*] not only for having sinned but insofar as he is capable of sinning." The faith in this incomprehensible mystery is the basis of religion, and what is most important is that the content of this belief is bound up "with the one who opened our eyes to this faith." The author also faithfully followed Christian doctrine in assigning a place in the historical process to Jews and Judaism. The Jews had indeed been the chosen people in times gone by. Even to this day, they constituted a nation which had not yet been relieved of its obligation to observe the precepts of the Law of Moses. There was only one way for them to free themselves of that burden, and that was to accept the New Testament. Medieval Jewry had refused to hearken to the Gospels because their hearts had been hardened by Christian persecution. Now that these persecutions had ceased, Jews were free to discern the Christian truths which were hinted at in the Hebrew prophecies. Such premises led the author to conclude that political emancipation should not be conferred upon Jews and, even more so, that they should not be accepted as Freemasons. A Jew faithful to his religion could not participate in Masonic activities. In any event the Jew never regarded himself as united in a covenant of brotherhood with others not of his own kind. He could never find his place among the Masons because he lacked that element which united them. "Only one who brings with him the belief in the founder of this covenant of love can enter it; whoever does not acknowledge the founder remains outside of it, since his love reaches no further than his self-love and the benefits it will allow him." The author did not dare deny that non-Christians were capable of disinterested love. Only the merest few, however, had acquired this trait, and the foundations of the Christian covenant of brotherhood should not be undermined because of them. "For them, the way lies open through the Church." [16]

The author deliberately cloaked his words in theological garb. He was quite familiar with the attempts to provide rationalistic, philosophic foundations for Freemasonry and to interpret its attitude to Jews accordingly. Such attempts, in his view, constituted a retrogression to a more primitive, pagan state which both Judaism and Christianity had been destined to supersede. Masonry deprived of its Christian basis was no more than the social embodiment of that paganism. "According to this [conception], only rationalist Jews and rationalist Christians could find common ground within the Masonic brotherhood. Whether the State should sanction such a meeting ground for those devoid of faith deserved serious consideration." [17] Here before us is a reconstructionist system of thought which, while recognizing the existence of rationalism, sought to reject and disqualify it by deliberate recourse to theological modes of thinking.

These currents of thought nourished the opposition to repeal of the paragraph barring Jews in the Eclectic Covenant. A member named Johann Jacob Scherbius, an active participant in the struggle, summed up this point of view as one of principle. Ancient Christianity, the common element of all its denominations, was the foundation of Masonry. "The Gospels are the cornerstone of our obligations; disbelieve this and you have ceased to be a Mason." The humanistic interpretation created a dualism in Christian Masonic life. If Christianity were true, then no one could "overcome the fear of death and attain salvation except through the merit of the Savior and the faith in Him. Is it permissible then, I ask, for the lodge, in contradistinction, to teach that we are worthy of this also by virtue of our humanistic attitudes and strict observance of the moral law?" [18]

A similar train of thought can be followed in the remarks of Karl Strauss, editor of the periodical *Archiv für Freimaurerei*. In an article published in 1844,[19] he justified the exclusion of Jews on the grounds of the close dependence of Masonry on Christianity. The reference here is to Christianity as distinct from the Church, yet governed by dogma and deriving its meaning and power from its dependence upon its founder, since Christianity "is an empty concept without Jesus, our master, who revealed himself to save man." From Christianity in practice stemmed that humanism which, de facto, had affected even Jews. Yet that humanism had not as yet rendered them completely fit to unite with those "attached to the source of humanism." Strauss justified Jewish demands for civil rights in the political sphere, since Jews were required to discharge their obligations to the state. The Masonic lodges, however, were voluntary associations which could choose their members as they saw fit.

One year after the appearance of Strauss's article, a third writer added his support to the view expressed in the *Archiv für Freimaurerei*.[20] Dr. Ernst Gottfried Adolf Böckel, superintendent and court preacher in Oldenburg, based his argument on a simple faith in Christian truth. He introduced himself as having defended Jews against their enemies during the "Hep, hep" riots of 1819. In the Danzig church, his had been the only voice speaking out against the anti-Jewish excesses ("without taking into consideration that I was perhaps alone in the whole German Fatherland"). Yet defence was not to be equated with religious compromise. Christians were duty-bound to strive to convert Jews. He related how he had rejoiced to see Jews entering the fold of the Church when he was still a student in Königsberg, apparently at the very beginning of the century. No thought had entered anyone's mind as yet of "building new temples out of the ruins of synagogues," of introducing reforms in Judaism so as to prolong its existence. Böckel would not countenance any dilution of either Judaism or Christianity, and could never agree to the excision of the Christian references in the accepted Masonic ceremonies. Generally everyone inducted into a lodge took his oath on the Gospel of John. Some lodges, however, placed a closed Bible before the initiate, thereby hoping to make the ceremony more palatable to Jews. Yet the New Testament constituted an integral part of the Bible, and the person taking the oath could not ignore this fact. "How can we invite the sons of Abraham to become sons of John without them at the same time becoming disciples of Jesus?" In the thirties Böckel was a resident of Hamburg. There he founded a lodge, and he maintained contact with it even after he had moved to another city.[21] His remarks were by no means the opinion of an isolated individual, but were representative of the views of many Masons throughout Germany. What distinguished them was their total commitment to Christianity and their attempt to extend that climate of belief to the world of Masonry as well. For them, whatever applied to Christianity applied to the lodge, and neither institution was open to Jews except at the price of conversion.

Jews endeavoring to gain admission to the Masonic association or seeking to consolidate their positions within it regarded their efforts as essentially a social struggle. On the other hand, non-Jewish Masons looked upon this struggle primarily as an ideological conflict between two wings of the movement, the Christian and the humanistic. Meanwhile, the number of Jewish Masons increased. Among them were several individuals of high intellectual caliber, who now began to air their views in public. Their position in the controversy was obviously on the side of the humanists.

On its semi-jubilee in 1833, the Frankfurt Jewish lodge published in printed form the speeches delivered by its members to mark the occasion. Among the speakers were Michael Creizenach, Jacob Weil, Michael Hess, and Ludwig Börne, all known as doughty fighters in the struggle to abolish the general, political, and social disabilities of Jews. Their commitment to the ideal of equality is clearly evident in their conception of the nature of Masonry. Creizenach admitted that he had found it impossible to discover any moral or religious function in Masonry which was not fulfilled equally well by other institutions. From where, then, stemmed that warm enthusiasm felt by so many for the order? He could find only one answer: "This holy and exalted order . . . is appointed to join together those who, without it, would never come close to one another." Michael Hess added that the "pure, human refinement of man" was the purpose of Masonry. Yet, in the eyes of all of them, the beginning and end of Masonry lay in the removal of the barriers dividing the classes of human society from one another.[22]

Jewish Freemasons were less fortunate than their Christian colleagues. Gentiles, even if they were humanists by conviction, could read any meaning they saw fit into the Christian concepts and symbols, and so accept them. The Jewish brethren were compelled to eliminate all these references and to fill the void with abstract formulas derived from the rationalistic culture they had absorbed. Only here and there did vestiges of Jewish traditions which accorded with Masonic strivings creep in. "When the night of idolatry enveloped the earth, the worshipers of the *One and Only* [italics mine] were able to gather secretly in their catacombs and pyramids." [23] Such scouring far and wide to seek some genealogical tree was very common among Masons. Yet to trace the source of Masonic mystery to the clandestine cultivation of absolute monotheism can only be explained as deriving from the influence of the Jewish—especially Maimonidean [24]—picture of the role of Abraham in an idolatrous environment. One of the members expressed his views in verse. The couplet:

Er ist's, den alle Völker meinen
Wenn auch in anderen Formen stets [25]

reads like a translation of Solomon Ibn Gabirol's *Royal Crown:*

> Yet is not Thy glory diminished
> by reason of those that worship aught beside Thee
> For the yearning of them all is to draw nigh Thee [26]

This game of hide-and-seek the Jewish Masons played with their Judaism could not continue. Some found it necessary to bring the connection between Masonic teachings and Judaism into the open, or at least to take issue with the attempts to tie Masonry to Christian symbols. In 1844, in another address on "Current Masonic Problems," delivered before the Frankfurt lodge, Jacob Weil quoted from King Solomon's prayer at the dedication of the Temple, and referred to him as *unser grosser Obermeister,* "our great Grand-Master." Here Weil was treading on firm ground, since Solomon's Temple had long been regarded as one of the central symbols of Masonry. He did not have recourse to the symbolism discoverable in the structure, but to the ideas expressed in the prayer: "Moreover concerning the stranger that is not of Thy people Israel, but cometh out of a far country for Thy Name's sake . . . hear Thou in heaven Thy dwelling place, and do according to all that the stranger calleth to Thee for" (1 Kings 8.41–43). Here, according to Weil, the father of Freemasonry had set down the cardinal principle of religious tolerance, which was afterward incorporated in the first English Masonic constitution.[27] In actual fact, however, the Freemasons had never accepted King Solomon as their mentor from whose lips instruction was to be sought. King Solomon's religious toleration was "discovered" by Moses Mendelssohn,[28] and from him the nineteenth-century Jewish preachers[29] learned how to put it to use to serve their ends.

Weil might have appeared to have chosen this verse at random to show the Jewish source of toleration. Yet the remarks do carry implications. He added to this verse a famous excerpt, with a slight variation, from the initiation ceremony of the Eclectic Covenant. The candidate for admission would be asked: "Do you acknowledge the religion which was the first to open the heart of man to brotherly goodwill toward all men and which we call by the name of its sublime founder, Christianity?"[30] This formula had provoked earnest discussion and debate among the Masons, for it had constituted the barrier preventing Jews from joining the Eclectic Covenant. Weil emphasized the first half, which mentions the opening of human hearts to universal brotherhood, but conveniently ignored the latter half which credited Christianity with producing it. Solomon had anticipated the founder of Christianity and so had Malachi in his sublime proclamation: "Have we not all one Father? Hath not one God created us?" (Mal. 2.10) [31] Any Mason reading this assertion would immediately have understood that the author wanted to cut Masonry loose from its Christian moorings and to anchor it in ancient Jewish doctrines.

A direct frontal attack aimed at splitting Masonry from Christianity was launched by Gotthold Salomon, the first preacher of the Hamburg Reform Temple. Having been initiated into the Frankfurt lodge in 1837, he subsequently visited other lodges where he delivered his addresses wherever and whenever he found an audience. He was considered a brilliant orator. His Masonic addresses were published in book form in 1845.[32] Most of the speeches contain no overt reference to Judaism and are devoid of any special Masonic train of thought. Like Creizenach, Salomon believed that the Masonic order possessed one primary function and this was the criterion by which it was to be judged. Its task was to unite what Church, state, custom, and human selfishness had rent asunder. What these had split apart, Masonry was to join together. Symbols and ideas were of no consequence. Salomon was prepared to accept John as the patron saint of all Masons, and indeed the lodges were named after him. But the symbolism inherent in his personality was not to be taken as the heritage of Christianity but of mankind as a whole. John gave his life for truth, and every Freemason was obliged to do the same. Vestiges of other Christian symbols were summarily disregarded by Salomon. "Why does the entire Masonic rite contain no trace whatever of Church Christianity? Why is Christ's name not mentioned even once, either in the oath or in the invocation recited at the opening of the session or at the Masonic repast respectively? Why do Masons date their chronology from the creation of the world like Jews and not from the birth of Christ? Why has Masonry no Christian symbol? Why the compass, triangle, and scales? Why not the cross?" Salomon's exuberance and his hom-

125

iletical approach easily thrust aside all objections to the participation of Jews in ceremonies alien and even contrary to their tradition.

Another Reform rabbi active in the Masonic movement strove to surmount the difficulties in these ideologically critical years, in even bolder fashion. He was Samuel Hirsch, the most prominent Jewish philosopher of the Reform era. We have earlier identified him as the orator, referred to as Kirsch, who had delivered a vehement denunciation of the exclusion of Jews before the Metz lodge.[33]

Hirsch, too, began by quoting a verse of Solomon's prayer. He then proceeded to ask whether the descendants of Solomon, Hirsch's Jewish contemporaries, should be entitled to less consideration than the stranger who had been invited by the tolerant king to pray in his Temple. "Is not he [the Jew] a Christian as well by virtue of his belief in the unity of God and in the survival of the soul, and especially in his ethical conduct [*moral pratique*]? True, the Jew disagreed with the Christian in questions of dogma: in regard to the nature of Jesus and the relation between the Father, Son, and Holy Ghost. Nevertheless, "apart from this, does not the Jew follow in the footsteps of John and Jesus? Was not Jesus, who died on the cross, the most noble example of self-sacrifice for the Jew as well as for the Christian, throughout his entire life? Does not this holy example represent to both man's enduring self-sacrifice for the benefit of his brother?" [34]

Coming from a rabbi, such observations seem utterly astounding. They appear to imply that Hirsch was prepared to accept the religious and moral authority of Jesus over himself and his congregation. Yet such remarks become intelligible once attention is directed to the philosophical system which Hirsch had developed in his *Die Religionsphilosophie der Juden*,[35] even before he had joined the Freemasons. Hirsch assigned the same position to Judaism and Christianity vis-à-vis paganism which they were both destined to supersede. Any contradictions between Judaism and Christianity were the results of later developments. As for the doctrines of Jesus himself, these had sprouted in Jewish soil and were by no means alien to the original Judaism. Hence Judaism had no reason to reject Jesus. In fact Judaism was entitled to demand him for herself and restore him to the bosom of Jewish history.[36] In presenting such a demand, Hirsch was not alone. Others expressed similar sentiments before and after him.[37] What was unique was that Hirsch had discovered a place where he could put his theory into operation: the Luxembourg lodge, where he occupied the office of *Orateur,* or permanent preacher. In his addresses delivered in 1854,[38] he developed the idea of a Masonic religion which was the purified essence of Judaism and Christianity. Here Hirsch was not speaking as the philosopher who had discovered common features in the two religions. His function as lodge preacher required him to instruct his listeners in Masonic truths. These he discovered in Jewish and Christian sources, and from them he compounded one obligatory religion. This was not a religion of reason which rationalist philosophy had regarded as the foundation of all religions, but the spiritual, progressive revelation which advances step by step in human history. Judaism and Christianity constituted steps of equal height in this ascent, and in Freemasonry the adherents of both were equal and identical by virtue of their common religion.

By propounding this theory, Hirsch accorded equal status to Jew and Christian in Freemasonry, yet he excluded anyone who was neither Christian nor Jew. Just as the supporters of the Christian viewpoint argued that there could be no true humanism which was not based on Christianity, so Hirsch contended that humanism could only be attained through Judaism or Christianity. Hirsch's particular philosophy was a personal theory, an outgrowth of post-Hegelian German idealism. At the same time, his conception gives clear evidence of the intellectual effort a thinker of his caliber was willing to exert in order to assure equal status for Jews in the Masonic world.

127

IX   Partial Emancipation and Subsequent Reaction

Despite growing fervor for the ideals of liberty and equality in Germany during the period of liberalism, no tangible results were achieved. Then came the Revolution of 1848. It seemed as if the dam had burst, as if all conservative restraints had collapsed, and a mighty flood would soon sweep away all the existing political and social foundations of state and society. The Masonic lodges were not passed by. As we have seen, the last remnants of opposition to the entry of Jews into the Eclectic Covenant in Frankfurt had been removed.[1] Even the gates of the Mother Lodges in Berlin were powerless to withstand the pressure. If the lodge heads were reluctant to conform to the spirit of the times, the daughter lodges in the provinces compelled them to awaken to the necessity for change. Even the affiliates of the Landesloge demanded a reappraisal of its attitude toward Jews. The three Mother Lodges deliberated among themselves—yet reached differing final decisions. In a statement of policy issued in 1849, the Landesloge openly declared that it was neither ready nor willing to yield "to the urge for changes in Freemasonry which had revealed itself as a result of the contemporary craving for reform [*Umgestaltungstrieb*] even among some of our own daughter lodges. . . . The entire Masonic world realizes that the doctrine of our Order is based on the immutable foundations of Christianity." In this view, just as no Jew, be he ever so noble, could belong to any Christian church, so too was it impossible for him to be a member of a Masonic lodge. Hence, though an increasing number of Masonic societies had appealed to the Landesloge to include their Jewish members in its work, it refused to accede to their requests. By this time apparently the government was no longer maintaining its surveillance of Mother Lodge activities. The Landesloge therefore conceded that the Royal York and Mutterloge were entitled to take independent action. It gave its assurance that, whatever steps might be taken by others, cordial relations between the three would not be impaired.[2]

The Landesloge's misgivings in regard to the actions of the other two Grand Lodges proved justified. The Mutterloge refrained from imposing its own will upon its affiliates and called instead for a poll of opinion. From among seventy-one lodges, fifty-six voted to allow members of other lodges, even if they were Jews, to participate in their activities; only fifteen voted against. In the Grand Lodge in Berlin, the resolution passed by a narrow margin, nineteen to sixteen. This majority was deemed sufficient, nevertheless. It was decided that from now on all doors would be thrown open to Jews belonging to recognized lodges. At the same time, the prohibition against accepting Jews or allowing them to join still remained in force.[3] A similar resolution was adopted by the Royal York.[4]

Viewed in historical perspective—against the background of the obdurate and protracted opposition of the dominant forces in Prussia—the opening of the lodge doors to Jewish visitors constituted a substantial gain. Yet it fell far short of placating the many who clamored for the removal of all barriers religious difference had interposed. Among the dissatisfied were adherents of the Prussian system, as, for instance, the members of the two Cologne lodges, the Minerva and Agrippina. They did not wait for authorization from Berlin, and, in 1848, decided to admit Jews. In the Minerva, Jews were elected to high office, one, Blankenburg by name, becoming the Grand Master.[5] The population of the Rhine district and of Cologne especially had been the torchbearers of the 1848 revolution, and so, in the eyes of the local lodge members, implementing the principle of equality had become the order of the day. They paid no attention at all to the formal aspects of the issue, that the admission of Jews had been proscribed by the constitution and that any amendment to it required the ratification of the Berlin Mother Lodge. The Minerva, on the other hand, was affiliated with the Mutterloge which had refused to retreat from its previous position —restriction of membership to Christians only. Yet the time was certainly not auspicious for insisting upon absolute conformity to this principle, and a compromise was proposed. Such Jews as had already been admitted to the Cologne lodge would be allowed to remain as permanent visitors; as for officeholders, the lodges were to hold new elections and appoint Christian brethren to these positions.[6] The Cologne Masons refused to compromise, and so committed a grave infraction of the rules of the Masonic union to which their lodge belonged. It was now liable to punishment in one of

129

two ways: either by being deprived of the Mother Lodge's patronage, and this was tantamount to ordering its dissolution as a Masonic unit; or by the suspension of its activities until it repented its
deviation. The Mother Lodge was content to impose the lighter
punishment. The Minerva brethren, for their part, were in no
mood to yield. They considered themselves no longer dependent
upon Berlin. Mother Lodge authority over the individual societies
in the Prussian cities had previously derived from a state law of
1798 which prohibited all secret societies, but specifically exempted
Masonic lodges affiliated with an authorized Mother Lodge. In
April 1848, however, in the midst of the revolution, the right of assembly became formally recognized and this change was hailed as
one of the concrete achievements of the revolution in Prussia. Accordingly, the Minerva brethren concluded that the individual
lodges no longer needed to depend upon the authorization of the
Prussian Grand Lodges for their functioning and this became the
accepted view not only in Cologne but even in Berlin. The Cologne
Masons could now afford to hope that even in the event of their
connections with the Berlin Lodge being severed, they would be
able to find some other Grand Lodge which would grant them affiliation. On November 23, by a majority of forty-eight to forty, they
resolved to break off relations with the Berlin Lodge. Their executive thereupon applied to the Frankfurt Eclectic Covenant, and,
after a lapse of several months, received an affirmative answer. In
adopting this motion to transfer the lodge's allegiance from Berlin
to Frankfurt, Jews played an active, if not the decisive, part. Several
senior members, however, looked askance upon the change of
affiliation—they even disapproved the admission of Jews—and resigned. The Agrippina was an affiliate of the Royal York. I have no
detailed information on its history, but what is known is that it
achieved the same results as its sister lodge. It also saw fit to disaffiliate from Berlin and it submitted its application for affiliation to
the Hamburg Grand Lodge.[7]

This state of affairs did not endure. As has been stated previously, the Berlin lodges had acknowledged during the revolution
that the freedom to organize applied in full to the Freemasons. Yet,
once the initial enthusiasm had subsided, reaction set in. The members of the Berlin Mother Lodges repented their hasty action in relinquishing their monopoly over the authorization of the lodges in

130

the provinces. They once again sought the help of a protector, namely, the Prince of Prussia. Through his intervention the authorities were apprised of the dangers threatening the state by allowing unauthorized lodges to exist. The ruling bodies took the hint. After some deliberation they declared that, although the right of assembly had not been abrogated, the ordinance of 1798 still remained in force. Accordingly, no Masonic lodge could function in Prussia unless it was an affiliate of one of the local Mother Lodges.[8] This directive was brought to the notice of the Cologne lodge by the police.[9] The lodges understood the warning: they were either to reaffiliate with Berlin or to disband. Nolens volens they submitted. The groups severed their connections with the humanistic Mother Lodges and returned to the Prussian fold.[10] The Christian members who had resigned, rejoined.[11] On the other hand, the Jews were compelled to leave. The Minerva lodge bade a sad farewell to its Jewish members. It awarded them certificates of honor so that their leaving should not be construed as a blemish on their character. Their former lodge commended them to such lodges as admitted Jews. We know that at least one of them was accepted by the Apollo of Leipzig, which had long been in the forefront of the struggle for tolerance.[12]

131

The restoration of Mother Lodge control may be taken as a reflection of a trend that had become especially prevalent in postrevolutionary Prussia. Having been buffeted by the turbulence of those confused days, people were now constrained to re-examine the liberal ideals which had threatened to overthrow the stable foundations of law and order. They reached the conclusion that the older institutions with their tried and tested principles deserved to be strengthened. As for the Church, its representatives girded their strength and threw themselves into their tasks with renewed vigor. The Mother Lodges considered themselves central pillars upholding law and order, and they believed that these pillars would be reinforced if the state would reinstitute its direct supervision of all the Masons. Yet, if they thought such actions would satisfy the new conservatism they were mistaken. Guardians of the Faith and witchhunters in society turned upon the Freemasons as subverters of the stability of state, society, and Church.

The first among the critics was Eduard Emil Eckert, a Dresden lawyer, later active in Berlin, Prague, and Vienna. During the revolutionary years he issued a newspaper which was distinctly conservative in outlook.[13] His first book came off the press in 1852.[14] He honestly believed that he had discovered in Masonry the source of the curse that had rained down upon the earth and destroyed law and order during the past generation. The perfect stable world of former times rested upon the division of society into estates, each occupying its proper station, the lower subservient to the upper, all submitting to the authority of the king or duke who ruled by Divine right.[15] The Church was the source of grace upon earth [16] and in its shadow all men and institutions constituting the realm of active, human society took refuge. This ideal order was shattered, in his view, when Freemasonry, some type of pagan church, entered the world.[17] The Prussian Freemasons' contention that their Order was identical with Christianity was patently absurd.[18] It was a "secret society which had, for the past three hundred years, plotted, instigated, and carried out the revolts against all churches and states, destruction of private property and the overthrow of estates and guilds." [19]

132

Eckert was an outstanding representative of that "conspiracy" outlook on the course of history which holds that the destiny of the world is controlled by clandestine forces. Such were the Freemasons who, according to some scattered references in his writings, were aided and abetted by Jews. We shall see more of this sinister conception and its development, fraught with such dire consequences, in the next chapter. At that time, however, the Jewish aspect of his writings attracted no special notice. His own attention was concentrated mainly on the Freemasons. He fulminated against them in his books and pamphlets distributed among the general public and in the memoranda he submitted to the state authorities in Saxony, Prussia, and Austria. He tried to persuade the rulers to banish the movement from their territories. All symptoms point to Eckert's having been psychopathic; indeed, he ended his life by suicide in Vienna in 1866. Those who met him probably noticed his condition. At all events, no one listened to him; he was expelled from Berlin by police order in 1856. The Freemasons accordingly made little effort to refute his arguments. Even an opponent of Freemasonry, the editor of the important Munich Catholic monthly, *Historisch-politische Blätter für das katholische Deutschland*,[20] found it necessary to dissociate himself from Eckert's views, since he did not want to be associated with Eckert's demented ravings.

The attack launched against the Masons from the pages of *Die evangelische Kirchenzeitung* possessed an altogether different significance. The editor of the newspaper, Ernst Wilhelm von Hengstenberg, was a devout representative of orthodox Protestantism, and he waged an uncompromising and relentless battle for its preservation. Articles appearing in his paper from January 1853 onward denounced Freemasonry as a deistic movement, inimical to Christianity, and its creed and worship. Hengstenberg's paper arrived at the conclusion that Christian clergymen had no place in Masonic lodges, and that Church authorities should compel them to leave. The generalization was drawn that Masonry had reared its head during the period of rationalism and had, in any event, already existed too long.[21]

Whether clergymen could participate in the Masonic movement was by no means a new issue. Readers of the present attacks recalled that the question had been raised in the *Kirchenzeitung* itself some ten years before.[22] At that time the question was left open. Now, however, the newspaper had made up its mind unequivocally. Realizing that they could not afford to underrate their present adversary, the three Mother Lodges hastened to issue a public statement denying the allegations against their principles. "We only accept Christians into our covenant . . . according to the doctrine of the Order and the constitution of the three Prussian Grand Lodges, our principles are specifically Christian. We believe in Christ the Redeemer, who atoned for the sins of mankind, and in our holy Gospels."[23] Such language had until then only been used by the Landesloge. It apparently had been responsible for the framing of the declaration, and the other two lodges merely concurred in its wording. The doubts cast on their Christianity had impelled the Grand Lodges to issue a statement in which the signatories went further in protesting their loyalty than they themselves thought justifiable.

The attempt to placate their antagonists did not produce the desired effect. Hengstenberg persisted in publishing his detailed, polemical articles, which he subsequenty issued in pamphlet form. To him, Freemasonry, even in its extremest Christian form, was merely a blind for freethinking, the denial of Christian dogma. The Chris-

133

tian symbols and concepts incorporated in Masonic ceremonies and systems merely served to reinforce his doubts. He regarded all of these Christological references as deceptions practiced by the earliest Masons to lead the naive and innocent astray. In reality, Christian symbols and ideas in Masonry represented a deviation from the basic tenets of that religion. Masons used the Gospels as a symbol, for the purpose of inducing the desired solemnity, but not to command belief in what they taught. Why did the Masons choose John the Baptist as their patron, if not to indicate that they were content with the precursors of Jesus and would not extend their faith to him? Even the concept of "the Noachides" rendered the Masons suspect in Hengstenberg's eyes. He knew that this concept had its source in Judaism and therefore inferred that the Masons regarded it sufficient to observe "the three cardinal principles" of Noah and had no need of Church dogma and salvation. He derided the attempt to prove the Christian character of the lodges by their exclusion of Jews. "If they are indeed Christian, let them affirm their faith in all the articles of Christian dogma; they will not need to adduce circuitous proofs." [24]

134

Obviously the Masons were not cowed into silence. A miniature literature was compiled in consequence of Hengstenberg's attacks.[25] Relations between Freemasonry and Christianity were re-examined and the various positions restated. The representatives of the Prussian lodges reiterated that Freemasonry and Christianity were identical, and that only through Christianity could genuine humanistic principles be cultivated.[26] It will be recalled that this assertion afforded Samuel Hirsch the pretext for the detailed presentation of his Religion of Humanity, *the* religion which, basically, united Judaism, Christianity, and Freemasonry. Others, on the right and on the left, merely restated their old positions. Some demanded a special status for Christian Masonry which differed essentially from the deistic variety.[27] Others maintained that the originality of Masonry lay precisely in its neutrality to all religions.[28] Hengstenberg aroused a furor of anger among the Protestant clergy against their colleagues who had become Freemasons.[29] As for the Freemasons themselves, his concentrated attack only strengthened the tendency to emphasize their loyalty to Christianity, the outward expression of which was their refusal to permit Jews to enter.[30]

During the Hengstenberg controversy the representatives of the Prussian lodges redefined their attitude, in practice, toward Jews: "Every foreign Freemason who presents proper credentials will be granted very limited permission to pay a visit without his being questioned on his religion or creed—so that individual Jews will, in this way, be able to take part in the meetings. . . . Jews residing in the Fatherland, who had become members of a lodge conducted in accordance with general humanistic principles will neither be accorded membership in, nor granted permission to pay a visit to, the local lodge." [31] In effect, the visiting privileges granted during the year of the revolution were not revoked, but given a narrower interpretation. Foreigners were to enjoy the privilege; local Jews to remain outside.

How long and how strictly the rule was enforced is not known to us. Possibly the exclusion was rigidly enforced only during the Hengstenberg controversy to demonstrate the Christian character of the Prussian lodges.[32] The period of reaction once again opened the way for the New Era, and the change made itself felt in the history of the Masonic movement as well. We hear, in 1858, of a lodge in Posen, affiliated with the Berlin Mutterloge, which persisted in denying membership to Jews, yet would "no longer ask any guest knocking at our door his religion." [33] In following this procedure, the Posen lodge was by no means exceptional. Lodges of other cities instituted the practice as well. Visits by Jews holding membership certificates issued outside of Prussia became a daily occurrence, until the habit became so widespread that the Mother Lodge felt constrained formally to sanction some type of procedure. A twofold problem had to be faced.[34] Lodges were generally meticulously selective in accepting new members; veteran Masons rejected anyone considered unworthy to mix in their company. The senior Masons could now contend that their powers had been drastically reduced, precisely in regard to Jews, since the latter would obtain membership in lodges beyond the boundary of Prussia and then return and participate as permanent visitors in the transactions of the lodge without the approval of the local Masons. A solution was arrived at by the joint agreement of the three Grand Lodges of Berlin and the three non-Prussian Grand lodges: Hamburg, Dresden, and Frankfurt. Henceforth, any Prussian Jew applying to a lodge not affili-

135

ated with Berlin would not be granted membership unless and until an inquiry on his suitability had been addressed to the lodge of his own city. The agreement was concluded between the Royal York and Mutterloge on the one hand and, prior to 1863, the non-Prussian Mother Lodges on the other. In 1863 the Landesloge also subscribed to the agreement upon the request of its Breslau branches.

Financial considerations also played a part in these matters. The member paid initiation and membership dues to his lodge; the visitor was exempt. A Jewish member belonging to a lodge outside his city paid his fees to its treasury, while the lodge which constantly extended hospitality to him as a visitor got nothing. The Royal York found a solution to this anomaly as well. Its constitution gave formal recognition to the status of "permanent visitor," which was defined as referring to a member who constantly attended the meetings of one particular lodge while belonging to another. Although such a visitor did not enjoy all the rights and privileges of the members, he was obliged to pay the equivalent of membership fees to the lodge where he was a visitor. This practice was already followed in 1859. Jews became permanent visitors and the lodge coffers received their just share. In 1869, under the pressure of one of its affiliates, the Mutterloge protested against this arrangement. The members of the daughter lodge saw that the affiliates of the Royal York were benefiting from the contributions of Jewish visitors, while they were not. They demanded that the Mutterloge institute a similar arrangement, threatening that, if their demand was not met, they would seek affiliation where they could benefit from the more advantageous conditions. Instead of yielding, the Mutterloge demanded that the Royal York abolish the special "permanent visitor" category.[35] The latter upheld its previous decision, and refused to yield to the pressure of the Mutterloge. Several years later the Mutterloge gave way and reluctantly introduced the same procedure.[36]

The accommodations for the benefit of Jews were tantamount to a full acknowledgment that there was no real justification for the exclusion of Jews from the Masonic lodges. The Protector was fully informed of the procedures. In the meantime he had succeeded to the throne of Prussia, yet even he was unable to take a stand against the advocates of greater leniency. The quarrel between the two

136

Grand Lodges over the "permanent visitor" status was submitted to his jurisdiction. On this occasion, he did not insist on any uniform practice but allowed each lodge to act as it saw fit.[37]

The heads of the lodges themselves encouraged the circumvention of the prohibition against Jews. They recommended Jewish acquaintances for membership in lodges outside Prussia so that these individuals could attend the local lodge meetings as "permanent visitors." [38] Nor were these isolated acts. The sixties constituted the period of the greatest decline of anti-Semitism in Germany. At that time the generation growing up after the Revolution of 1848 was finding its way into adult society and, even though full emancipation had not been achieved, saw no reason to fight over it. The final episode occurred as the result of an internal, political struggle—the union of the northern provinces in 1866, and the German Unification of 1871. Public opinion at that time was focused primarily on political and military events. Attention was diverted from social affairs, and so from the Jewish problem as well. The Jew who conformed ever more closely to the cultural patterns prevailing in the country, became a more frequent phenomenon and those seeking admission to the lodges were no longer single individuals. A significant section of the Jewish community was now comprised of men of this type of social standing, cultural achievement, and behavior pattern. Apparently the arrangements allowing Jews entry to the Prussian lodges was in effect an admission of the prevalence of this Jewish type which had become completely acclimatized to the social environment.

137

Needless to say, this circumvention did not constitute a complete and final solution, not even de facto and certainly not de jure. To attain the status of an ordinary permanent visitor, the Jew had to travel abroad and to provide himself with a recommendation to a lodge where he was unknown. Only men of means or with influential contacts were able to achieve this objective; the rest had to suffer discrimination. Pressure to enter the Masonic lodges had steadily grown among segments of Jewry which had become fully acculturated and, with the restrictive conditions obtaining in Germany, could not find its proper outlet. This situation is well illustrated by an incident which the Mother Lodges of Berlin were forced to deal with.[39] In 1860 a Jewish merchant named Hermann Bloch was caught distributing spurious Masonic membership certificates, purported to have been signed by one of the London lodges. The holders of these certificates had paid membership dues for their so-called affiliation and had hoped in this way to gain access to the local lodges as visitors. According to the sources, the majority of the victims were Jews, and the list of names confirms this conclusion.[40] And no wonder! Jews were the only ones who needed to traverse these circuitous paths to reach their goals.

Viewed as a matter of principle, the situation was quite anomalous. The practices in the lodges bristled with inconsistencies, which were easy to hide but difficult to resolve. It was not surprising that the situation was challenged even within the lodges themselves. We have detailed evidence of the deliberations of the Mutterloge, which we shall examine presently, but know nothing of what took place in the other lodges except for the results. The Royal York accepted the logic of the situation, and in 1872 repealed the restrictive clause. Henceforth Jews were formally entitled to election as full members.[41]

For its part the Landesloge refused to allow any debate on the issue. Although Jews were freely admitted as visitors, it remained adamant in its insistence that formal membership was forbidden to them because of the contradiction between adherence to the Jewish faith and Masonry as interpreted by the Landesloge. One of the leaders of that lodge, a well-known author in his time by the name of Adolf Widmann, undertook the defense of this position in his article: "Brief an einen Juden und Freimaurer" (Letter to a Jew and a Freemason).[42] Widmann here explained to his Jewish colleague—and this may not have been just a literary device—that there were two currents in Masonry, each following a different course in its attitude toward Jews. The English current, which took in the Royal York, for instance, viewed the basis of Masonry as primarily humanistic, while the Christian elements which had attached themselves to it were secondary. Hence the latter were reducible to such minor proportions that a Jew could belong to such a lodge without compromising his conscience. By contrast, Landesloge Masonry was firmly rooted in Christianity and its humanistic elements were merely an outgrowth. No deviations from Christian symbols and content could be countenanced. Anyone joining these lodges had to accept Christian doctrine in its entirety and to acknowledge the implications of obviously Christian symbols. Could any Jew do so without at the same time undergoing a Christianizing conversion in "acknowledging the historical process and the power of Christ in this history," that is, that with the advent of Jesus, Christianity had superseded Judaism?

The Landesloge cast about for a refuge secure from the vicissitudes of the times, and left it to others to effect the changes the times demanded. Widmann explicitly welcomed the action of the Royal York, which, at the time his "Brief" was written, was about to grant formal entry to Jews. He expressed the hope that their differences in practice would not strain the friendship of the Berlin Grand Lodges for one another. On the contrary, "by this means the obstacles which constantly keep Jews restive would be removed, since they had to fetch their Masonic credentials from non-Prussian districts even though they are as much citizens as we are." Finally Widmann earnestly appealed to his real or imaginary Jewish Mason to rest content with this compromise: "If the sons of your tribe will be able to control themselves and in conformity with Masonic morality restrain their propensity to exaggerated exuberance at their victory, to pay respect to their reason alone, and to regard each success a stepping stone to further progress—then all will be well." Widmann's attitude, which was quite typical for these times, was not free of prejudice against Jews and Judaism. Nevertheless, he saw himself and his like forced to retreat and looked for a dignified way out to new positions where he hoped to fortify himself and hold his ground.

An open struggle broke out between the two factions within the Mutterloge. In 1870, two affiliated lodges in Osnabrück and Gotha proposed that the restrictive clause be repealed by the action of the Mutterloge itself. In addition to the regular arguments, which had been aired for some time, the Osnabrück Masons pointed to the lack of consistency in the existing situation. "If a recent majority decision of the meeting held . . . in the year 1868 . . . permitted the entry of Jewish members in our lodges as permanent visitors, it would be only consistent to waive the acknowledgment of the Christian faith as a precondition for entering the Masonic league." [43] The Gotha lodge proposed that in preparing for 1872, the year appointed for the periodic review of the constitution, the affiliated lodges be polled on their attitude to the Christian restriction: whether it should be retained or whether the first three degrees be-

139

come open to all men. This proposal was seconded by other lodges.[44] It was even placed on the agenda and considered by the various affiliates of the Mutterloge.[45] The referendum requested was held in 1872, and the results became the basis for ensuing discussions.[46] The minutes of these deliberations provide an important historical source for assessing the position of Jews both within and without the Masonic brotherhood.

At that time, one hundred and eleven lodges with a combined membership of 12,265, were affiliated with the Mutterloge. Of these, 7,575 Masons had attained the degree of Fellow of the Craft, the prerequisite, according to the constitution, for the right to vote. For the referendum, 2,787 members registered as present, and the commission tabulating the results confirmed that distance had prevented about a third of those possessing the franchise from attending and voting. Just a few more than half the membership, then, were responsible for the final decision: 1,390 voted for repeal; 1,-397 favored the retention of the Christian clause.[47] Opinions were equally divided and the formal decision to retain the restriction can only be regarded as accidental.

140

The members of the commission did not consider their task completed with the mere tabulation of the votes. They tried to determine its meaning by a breakdown of the various components. The ayes and the nays were far from being evenly divided in each lodge. In sixty-five lodges, the majority favored repeal; in forty-three, the majority voted for the status quo, while in two, opinions were about equal. It appears that in the smaller lodges the majority generally desired repeal, but it was not so in the larger. It was clearly shown that in the populous lodges of the large cities—Danzig, Königsberg, Stetin, Breslau, Magdeburg, Münster, and especially Berlin ––large majorities had voted against the repeal. Even in Cologne, where sentiment for repeal ran high, the resolution was carried by a small majority. That a larger number of lodges voted for repeal than for retention was due to the smaller cities. Having observed the situation at close quarters, the members of the commission had an explanation for this phenomenon: "The lodges belonging to the majority have been granted sufficient opportunity to see the situation in actual practice. Many non-Christians participate devotedly as permanent visitors in the workings of the lodge and they are indistinguishable from the members of longer standing, but in respect to Masonic activity and brotherly love. Now, if these brethren had been compelled to seek admission to other lodges, the absurd result would follow that the examination of the candidates and their membership dues would be transferred to these other lodges, while in reality the accepted candidates would, under the guise of visitors, become members of the lodges of our League and fulfill the functions of regular members." [48] One of the representatives of the minor lodges, brother Nebel of Neustadt Eberwalde, testified to the peculiar situation obtaining there in these terms: "The brethren of the smaller lodges find themselves in a painful predicament, since they come into intimate contact with their Jewish brethren. . . . It is almost impossible to maintain relations with them in amicable fashion and this vacillation is intolerable." [49] Evidence of the close relations between Jews and non-Jews in these lodges was furnished by others, among them the representative of the Posen lodge.[50] Most of the electors, however, had not had the benefit of such experiences and their decisions were influenced by other considerations.

The distinction between the large and small lodges was not the only demarcation line dividing the voters. There was also a regional factor. In the Rhine district, the majority supported the repeal (243 to 62 in fifteen lodges); in Westphalia 94 to 26 in eight lodges; Posen, 125 to 64 in six lodges; and Prussia 142 to 116 in ten lodges. In Pomerania, the overwhelming majority voted for the status quo (201 to 72 in ten lodges); smaller majorities favoring the retention were obtained in Saxony (354 to 204 in sixteen lodges); Brandenburg (363 to 237 in twenty-two lodges) and Silesia (153 to 133 in eleven lodges).[51]

An unequivocal explanation can be advanced for the liberal tendencies of the western areas. In a discussion held earlier, in 1870, the Master of the Cologne Lodge declared, according to the minutes: "In my birthplace there are many Jews who have been accepted across the border, and the same applies to other lodges on the boundary. We would have avoided many unpleasantnesses had we too accepted Jews." In the final discussion the Düsseldorf representative protested against the opponents of change: "The brethren have not made themselves fully aware of the extent to which the western lodges have to grapple with this problem." [52] The relatively improved social status of the Jews in the western areas is also attested to by other sources, and we have here a concrete example of how the proximity of the border affected events in the vicinity. Whether the voting reflected a favorable or unfavorable attitude toward Jews in general cannot be determined without corroborating, documentary evidence from other areas of society. Nevertheless, a clear decision within a small group which possessed standing and influence indicates that a similar mood prevailed even beyond its periphery.

The poll of the lodges had no legal force. It could only offer guidance to the constitution commission in submitting recommendations to the Grand Lodge. The committee saw no further prospect of achieving any change in the status quo and recommended that a decision be deferred to a later date. The Grand Lodge gathered together on April 21, 1873. It consisted of seventy-five members, forty-seven of whom were chosen by the central body and twenty-eight of whom were delegates appointed by the affiliated lodges.[53] The inclusion of local representatives was a recent innovation, a concession to the prevailing parliamentary spirit.[54] Here the negative decision was much more clear-cut than in the lodges themselves. The recommendation to defer action was disregarded, and an immediate decision demanded. Only thirty of those present voted affirmatively—and these were divided evenly between the Grand Lodge members and the delegates—while forty-five voted to retain the status quo.[55] The awakening of the seventies had also proved abortive.

142

It may appropriately be asked: what were the factors that determined the present decision? There was no indication of any direct influence exerted by the House of Hohenzollern in this instance. Wilhelm still held the title of Protector, but as soon as he ascended the German throne he appointed his son, later Frederick III, as his deputy and the latter was considered sympathetic to the liberal cause. We do not know how the two personally felt toward the resolution on the Jews, but at all events, once the Reich had come into being, a certain change was noticeable in the attitude of the monarchy to the Freemasons. Already in 1866, when the northern provinces united, questions were raised about the future of the lodges in Frankfurt and Hessen-Kassel, now that these two localities had come under Prussian hegemony. The humanists among the Masons feared that they would now become subject to Prussian regulations which only permitted lodges authorized from Berlin to function.

There had been public discussion on the course to be followed if the humanistic lodges were forced to act contrary to their convictions and cancel the membership of their Jewish brethren.[56] These fears were not idle fancies. The Berlin circles sought to persuade the government to permit their Christian approach to prevail throughout the greater Prussian territory.[57] Negotiations were protracted and, before these could be brought to any conclusion, the Franco-Prussian war had broken out and the German Empire had emerged. Now all the German lodges, including the Grand Lodges of Hamburg, Saxony, and Bayreuth, came under Hohenzollern dominion. Had the rulers desired to be consistent, they would have forced all of these lodges either to accept the Prussian, Christian version of Masonry or to go out of existence. Such a step, however, would have been branded as a Prussian attempt to dominate public life in the small federal states, and political expediency at that time dictated that no such impression be created. The Kaiser accordingly addressed an inquiry to the union of Grand Lodges in Berlin: did they still recommend that the Prussian practice be imposed on the lodges in Frankfurt? At the sessions of the *Grossmeister-Conferenz*, which consisted of delegates of the three Grand Lodges and was presided over by Crown Prince Frederick, it was decided to reject the recommendation and to permit all the Masonic unions outside of pre-1866 Prussia to continue as before. Only one condition was stipulated: the lodges had to be affiliated with a German Grand Lodge. The Alsace Masons were ordered to cut loose their ties with the Grand Orient of Paris, and the time came too for the Frankfurt *Judenloge* Zur aufgehenden Morgenröthe to take its leave of the Grand Lodge of London.[58] The *Grossmeister-Conferenz* even petitioned the Kaiser to consent to confer his protection on the Grand Lodges outside of Prussia if and when these made application.[59]

In rendering such decisions the Prussian lodges not only conceded that the humanistic lodges outside of Prussia were entitled to exist but that they possessed the same Masonic standing as the Prussian. In their own debate on the retention of the restrictive clause, the Prussian lodges argued for their right to differ with, rather than to oppose, the liberal approach. The reason for their disagreeing was their particular attachment to positive Christianity. Their symbols, signs, and ceremonies possessed Christian connotations, and the presence of Jews in their activities would only vitiate the power

143

and meaning of the ceremonies and at the same time compromise the conscience of the Jews. The Prussian lodges had introduced higher degrees, above the three basic ones, and these were plainly Christian in character. At least one of their brethren argued that it would be deceitful to accept a Jew in a lodge when he could never be raised to the higher degrees.[60] This fervent attachment to Christianity also revived some remnants of anti-Jewish prejudice. There was talk of the superior morality of the Christian, not as evinced in actual behavior but as the conclusion drawn from the theological premise that only Christianity could raise man to the pinnacle of ethical conduct.[61] Yet, even those who openly subscribed to this view admitted that there were exceptional Jews who had become adapted to Christian principles, but for them it would have been better to have embraced Christianity in toto. The general tendency was to separate any positive attitude toward Jews from the question of their acceptability in the Prussian lodges. Brother Meyerdorff of Berlin, an honorary member of the Grand Lodge, testified in 1870 and again in 1873 that he himself had recommended Jews for membership in those lodges which could legally accept them, but not in the Prussian lodges where they had no place.[62]

144

Despite the negative outcome of the debate and the vote, the tone and content of the arguments reflect a decline in animosity against Jews, a decline characteristic of the sixties and early seventies. Brother Bauer, Master of the Posen Lodge, took the floor during the opening of the discussions in 1870. As a result of what he had experienced in his own lodge, he was in favor of admitting Jews. He also made a statement of general significance for the whole of that period: "During the past decade, a powerful change has come about in the appraisal of Jews. We also have to submit to that change." [63] Actually many of the debaters, both pro and con, believed that the opposition was only strong enough to defer, but not to defeat, a final, favorable decision.[64] Time, it seemed, was on the side of the Jews.

Certainly the protagonists of change did not give up in despair after their setback in 1873. Three years later the question was once again placed on the agenda of the Grand Lodge.[65] Once again the resolution failed to obtain the requisite two-third majority for its passage, but the breakdown of the votes revealed a decided shift of opinion. Of the one hundred and forty-five present, eighty-eight supported repeal and only fifty-seven voted against. The distribution of the voters, too, was different this time: ninety-three of the one hundred and forty-five were delegates appointed by the affiliates and sixty-five of them voted in favor of repeal. The negative decision was due to the members of the Grand Lodge who did not represent any affiliated lodge but had been chosen from among the Berlin lodges on account of their personal qualifications and social standing. Understandably, the majority of the delegates from the province were in favor of the repeal—these would have been the people most anxious to come or the ones most urgently pressed to come by those eager for a positive decision.[66] In any event, the protagonists of change were convinced that, had the decision depended only on the delegates representing lodges, they would have had the upper hand. They therefore now directed their efforts toward effecting a change in the constitution that would weaken the hold of the members chosen by the Grand Lodge.

What is of primary interest in the 1876 assemblage is not the distribution and character of the voters or the final results. The novelty lies in the arguments advanced by the opponents of change. The guardians of Christian Masonry had now become imbued with the new, critical attitude toward Jews which had begun to permeate Germany some few years after the establishment of the Empire. The person summing up the debate for the opposition explicitly brought up the Jewish participation in the *Gründerzeit*,[67] the business speculations that had flourished soon after the war and that had ended in the financial disaster of 1873.[68] The *goldene Internationale*,[69] the allegation that there was international cooperation among Jewish bankers, also received mention. Accusations of "alien" and "harmful" elements, with both biological and social connotations, reared their heads. It was argued that the Jews would constitute "the fertilization of the soil with foreign elements." "Jews are knocking everywhere, trying to enter polite society." "They are nevertheless rebuffed everywhere, because these elements are nothing but repulsive to us on account of their mode of life and their social conduct." In support of his last assertion, the author cited the experience of the Royal York. This lodge had decided, in 1872, to permit the acceptance of Jews. Yet all candidates for admission had been voted down as socially objectionable.[70]

145

These minutes are not the only item of evidence revealing that a new spirit had penetrated the lodges, some years before Stöcker's provocative speeches and Treitschke's accusing articles had inflamed public opinion.[71] As a result of the Berlin deliberations, four articles appeared in the *Freimaurer Zeitung*. Previously this newspaper had been one of the most ardent supporters of the Jewish cause. Three of the articles upheld its former views; the fourth, however, the longest of them all, was entitled "Die Gründe der Abneigung gegen die Juden" (The grounds for aversion to Jews).[72]

According to the author, the Master of his lodge (he did not specify which) had included the Jewish question in the agenda of the sessions devoted to current affairs. He had taken upon himself to submit this topic to the brethren, and he had done so in an utterly unusual manner. Instead of dealing with the application of Masonic principles to other religions, he decided to "rally the anti-Jewish voices that had made themselves heard in the non-Masonic world." He had hoped in this way to penetrate to the root of the problem. This was to be found, according to the sources which he relied on, not in religious differences (since the modern era had achieved unqualified tolerance in religious affairs) but in the different nature of the Jews, which could be discovered through the anthropological study of ethnic groups. He cited the findings of this type of research in respect to Jews—findings which, to him, seemed clear and authoritative beyond all doubt. The basic thesis of this theory is that "the Jew is equipped with all the virtues but also with all the vices of the Semitic race. . . . A deep abyss separates them from the German tribes with regard to racial fitness and ability in certain patterns of ideas, thought processes, and *weltanschauung.*" Then as now this difference is unbridgeable. "Perhaps some brother or other is now, for the first time, becoming aware of the immutable nature of national spirit and still doubts the permanence of the social phenomena it creates." The author therefore mustered historical facts ranging from the days of ancient Egypt to his own times. And, if this difference is so firmly anchored in ethnic elements, it is no wonder then "that we feel almost instinctively that the Jew is a son of alien seed." No one can escape this feeling of strangeness—neither the highly educated nor the completely enlightened. And this difference cannot be ascribed to environmental influence alone; the Jews are inferior to Aryans in their moral conduct as they have shown in the *Gründungsjahre*. They are greedy for profit, usurious, and the instigators of quarrels. Above all, Jews despise others and withdraw from them out of snobbish pride. It is no wonder they have been repaid in kind by their non-Jewish neighbors. The gentile's hatred for the Jew was merely a reciprocal reaction to the Jew's hatred of the rest of the world. An editorial note appended to a rebuttal appearing in the next issue stated that the article was not intended as an attack upon Jews and was, from the beginning, merely "an objective description of the causes of a situation which undeniably exists." [73]

The increasing appeal to racial justification of the social exclusion of Jews shows how deeply the new conception had encroached into social attitudes. When Treitschke stepped forward in 1880 with his public denunciations of post-emancipation Jewish participation and behavior in social and political life, he too used arguments totally unrelated to religious conflict. He maintained that he was merely stating aloud what others were whispering.[74] Masonic sources confirm his assertion, and even narrow down the determining of the period when the change occurred, when the expectation of Jewish integration gave way to anti-Jewish hostility. This change took place during 1874–75.

147

X   The Source of "Jews and Freemasons"

Although the Jewish struggle for the right to enter the Prussian lodges had been confined within the Masonic brotherhood it had become public knowledge since news of happenings within the lodges often leaked out to the general press. Hence, if it was at all conceivable at the time for the two names, Jews and Freemasons, to be linked together in the public mind, it could only have been in contrast and in conflict—as two camps arrayed against each other. True, both Jews and Freemasons had been the targets of attacks by their respective opponents. Animosity against Jews hardly requires any explanation; it was nourished by ancient religious, national, and cultural traditions. Yet, as far as the generations of the 1830s and after were concerned, anti-Jewish discrimination seemed in headlong retreat, although vestiges of the hostility of the past were still sufficiently strong to set the Jews apart as a group burdened by an alien and doubtful nature. We have encountered examples in Masonic history of the relaxing of restrictions against Jews and of the doubts concerning them. At any rate, whatever occurred within the seclusion of Masonic chambers was only a reflection of what was taking place in society as a whole.[1] If, on the one hand, a critical attitude toward Masonry manifested itself among the general public, the front was drawn along different lines than the opposition to Jews. As yet there was no connection between the antagonism toward Masonry and the animosity toward Jews either in regard to the ideas or the persons involved.

The earliest signs of the coalescence of the antagonism toward the two appeared in Germany and France during the sixties and seventies. As early as in 1848, there had come off the press a series of anonymous pamphlets entitled *Zur Aufklärung der grossen Freimaurer-Lüge* (On the disclosure of the great Freemason lie),[2] which attributed the misfortunes of the revolution to the activities of the Freemasons, and accused them of being influenced or directed by Jews, the latter contention being based on the fact that all the Grand Lodges (except the Prussian) accepted Jews. The author concluded that "in the republican aspirations of the Masonic league Jews constitute the driving force." [3] He fused his hatred of Jews and Freemasons and seized upon every means at his disposal to attack the two targets. In one of the issues, he reprinted Johann Christian Ehrmann's 1816 pamphlet, *Das Judenthum in der M [aurere]y*.[4] As will be recalled, Ehrmann was a Freemason and at the same time violently anti-Semitic.[5] In his day he had warned the Masons against admitting Jews to their brotherhood, since Judaism and Freemasonry were essentially and innately antagonistic to one another. As for the anonymous author, he noted that since that time Jews had conquered the lodges and now quite openly controlled them.[6] To prove his assertion, he cited the remarks of the Frankfurt Jewish Masons Hess, Weil, Goldschmidt, and Börne.[7] As has been shown, these men had contented that Masonry had emerged into existence to fulfill the humanistic ideal which stood above any individual's adherence to a particular nation or religion.[8] Such a definition of the nature of Masonry was, in the eyes of the author, identical with the aspiration to found a world republic.[9] The Jewish Masons' affirmation of their faith that the Masonic ideal, as they understood it, would ultimately prevail was construed by him as their confidence in eventually seizing control of the reins of government.[10]

149

These leaflets were printed during the turbulent days of the revolution. They failed to attract attention and disappeared. There is no mention of them in Masonic bibliographies.[11] Yet they did leave an impression on one person at least, on Eduard Emil Eckert of Dresden. His books betray the influence of this double-edged propaganda. In presenting his arguments against the Jews, Eckert quoted the same sources and followed exactly the same order as the author of the leaflets.[12] At times he even transcribed the author's notes.[13] Eckert's works did not fall stillborn from the press. It would be of interest to see how his anti-Masonic propaganda was dovetailed into his anti-Jewish antagonism.

In opposing the Masons, Eckert's point of departure was his fear lest the patriarchal social order begin to disintegrate. His propensity for suspecting conspiracies moved him to believe that the transformations occurring before his eyes were the outcome of deliberate plots by sinister forces lurking within the closed lodges of the Freemasons. Now this process of disintegration had also affected the Church's position in the state and damaged the Christian character of society. Eckert was convinced that those directing the destructive process were also bent upon eradicating Christianity from the world. To him, the Freemasons appeared as some kind of profane and pagan church.[14] Hence it was easy to clutch at this straw, that the Jews, the one people that had consistently rejected Christianity, had moulded the character of Freemasonry. He adduced the statements by Jewish Masons quoted in the anonymous pamphlets and added excerpts from Gotthold Salomon's book [15] in order to ridicule the foolish who believed that Freemasonry was interested in the welfare of Christianity. By its very nature Freemasonry was a rival institution to the Church.[16]

Although his primary concern was with the Masonic movement, Eckert's dread of the impending disintegration of the old order impelled him to deal directly with the Jewish question. The anti-Semitism of that period—when emancipation was progressively becoming actualized—was nourished to a great extent by the challenge to the fixed and accepted patterns of life. As the Jews continued to become integrated into society, they appeared to be tearing down the fences and weakening the structure of ancient institutions.[17] Eckert explicitly stated his position on Jewish demands for equality in the political, social, and economic spheres. He rejected their claims, not, he asserted, out of hatred, but in order to protect the indigenous population against being overpowered by an alien, aggressive, and greedy nation. These sons of a foreign race, scattered over the face of the earth, had entered into an alliance with the Freemasons, those other agents dedicated to the undermining of society. Eckert joined together the two enemies of the old order, and fashioned them into a hydra-headed monster. "Moreover, the world Jewish community has a concrete, dangerous, and sinister ally in the world league of the Freemasons, since the latter aims at the destruction of the Christian faith and its replacement by ancient paganism; and since Freemasonry, too, does not acknowledge any Fatherland, it becomes the natural ally of the Jew against Christianity and the state." [18]

Summarily dismissed even by those who were in principle antagonistic to Freemasonry, Eckert's arguments did not, nevertheless, disappear entirely from the world. He had not been the only one who had accepted as reasonable the premise that the Freemasons were the source of all evil in the world. A Catholic writer, well known in his time, named Alban Stolz set up the Jews and Freemasons as the common target of his criticisms whenever he had the chance. He made good use of the leaflets of an anonymous Berlin author who claimed to have been a Mason in the past but had now emerged into the open to reveal their secrets. According to that author, the activities of the Masons were controlled by a certain secret society comprised of Jewish members, and these Jews were the instigators of the periodic revolutions that threw the world into convulsions.[19]

Ten years after Eckert had died, Georg Michael Pachtler, a Jesuit, opened his barrage of critical anti-Masonic writings.[20] In temperament, Pachtler was Eckert's direct opposite. He stated his case with calm deliberation; his claims, however, were no less extreme than those of his predecessor. He, too, attributed the decay of his own generation, the undermining of the social order, the abandonment of faith, and the challenge to the authority of the Church to the surreptitious activities of the Masons.[21] The seventies were the years of the *Kulturkampf* in Germany and the period following the abolition of the Pope's temporal sovereignty in Rome; and so the Jesuit's accusations appeared to rest on incontrovertible facts. Naturally his assertion that the Masons were responsible for all these evils was empty talk. Pachtler himself conceded that the Masons did not constitute the only factor in the corruption of the world; yet, in his eyes, the Masonic lodges appeared as the focal point of all evil, since they had from their very inception been founded on humanistic principles, natural morality, and the bare, deistic creed. To be content with such beliefs seemed to be a clear and complete repudiation of Church doctrine and authority. To prove that this was the trend of the lodges, Pachtler adduced quotations from Masonic literature and here, he relied, as did Eckert, on the pronouncements of the Jewish Masons who had emphasized that Masonic doctrine was distinct from and independent of Christianity. Pachtler did not distinguish between those lodges which had openly espoused humanistic principles and the Prussian lodges which had proclaimed themselves Christian institutions. Such protestations of loyalty to Christianity seemed to him nothing but lip service.[22]

In the seventies, when even in the Prussian lodges the number of Jews admitted as permanent visitors had increased considerably, this allegation did not appear entirely unfounded. The fact that

151

Jews were formally accepted as members in Hamburg and Leipzig but not in Berlin or Breslau evoked his derision.[23] He even went so far as to predict that the last barriers to Jewish equality would soon come down;[24] in fact he had at one time mistakenly believed them to have been removed already.[25] It was only logical for Jews to be admitted to the lodges since Masonic doctrine was, as far as he was concerned, identical with Judaism especially in its Reform manifestation. At any rate, Jews and Freemasons were natural allies, since both espoused the same cause, the abolition of Church authority and the eradication of the belief in Jesus. Pachtler believed that even an orthodox Jew would be prepared to join the Masonic movement, if only to attain his one, holy objective—the destruction of the Christian faith. What appeared to him first as a logical necessity, he afterward asserted as an established fact: "Long experience has taught us that, relatively, it is Jews who participate to the greatest extent in Freemasonry. Indeed, there are some who believe that in the composition of its members the Grand Orient of Paris is two-thirds Jewish."[26] The identification of Freemasonry with Jewry had now taken a significant step forward.

Opposition to Freemasonry as such was not merely a local phenomenon; it had manifested itself all over Europe, if not internationally. Propagandist writings, pro and con, in large numbers were translated from one language to another. Eduard Emil Eckert's magnum opus, *Der Freimaurer-Orden in seiner wahren Bedeutung* (The true significance of the Freemason Order), enjoyed the same fate, its French version appearing in Liège in 1854.[27] So the seeds of common hostility to Jews and Freemasons were first sown in France. There the soil was more fertile than in Germany where Jews still had to fight, in the fifties, for their rights to gain entry to the lodges as equals. In postrevolutionary France, however, all barriers against Jews with regard to Masonry had once and for all been removed. In 1848 the doubt had arisen in one of the French lodges as to whether a Jew was eligible for elevation to the fourth degree, the name of which was in some way tied to a Christian symbol. The case was referred to the Grand Orient, which ruled that a Mason's religion was in no way connected with his Masonic rights. Nor was he ever to be asked about his religion.[28] Jews were certainly represented in the French Masonic leadership. The most prominent figure in all French Jewry was Adolphe Crémieux. He was known as an active participant in the brotherhood, and by the end of the sixties he had become the head of the Scottish rite.[29] If anyone wanted to combine his hatred of Jews with his antagonism to the Freemasons, he would not be confronted by evidence to the contrary.

Eckert's remarks elicited some favorable responses in French anti-Masonic writings. One such book published in 1857 followed him in quoting the Jewish preacher Salomon's assertion that Freemasonry had no Christian roots. The author adduced this remark in support of his thesis that Freemasonry aimed at demolishing the structure of the Church.[30] The Freemasons had become accustomed to such attacks and a Masonic organ in France, *Le monde maçonnique,* included this polemic work in the list of those not worth answering.[31]

The Jewish-Freemason "combination," viewed as the archenemy of Christianity, did not emerge in the world as some chance variation produced by literary fertilization. The causes lay deep in contemporary social reality. The same motives that impelled Eckert to search for the culprits guilty of subverting the old order that had been erected upon the foundations of Church and state animated many others as well. Everybody was aware of the historical and theological tradition of Jews' being burdened with guilt. And in the Catholic countries especially, a grave indictment—though perhaps less firmly impressed upon the consciousness of past generations—was widely leveled against the Freemasons. Groups and individuals were caught up in the anti-Jewish animosity or the anti-Masonic struggle with varying intensity, but what was common to all of them was their readiness to thrust the responsibility for the unrest of the times on some identifiable scapegoat. It was quite easy, then, for anyone set upon attacking the Masons to hold up the Jews as a secondary target; while anyone accustomed to blaming Jews for all the ills of the times could quite readily swallow the accusations against the Masons. The outcome of this process was that Freemasonry was depicted as an end-result of Jewish machinations.

The first example of the latter type of individual was Gougenot de Mousseaux, whose *Le Juif, Le Judaïsme et la judaïsation des peuples chrétiens,* published in 1869,[32] is a classic anti-Semitic work. It mentions Masonic affairs with some frequency, but only incidentally. De Mousseaux was a Catholic theologian. He had drawn the

153

essentials of his views from the stores of ecclesiastical tradition.[33] The history and destiny of the Jews are explained as the wages of sin: the sin being the rejection of Jesus; the wages, the exile and humiliation visited upon the seed of the deicides.[34] De Mousseaux would not omit anything from his vehement indictment of Judaism. He repeated all the charges hurled at Jewry throughout the Middle Ages, from the Jewish preoccupation with usury [35] to the blood libel, the truth of which he did not at all doubt.[36] The cause of Jewish vice and deceit was to be found in the Talmud, which he held responsible, following accepted anti-Semitic tradition, for inculcating hatred and injustice against the entire world.[37] Such explanations could provide a satisfying understanding of Jewish-gentile relations as long as the two had faced each other as hostile camps. Yet, ever since the outbreak of the French Revolution the status of Jews had changed. The emancipation apparently had put an end to their political disabilities, while the rise of an enlightened class of Jews and the introduction of religious reforms in their congregations seemed to augur a new chapter in their history. De Mousseaux's primary purpose was to convince his readers that these transformations in the status and condition of the Jews had in no way cut them off from their tradition and by no means healed them of their religious and moral corruption.[38] If Jews claimed to have given up their hopes of returning as a nation to their homeland, they were merely dissembling.[39] They were still a nation apart which had not, by any means, discarded its belief in a messianic future when the hegemony over the whole world would pass into their hands. The new political, social, and intellectual metamorphosis of Jewry only increased the threat to the nations in whose midst they dwelt. The new Jew had become the protagonist of freethinking which was tantamount to the denial of Church doctrine and the undermining of the accepted and blessed social order.[40] Jewish organizations—the Consistoire, which united all French Jewry, and the Alliance Israélite Universelle, which sought to unite all of world Jewry—tolerated or even actively encouraged those elements that were casting off their faith and undermining the stability of church and society.[41]

This train of thought led De Mousseaux to the subject of Freemasonry, the lodges of which he conjured up in his mind as societies clandestinely carrying out the nefarious Jewish subversive designs.

That the Masonic movement was a Jewish secret society was borne out, in his view, by many proofs and allusions in literature and life. He had certainly been impelled to think along these lines to some extent by Eckert, whose book he quoted with special emphasis.[42] He adduced Eckert's testimony to the fact that "all the world-shaking anti-Christian and antisocial outbreaks were the handiwork of the Freemasons and Jews." [43] From Alban Stolz, De Mousseaux acquired the conviction that the underground activities of the Freemasons were directed by their appointees, the vast majority of whom were Jews.[44] In Eckert he found allusions to the fact that the Masonic ideology had been drawn from Jewish sources.[45] By their nature these sources often seemed identical with rationalism which was, as we have seen, in Eckert's eyes the principal characteristic of the modern manifestation of Judaism. On the other hand, De Mousseaux maintained that Freemasonry was tied up with Jewish Cabalistic teachings. Such an assertion was not altogether groundless—but he inflated the influence of these teachings on the Masonic movement out of all proportion. He was induced to draw this conclusion by the works of a certain Eliphaz Levi, a former Catholic monk and intellectual dilettante, who had, during the sixties and seventies, propagandized on behalf of some eclectic-theosophic teachings into which he had injected liberal doses of the Jewish Cabala.[46] Levi had looked upon the Cabala as the fons et origo of all mystic, salvationist doctrines, and contended that Freemasonry, too, had derived its principal teachings from there. He wanted to enhance the value of his theory by this assertion. In De Mousseaux's hands, it became a weapon to fight Masonry. From these remarks he extracted decisive proof that the Cabalists, the Jewish guardians of mystic secrets from ancient times, sat in the secret councils of the lodges and presided over the insidious plot to destroy Christendom.[47]

In addition to literary sources, De Mousseaux was influenced by information drawn from life itself and interpreted by him as evidence that Freemasonry had, from its very inception, been a Jewish movement. He was well aware that Jews were streaming into the lodges and argued that they were the world-wide sympathizers of the Masonic brotherhood. At the very time when Catholics were being threatened with excommunication for belonging to the Masons, Jews were being encouraged by their spiritual leaders to join.

155

This gibe came in consequence of an incident publicized in the Jewish press. A certain Michael Berend had died in Brussels. Although he had been reputed to be a freethinker and a Freemason, a eulogy was delivered over him by the Chief Rabbi, Astruc, who explained, in justification of his tolerance, that, despite Berend's heretical ideas and Masonic membership, he had nevertheless remained a Jew. No wonder that Jews flocked to the lodges when their rabbi's blessing escorted them on their way! De Mousseaux was fully aware that some lodges were closed, or had been closed in the past, to Jews. He attributed this fact to the lack of sympathy for Jews prevailing in the general community and in Masonic society in particular. But he immediately added that Freemasonry was not to be judged in terms of its overt leaders and members. These might not have been Jews and might perhaps have been hostile to Jews. He, however, had reference to the anonymous, covert leadership. "The Jews are obviously and, we add, necessarily, the soul, the head, the true Grand Master of Freemasonry. Those who perform its public functions are merely the deceptive and deceived heads of the Order." [48]

156

To give this theory a secure foothold, De Mousseaux seized upon Adolphe Crémieux, in his personal and communal capacities, as an example. Crémieux, who stood at the head of one of the most important rites in Masonry, was also regarded at that time as a key figure in French Jewry, and was known, from 1860 onward, as one of the founders of the Alliance Israélite Universelle. The goal of the organization—to organize world Jewry for the advancement of their rights—aroused the countersuspicions of a man like De Mousseaux. That the Catholic Church had grounds to be apprehensive of organized Jewish activity is borne out by the Mortara incident: a Jewish child had been baptized under the auspices of the Catholic hierarchy in Rome; the indignation of the Jewish community expressed itself in widespread and vigorous protest and gave the final thrust to the efforts to establish the Alliance Israélite Universelle.[49] De Mousseaux's suspicions, on the other hand, were not confined to the overt acts in this instance either. The Alliance loomed before his eyes as a smokescreen for the secret society of the Freemasons whose activities in undermining the Church and all it cherished seemed a far more dangerous threat than the visible struggle of the Alliance to achieve its avowed aims. The identity of the Freemasons and the

Alliance was clearly demonstrated in the person of Crémieux who stood at the head of both groups.[50] Moreover, De Mousseaux discovered even further evidence in the ideological platforms of the two movements. The Alliance propagated the idea of a world union of Jewry, and the same type of hegemony happened to be the secret goal of Freemasonry. Who could deny that the two were essentially the same? [51]

Jewish Freemason connections did not occupy the center of De Mousseaux's attention. Passages referring to the topic appear sporadically throughout the book. After a lapse of eleven years, in 1880, another book was published. This one was devoted in its entirety to the topic, its title openly proclaiming the fact and the intent. It was *Franc-Maçons et Juifs, sixième Age de l'Église d'après l'Apocalypse,* by C. C. de Saint Andrée, a pseudonym for E. H. Chabouty, a village priest of the Poiton district.[52]

Like De Mousseaux, Chabouty was steeped in Catholic tradition and even surpassed his predecessor in his propensity for apocalyptic speculations. His calculations indicated to him that, with the emergence of Freemasonry in the eighteenth century, the world had entered the sixth era of the Church. The period was obviously one of decline, of challenge to the foundations of faith and the social order erected upon them. This challenge was the work of the devil,[53] Chabouty using that term in its plain, literal sense. Who were the agents of the devil? Here Chabouty became somewhat confused. He had uncovered conclusive evidence that both the Freemasons and the Jews were directing the work of destruction, of driving the Church from its entrenched positions and of diverting people from the holy discipline of the Church to secular licentiousness. Both Freemasons and Jews were in the process of gaining control of the world. Yet the two could not possibly wear the same crown. Chabouty formulated his dilemma in these words:

157

> From all the evidence accumulating from a variety of quarters, it becomes absolutely certain that the Jews instigate and direct everything: politics, finance, commerce, industry, economics, philosophy, science, and art, on both continents and especially in Europe—in a word, they are "the kings of the age."
>
> Yet, on the other hand we are convinced that Freemasonry in-

stigates and directs everything, and it, too, in all the world and especially in Europe.

To which of the two, the Jew or the Freemason, do the direction and the control belong? Here we are on the horns of a dilemma: either Freemasonry has overpowered the Jew and utilizes him and propels him forward—or else it is the Jew who has prevailed over Freemasonry and made it the footstool for, and the instrument of, his designs.[54]

His verdict declared the Jews the guilty party, since they held in their hands the means to power: the money and the genius.[55] They had constituted a secret society for hundreds of years. In their midst were energetic and aggressive individuals, who could keep secrets, and such persons formed the stable cells for all clandestine organizations. The Jews were power-hungry, consumed by an exaggerated greed for rule. They aspired to power in every country and, in addition, desired to restore their ancient land to themselves, since they had by no means abandoned their belief in a redeemer who would lead them back to the territories of their forefathers.[56]

Essentially this conclusion adds nothing new to De Mousseaux's arguments. These Chabouty merely repeated and amplified. Nevertheless, in his thesis that Jews were striving to seize control of the world through the agency of the Freemasons, Chabouty had given the subject a new dimension. By dealing directly with the relations between the two groups and in his explicit conclusion that the Jews gave the orders and the Freemasons carried them out, he purported to give a clear account of the division of functions and responsibility between them. Moreover, although Chabouty's arguments drew upon theological reflections and literary sources, they were not completely removed from the reality of events. Since De Mousseaux's work had made its appearance, several incidents had occurred which, in Chabouty's mind, confirmed his conclusions on the constriction of the Church by the secularists and on the seizure of world domination, both publicly and privately, by the Jews. The Holy Father in Rome had been deprived of his domain, and secular forces had raised their heads in the French Republic. Who were so vitally interested in snatching education from the hands of the Church and in instituting civil divorce, if not the Masons and the Jews? One society had already been founded with the aim of insti-

158

tuting the rule of secular principles; this was L'Alliance Universelle Réligieuse, which Chabouty placed in the same rank as the Alliance Israélite Universelle.[57] The thesis propounded by Toussenel,[58] the father of French anti-Semitism, that the Jews were the kings of the world received new support.

Chabouty's ears had caught the echoes of the anti-Semitic propaganda disseminated in Germany after the great economic collapse of 1873, propaganda directed primarily against the rise of Jews in the sphere of commerce.[59] No one in Germany could ever have conceived of concluding from these allegations that any ties existed between the Jews and the Freemasons. On the contrary, anti-Semitism gradually infused itself into the ranks of the Freemasons themselves. In France, however, the battle lines were drawn between the Catholics and the secularists, and there the Jew was portrayed as siding with the Freemasons, the outstanding representatives of secular ideologies. Here the Jews and the Freemasons could become associated in human minds. Chabouty's special contribution was his incorporation of this combination in the title of a book, by which means he assured that the association would be held up to public notice. The book itself was too prolix and too much encumbered with detail to win wide circulation. Two years later, however, Chabouty summarized his views in a shorter work this time bearing his full, true name.[60]

The two works accomplished their purpose: the combination, Jews and Freemasons, found a place in literature and became available for use as a propaganda slogan. In the beginning the Freemasons were mentioned first, the Jews, second. Later, especially in Germany, the order was reversed and the slogan rang out as "Jews and Freemasons."

159

XI The Extent and Limits
of the Slogan

The ideological and social struggle described so far took place within the closed society of the Freemasons. At times—and then by pure chance—its echoes reached the ears of the public at large. The frequently recurring attacks on the Freemasons did receive some notice in the press and literary media, but were only incidental in the public life of the various communities. Public attention was caught and held for only fleeting moments. At all events, the role of the Freemasons in the general community has been taken account of in this book only insofar as it affected the Jews in their struggle to enter the lodges.

Yet, as we have seen, an unexpected dialectical development was suddenly set in motion. Even before the Jews had achieved their goal of equality in the lodges, the Freemasons were accused of having close connections with Jews and being guilty of collaboration in their plotting. In France and the countries under its influence, from the eighties onward, these allegations began ringing in the ears of the populace as a result of an intense propaganda campaign, and this propaganda became a weapon in the political struggle between the various ideologies and parties in the state. As we follow the developments, we pass almost unaware from a portrayal of the history of ideas and their social background to an analysis of an apparatus to win souls in political contests.

The first stage of this development was reached when the Jewish-Freemason combination was converted from a hypothesis subject to proof into a slogan speaking for itself. The formula arose, as we have seen, as a by-product of the theoretical investigation into the functions fulfilled by Jews in the history of the Freemasons. Those who knew the truth dissociated themselves from the implications of linking Freemasons with Jews, despite their bitter resentment against both. The French convert, Joseph Lémann, published his *L'entrée des Israélites dans la société française et les états chrétiens* in 1886.[1] The book was written out of fear for the fate of Christian society. The ramparts of religion and morals which the Catholic

Church had erected to preserve the countries within its sphere of influence were being progressively broken down. And to him the entry of the Jew into French society was one symptom of this breakdown. Had French society preserved its Christian character, he believed, Jews could have improved their condition and raised their status, although they would have had to remain on the fringes of the community. A secular transformation, however, had opened the way for Jews to be ranked equally with Frenchmen as members of the same society.[2] For this state of affairs he blamed the free-thinkers —those who had cast off the authority of the Church—and, among the culprits, or at their head, stood the Freemasons who had aided and abetted the Jews in achieving emancipation during the Revolution and had paved the way for them to enter French secular society. The Masons' preoccupation with Cabalistic doctrines was, in his eyes, some sort of preparation for the admission of Jews into their society. As for the predisposition of the Jews and Masons to unite, this stemmed from their common hatred of the Church.[3] Both of them aimed at grafting French society onto secular roots and at severing the sources of Christian influence which had sustained that society through all its previous existence. Despite the severity of their criticism of Masonic and Jewish methods, Lémann's observations throughout maintained the tone of relevant, reflective argumentation. He explicitly dissociated himself from De Mousseaux's and Chabauty's wild assertions.[4] His writings were directed toward the intelligent reader and were likely to influence only narrow circles. In the same year that his *L'entrée des Israélites* came off the press, Edouard Drumont published his *La France juive*—the short and incisive title heralding the introduction of a new approach in this class of literature. The style addressed itself to the emotions of the masses, not to the calm reflection of the thinker;[5] and the book achieved a vast circulation—a hundred printings in a single year.[6]

161

The immediate success of this work astonished the author himself. It resulted from the forceful manner of his expression and his fiery conviction in the truth of his opinions on the functions Jews were performing in the life of modern France. This seemed to the author, and to many others who adopted the same position, to be corrupt and perverse on account of the greed for money, lust for pleasure, and craving for power over others, all of which had become rampant. These vices were exemplified to Drumont in the

areas of commerce, social life, legislation, and politics. In all these
doubtful affairs he found Jews taking a hand. Drumont himself was
in no way involved in business or social life. He had no real contact
with law and politics.[7] In all these matters, this member of the pe-
tite bourgeoisie relied on hearsay, except for his own additional
assertion—that the Jews were responsible for everything—faithfully
following the rule that faults are found for the damned.

As his title shows, Drumont's avowed objective was to attack the
Jews, and his work has been designated as an anti-Semitic classic. In
1886, however, it was impossible for any French anti-Semitic writer
to avoid including the Freemasons in his account. From the time
that Chabouty's works appeared on the scene, this mental association had become firmly established and regularly put to use by both
anti-Jewish and anti-Masonic writers.[8] Drumont, who was predisposed to give credence to any report of Jewish complicity in every
despicable act, was even more ready to believe that it was the Jewish character of the Masonic movement which was eroding the foundations of Christian society. Evidence of this destructive influence
had already been supplied by distinguished authors and sages.
Quoting liberally from Chabouty, Drumont concluded that "no one
can deny that the leadership of the lodges has long ago passed into
the hands of the Jews." From behind the scenes, the Masons, alias
the Jews, controlled legislatures. They held the keys to the royal
courts in their hands. Judges were appointed at their behest, and
woe betide any judge who dared convict a member of the Jewish-
Masonic league.[9] He scattered the designation *Franc-Maçonnerie
juive* throughout the entire book,[10] and since it became one of the
most widely read works in France, it must be regarded an important factor in impressing this combination upon the minds of the
people.

Drumont's work conditioned the public to react as they did during the Dreyfus trial. The Jewish-Masonic image as a diabolical
pair gave the anti-Dreyfusards one of their most potent propaganda
weapons while the controversy was raging. Drumont himself devoted a special tract to *La Tyrannie maçonnique,* which adduced
the well-known proofs of the Jewishness of Freemasonry.[11] This
work was one among hundreds dealing with the theme at the time.[12]
In substance, the allegations contained nothing new. Yet their wide
circulation demonstrates how provocative was the slogan *Franc-*

162

Maçonnerie juive, which purported to sum up in maximum brevity where the source of the evil lay, namely, in the secret alliance between the two groups joined together to the detriment of everyone else. Undoubtedly the propagandists of the French right deliberately put this catch phrase to use, but they could not possibly have exploited it so effectively had the targets of the expression not evoked hate associations in the public and mass mind.

The slogan "Jews and Freemasons" was not confined just to France. It had established itself, as we have seen, during the seventies and eighties when anti-Semitism had become rife in various countries of Europe. In 1882, the first international anti-Semitic conference ever to be convened took place in Dresden, and one of the chief speakers was Győző Istoczy, a member of the Hungarian parliament. He could boast that he had begun disseminating anti-Jewish ideas in 1875, when only the first shoots of the new movement had thrust themselves above the surface in Germany. Being a member of the Hungarian parliament, he had acquired an international reputation and maintained connections with like-minded individuals in foreign countries, including France.[13] It may reasonably be assumed that the idea of joining Jews and Freemasons together had reached him from there. At all events, at the Dresden conference he presented a manifesto appealing to the governments of all Christian countries to beware of the Jewish menace. One of his paragraphs condemned the Freemasons as the dangerous ally of the Jews. To Istoczy's surprise, this statement evoked the determined opposition of the German delegates. Several of them apparently had succeeded in reconciling their Freemasonry with their anti-Semitism and found no contradiction between the two. These delegates taught Istoczy that his accusations against the Freemasons were entirely unfounded, first, because most of the German lodges would not admit Jews, and second, because every Jew would feel out of place in Masonry, since its very name denoted construction while Jews by nature were a destructive force. The debate on the manifesto ended in compromise. The paragraph dealing with the Masons was amended to read: "In certain places Jews have succeeded in perverting and falsifying Masonry and have transformed it into a tool for gaining their ends." [14] Istoczy's manifesto was then adopted, published in hundreds of thousands of copies, and distributed far and wide.[15]

163

This ludicrous episode throws light upon a seemingly astounding historical paradox. In France the slogan spread with extreme rapidity, yet in Germany, the classic country of anti-Semitism, whence the initial impulses for the slogan had emanated, it failed to strike root. No trace of this formula appeared in Germany until the end of World War I.[16] The reason lies in the course traversed by Jewish-Freemason relations in practice within Germany during that period.

The rise of anti-Semitism in Germany visibly affected the attitudes of the Freemasons to the Jewish problem. While in the sixties and early seventies the tendency to open the lodge doors to Jews grew stronger, the situation deteriorated during the later seventies, when anti-Jewish overtones kept obtruding into the arguments of those opposing Jewish entry.[17] This trend gained ground during the eighties, the years of the high tide of the new political anti-Semitism. In 1884, a new constitution was presented for adoption in the Berlin Mutterloge, and the Jewish question once more came up for consideration. Again opinions were divided, but the final decision was in favor of maintaining the Christian restriction, the vote being eighty-five to twenty-three.[18] The radical alteration in the mood of the present as compared with the past was not lost upon the members. Only a few years earlier they had believed that time would bring about a solution consistent with the basic principle of Masonry. One of the members expressed his disappointment in these terms: "It is not the Jews who have changed, but the attitude of many of the lodge brethren. Such an about-face is no credit to the Masons." [19]

The new attitude produced repercussions even in those lodges which had until now been liberal toward Jews. From the eighties onward reports were bruited about that Jewish candidates had been blackballed by these lodges. Incidents of this nature increased to such an extent that no one could any longer doubt that the candidate's Jewishness was responsible for his rejection. Incontestable proof of the true state of affairs is furnished by the fact of the establishment of the first B'nai B'rith lodge in Germany. The founders were all former Masons, presumably belonging to affiliates of the Royal York, who had resigned from lodges whose manifestations of anti-Semitism they had found intolerable.[20] Sincerely believing in

164

the ideology of Freemasonry, they, with Julius Fenchel at their head, had given serious thought to finding some area outside the lodges where they could translate this ideology into practice. It occurred to them that they might follow the example of the American B'nai B'rith and become an independent Jewish order. Fenchel wrote to the leadership of the organization in the United States requesting permission to establish a lodge in Berlin. The American B'nai B'rith leaders, former German immigrants, heartily approved the spread of their organization into the land of their birth. The Berliners who addressed the petition, however, were hardly men of any consequence, and the Americans doubted whether they were capable of implementing their plans. Negotiations dragged on for two years. Yet, once formal authorization was finally granted, it became abundantly clear that time was indeed ripe for the founding Jewish lodges. Within the first year two more lodges sprang up in Prussia, as did lodges in other cities, among them Hamburg (1887), where the lodge doors had not closed down on Jews, and Frankfurt (1888), where the old "Jewish" lodges were still functioning. In these two localities, the founders of the B'nai B'rith lodges encountered the resistance of the Jewish Freemasons. The latter considered the creation of lodges intended for Jews alone as an abandonment of the Jewish claims upon the existing lodges to eliminate the discrimination between Jew and non-Jew.[21] The spread of the B'nai B'rith lodges proves that the number of Jews expecting the speedy fulfillment of this demand had declined substantially. Three years after the first German B'nai B'rith lodge had come into existence, twenty-nine lodges were in active operation and their membership had risen to 3,000.[22]

165

Direct evidence that Jews were gradually being driven out of the lodges can be drawn from the events transpiring in the Royal York of Berlin. This was the only Prussian Grand Lodge, it will be recalled, which had, in 1872, allowed Jews to join its affiliates. From that year onward, Jews had never absented themselves from these lodges, even though their presence did cause embarrassment. The Royal York had, from its very inception, committed itself to the humanistic principle in Masonry but had, in the course of time, absorbed distinctly Christian elements. In the third degree rites, the name of Jesus was expressly mentioned. Once the lodges began to admit Jews, it was felt necessary to base the ceremonies on concepts and symbols which would not offend Jewish susceptibilities. Again, there were brethren who, uninfluenced by any Jewish connections, still sought to restore the humanistic character of the lodge activities. Nevertheless, numbers still clung tenaciously to Christian symbols and ideas. In 1885 the struggle between these factions was resolved by a compromise. The name of Jesus was omitted from the script, but christological symbols and formulas were retained, thus indicating that only through Christianity could true Masonic perfection be attained. The delegate moving the adoption of the compromise resolution felt that pure Christianity, as believed in by its enlightened adherents, would also be acceptable to the conscience of the Jew who sought to join the society of the Freemasons.[23]

Possibly the proposer of the resolution may have been correct in assuming that the Jews clamoring for admission at the lodge gates had become reconciled to conceding a more elevated status and prestige to Christianity than to their own religion. Nevertheless, Jewish Masons could find no haven in the lodges during the ensuing years. If the Christian character of the ceremonies did not deter them, the quota on Jews made them painfully aware that they were merely "tolerated" in the Masonic brotherhood. Jews who were members from before were not expelled, but new candidates were unable to enter. Any Jew, no matter how highly he had been recommended, was sure to be voted down in the secret ballot.[24] Not only were Jews in the lodge aware of this fact, but liberally minded Christians, too, viewed with apprehension the predominance of the anti-Jewish attitude in Masonic ranks. One such Christian was Dr. Hermann Settegast, Deputy of the lodge from 1884 to 1889 and Master of it afterward.[25] By proposing that anyone objecting to the admission of a new candidate should be compelled to state his reasons and that the candidate's religion could not constitute sufficient reason for his rejection, he hoped to remedy the situation.[26] When his proposal was rejected in 1890, Settegast resigned his office and left the lodge.

His departure from the Royal York produced far-reaching consequences on the status of Freemasonry as a whole in Prussia. He had no desire to relinquish his Masonic connections altogether, so soon afterward he founded a new lodge under the Hamburg auspices.

Two years later, in 1892, he went even further and established, together with fifty other Masons, a new Mother Lodge in Berlin.[27] About half of these brethren were Jews.[28] It was called the Grosse Freimaurer-Loge von Preussen genannt Kaiser Friedrich zur Bundestreue. The choice of name was not accidental. Following the accepted practice of the House of Hohenzollern, Friedrich had been a member of the Freemasons since his youth. He was reputed to be in favor of liberal reforms in the state, and the humanistically minded Masons dared to hope that, upon his accession to the throne, his influence would assert itself on their behalf. His tragic death, after a reign of only one hundred days, put an end to these hopes, but his name lived on as a symbol of liberalism and tolerance.

Settegast's bold act was entirely without precedent and provoked a furor within and without the Masonic brotherhood. Difficulties were placed in his path by the authorities. They held that the law of 1798 was still in force, and accordingly no lodge could legally function in Prussia unless it had affiliated with one of the already existing three Grand Lodges.[29] Not to be deterred this time, Settegast and his colleagues took their case to court. As one of the parties to the trial, the three Mother Lodges also appeared. In the memorandum they presented to the court, they not only listed their legal arguments but also described the social and political functions of their lodges. It would therefore be interesting to make the acquaintance of this document. The representatives of the three Grand Lodges contended that the loyalty of their Masons was above question and needed no direct government surveillance. If, however, other, independent, Grand lodges sprung up, these could easily become converted into nests of propaganda and subversion threatening the stability of the state.[30]

The plea of the counsel for the Mother Lodges was not sustained. The court ruled that the act of 1848 granting the freedom to organize had automatically repealed the law of 1798. Even that public juridical status which the three Lodges had presumed to enjoy was now denied them by the verdict of the court. They were declared to possess the standing of private organizations, and therefore were no better in the eyes of the law than the Kaiser Friedrich Grand Lodge which had just been founded. As far as the government was concerned, the new Grand Lodge was as entitled to function as any of the Mother Lodges of longer standing.[31]

167

The founding of Settegast's lodge marked a radical change in the history of the Freemasons in Prussia. First, the three Mother Lodges had lost their government protection. At the same time, the royal patronage which they had enjoyed since their very founding in the reign of Frederick the Great in the eighteenth century was withdrawn. Breaking the family tradition, Wilhelm II did not become a Freemason. In the early years of his reign, the Mother Lodges had no royal protector whatsoever. On his accession, in 1888, the arch-conservatives, who were inimical to the Masons, rejoiced, believing that the influence of the movement on the royal family would cease once and for all.[32] The Lodges did, however, succeed in finding a patron, in the person of Prince Frederick Leopold, a distant cousin of the Kaiser, who accepted the office in 1894, soon after the verdict in favor of Settegast had been handed down.[33] On this occasion the initiative undoubtedly emanated from the Mother Lodges themselves and not from the royal family or the Kaiser.[34] His attitude toward the Masons had indirectly affected the founding of the new Lodge. Wihlelm I had, at least in his early days, looked upon the veteran Lodges as pillars of support for his rule. At that time Settegast might well have failed to obtain for his Lodge the same status the older Mother Lodges possessed. Wilhelm II, on the other hand, was ready to forego the solid support of the well-to-do classes and rely instead on the loyalty of broader circles, although he kept on changing his approaches, in his usual capricious fashion, from one group to another. Nevertheless, the Masons continued in his days, too, to give demonstrative expression of their loyalty to the reigning monarch. In many of their lodges, they continued to celebrate the King's birthday with the same solemn ceremony as before.[35] The Kaiser graciously accepted all the greetings proffered him, and refused to distinguish between one Lodge and another. When the Kaiser consented to accept the felicitations of Settegast's Lodge on the occasion of his birthday in 1894, they recorded his response as a signal victory over their adversaries.[36]

The gain for the Jewish Masons was rather doubtful. Together with Settegast, the Jewish members had resigned from the Royal York.[37] In the new Lodge, Jews and non-Jews were evenly divided in respect of numbers, but in its leadership the Jewish element preponderated,[38] and their numbers increased as time went on. The same situation obtained in the seven individual lodges affiliated with Settegast's Grand Lodge.[39] In consequence of the removal of all government restriction, two new lodges were founded in Berlin, one affiliated with the Hamburg Grand Lodge, the other with the Frankfurt Eclectic Covenant. It may reasonably be conjectured these also were comprised of Jews who had been denied admission to the older Prussian lodges. They at least possessed some guardian —their right to exist could never be challenged. On the other hand, although Settegast's lodges could not be forced to disband, they were disdained as wild, mushroom growths. They did not come into existence as the result of true Masonic illumination, as far as the veteran masons were concerned, but to constitute the battering-ram to break down the doors closed to Jewish candidates.[40] At all events, Jewish aspirations had always been concentrated on being accepted in the regular Masonic lodges and not in crawling into lodges where their own community predominated. In effect the same situation had come about in Berlin as had existed in Frankfurt at the turn of the century, when Jewish Masons had, for lack of an alternative, been forced to maintain lodges of their own.

It is impossible to determine with any precision the extent to which the tendency to exclude Jews prevailed in all of Germany. News of what transpired is rather fragmentary. Yet the information is of some significance. At the beginning of the 1890s a liberal lodge was constrained to ask a Jewish candidate to withhold his application at least until the wave of anti-Semitism subsided, out of fear that he would be voted down.[41] There can be no doubt that eighties and nineties marked a retrogression from the achievements of sixties and seventies. The exclusion of Jews became the regular procedure in every area of life,[42] and the Masons were no exception. Even those who had always taken up the cudgels on behalf of Jews now changed their minds. Joseph Gabriel Findel had, in the past, striven for the removal of anti-Jewish restrictions. Now he was outspoken in his opposition. Too many Jews, he contended, were attempting to storm the lodges, and most of the candidates were not fit to enter.[43] He deplored the acrimonious tones of the Jewish demands, couched as if each Jewish applicant was entitled to become a Mason,[44] when all of them knew that no one was ever granted this privilege unless his personal character had first been investigated by the existing members of the lodge.

These allegations were not pure fabrications. Jews undoubtedly streamed toward those organizations where admission implied acceptance in the general society. Similarly, often Jewish intellectuals raised vociferous objections against all failures to grant them full civil rights in practice. These two phenomena constituted the birth pangs of social emancipation which was farther from realization than its initial proponents and supporters had imagined. In the eighties and nineties we find ourselves in a counter-reaction which had taken the form of an organized anti-Semitic movement. At this stage, even the exclusion of the Jews from the lodges bore a distinctly anti-Semitic character. Findel did not attribute the rejection of Jews to religious difference. He subscribed to the opinion that the Reform Jews trying to gain admission to the lodges were not so far away from the acknowledgment of the principles of pure Christianity. The obstacle to their admission was their different nature. "The racial differences inherent in their nature" might possibly have resulted from historical development alone, yet, nevertheless, the Jews did possess traits which rendered them unfit for Masonic membership.[45] If any Jew claimed to be free of such undesirable characteristics, the burden of proof lay upon him.

This retrogression in the Masonic attitude toward Jews, the subsequent protests, and the ensuing controversy did not remain secluded within the Masonic community. What had occurred in the lodges was actually only one aspect of the recrudescence of anti-Semitism which had captured the attention of the people. Some of the struggles, Settegast's trial for instance, were by their very nature public property. He published a tract in 1892 in which he recorded the events leading to his resignation.[46] It was reprinted six times in a single year. The book was not issued as a private manuscript reserved for Masonic perusal only, but was printed by a Jewish commercial house which endeavored to promote its sale.[47] In the battle-lines drawn between the anti-Semites and the liberals, Jews and Freemasons faced each other from opposite sides. Even if there were individuals harboring hatred against both the Masons and the Jews, they could not fuse the two objects of their hatred, as had happened in France. Not that the association of the two had escaped all notice in Germany. French anti-Semitic tracts, chief among which was Drumont's *La France juive* had been translated into German,[48] and these works gave bold prominence to the catchword, *Franc-maçon juive*. Furthermore, every detail of the Dreyfus trial was closely followed in Germany, and, as the case continued, the use of the slogan became correspondingly more widespread. German anti-Semitism had not yet found the opportune moment for combining the two hate-objects, even though the mental association had first been formed in that country during the sixties.[49] At the very time that the cry sounded so reasonable and appealing to French ears, it could produce no echo in Germany. The contradiction between the two situations was too glaringly obvious.

The barrier standing in the way of the slogan was peculiar to Germany. In countries within the sphere of French influence, effects of the slogan could already be discerned in the eighties. Such effects appeared in the *Protocols of the Elders of Zion,* which were distributed in Russia at the beginning of the twentieth century. These writings are of particular interest in view of their later, vast circulation throughout the length and breadth of the world. These *Protocols* purported to be a verbatim report of secret decisions taken at the first Zionist Congress in 1897, where the plans had been laid for the Jews to realize their ancient ambition, the seizure of the reins of power over the whole world. The first version of the *Protocols* formed part of Serge Nilus' work, *The Great within the Small; the Anti-Christ as an Imminent Political Possibility.* As the title indicates, the reference is to a seer of apocalyptic visions who might possibly have believed in the truth of the *Protocols.*[50] Of course this does not answer the who? when? and why? of the work's composition. These questions have evoked ample literary interest but have never been solved. On the other hand, the literary sources serving as its models have been identified with all due certainty. The sources were two. In 1864 a delightful parody on Napoleon III's ambitions for world rule appeared in Paris. Entitled *Dialogue between Machiavelli and Montesquieu,* its author was Maurice Joly. It was confiscated by the French government and was in the course of time forgotten. Taking the work as his model, the author of the *Protocols* used it to depict a Jewish plot for world domination—the Jews being substituted for the single, ambitious emperor.[51] The alleged Jewish conspiracy was an old anti-Semitic theme, but the idea that Jewish leaders had convened to plan this seizure of power was the invention of a German author, Hermann Goedsche. One of the

171

chapters of his book, *Biarritz,* bears the heading "The Jewish Cemetery in Prague and the Council of the Representatives of the Twelve
Tribes." Here is where the author of the *Protocols* obtained the
idea of Jewish emissaries meeting to concoct their plot.[52]

For our purpose, only the establishing of one single fact is important: both sources make absolutely no mention of the Freemasons.
If we keep in mind the chronology fixed earlier in this book, the
fact becomes quite obvious. During the period when Joly and
Goedsche compiled their works, Jews and Freemasons had not yet
become linked in the public mind. When the *Protocols* were being
written, however, the slogan had become widespread, at least in
France. The author accordingly introduced this new theme, which
he had culled from anti-Masonic or anti-Semitic writings, like the
works of Chabouty and his followers. Research has already revealed
the close correspondence between Chabouty's ideas and those of the
Protocols.[53] It may therefore be assumed that his books were the intermediate, if not the direct, source for designating the Freemasons
as the agents of the Jews in their attempts at world conquest.

Jewish-Masonic cooperation was accorded close and detailed attention in the *Protocols*. There the Masons appear as the unwitting
tools of the Elders of Zion, unaware of the purpose for which they
are being exploited. "Gentile Masonry blindly serves as a screen for
us and our objects, but the plan of action of our force, even its
abiding-place, remains for the whole people an unknown mystery."
"Aims which are not even so much as suspected by these *goy* cattle,
attracted by us into the 'show' army of Masonic lodges in order to
throw dust in the eyes of their fellows." The Masons were actively
engaged in preparing revolts and insurrections but were, wittingly
or unwittingly, merely carrying out the missions of the Elders of
Zion. Should it ever occur that a gentile gain greater access to the
secret counsels than he was entitled to, the means would be found
to silence him. He would be banished to continents far removed
from Europe where his voice would no longer be heard. When necessary, the Elders even secretly carried out capital punishments.
More than one person had died at the behest of the Elders, who
knew how to condemn their adversaries to death without any suspicions being aroused of the victims having died of unnatural causes.
This was the fate that awaited anyone who knew too much about

the missions he had performed on behalf of the Elders, and had therefore become dangerous.[54]

For such a book the details on the Masons are not exceptionally fantastic. The work is such a tissue of falsehoods that it seems to be poking fun at the reader's common sense. The conjecture has been raised that the authors wanted to convince Czar Nicholas II of Russia that the Jews and Freemasons were undermining his throne.[55] At all events, the Russian community at large was not deceived by the forgery. There the *Protocols* did not achieve any wide circulation or produce any echoes. Their day was to come later, in the turbulent times following World War I.

XII Approaching Ostracism

In this chapter we reach the period adjacent to our own times, one marking the terminus in Germany, the main scene of the events forming the subject of our study. The Nazi regime's liquidation of German Jewry brought an end to all the problems of their relations to the Masonic movement. Yet the process of annihilation, as well as its preliminary stages, deeply involve the relations—more imagined than real—between the two groups. We have previously traced the emergence of the rabble-rousing cry, "Jews and Freemasons!" It became, with the rise of the Nazis to power, one of the most potent weapons of their propaganda campaign, which achieved the temporary suppression of the Freemasons and the total annihilation of the Jews.

Anti-Semitism once more raised its head in Germany while World War I was still raging. When hostilities initially broke out, the Jews were included in the surge of national enthusiasm sweeping the country. When prospects of victory seemed to recede and spirits became depressed by the ravages of war, the source for national unity vanished, and Jews were once more marked off as a minority whose every act required surveillance. A whispering campaign accusing the Jews of disloyalty to the Fatherland, alleging that disproportionately fewer Jews were fighting at the front, moved the Prussian War Office in 1916 to conduct a census of Jews serving in the German armies, to determine how many were actually on active duty and how many were hiding behind the lines.[1] As the fighting dragged toward its close, resentment against Jews grew more intense and, once it became clear that the war would end in a German defeat, there was talk that the whole conflagration had broken out in consequence of international Jewish plotting.[2]

Jews, however, were not the only ones likely to be blamed for the German disaster. At the sight of the nations of the world rallying together against Germany both during and immediately after the war, suspicion fell upon every group with any sort of international connection. The Freemasons were known as a world movement with branches and lodges in many countries. Attention was focused upon them as the news spread of anti-German actions by Freemasons abroad. According to these rumors, French Masons had induced their brethren in Italy to encourage its entry into the war on the side of the Allies. German Masons gave credence to these reports and censured their fellow Masons in the Romance countries for interfering in politics. When Italy did declare war in 1915, the German Masons decided to break off all relations with the Italian and French lodges.[3]

Nevertheless, dissociating themselves from the acts of foreign Freemasons did not clear the German movement in the eyes of their opponents. On the contrary, the slanders grew more strident. At first, the charges were spread by Catholic sources only. Books and popular articles scattered the gossip in all directions,[4] and even a monthly as serious as the *Historisch-politische Blaetter fuer das katholische Deutschland* brought its contribution to the general agitation.[5] The Catholics now seized the opportunity to pay off an old debt to the movement they hated. In their eyes, their opinion that Masonry constituted a threat to everything dear to a true Christian had been vindicated by the conduct of the Masons of the Romance countries. As far as the Catholics were concerned, there was obviously no difference between one Mason and another. All, even the German Masons, were under suspicion of complicity in the plot to overthrow the accepted world order.

The accusations did not emanate from Catholics alone. The subject was raised in all kinds of publications,[6] among others in Theodor Fritsch's anti-Semitic monthly, the *Hammer*.[7] He himself had written a booklet in 1916 which dealt with Masonic activities in Latin countries.[8] To a large extent he relied on Catholic sources but, in contradistinction to them, distinguished between the Masons in the Romance countries and in Germany; the latter he exonerated from all blame. His remarks, however, were pervaded by anti-Semitic overtones. He charged that others were standing side-by-side with the Masons of the Romance lands and these, too, bore a share of the responsibility for the confusion that had troubled the world. They were the money magnates and the agents doing their bidding through the medium of the press. They constituted the *Neben-Regierungen* (governments behind the scenes) of all countries and their members were in contact with each other across national boundaries. To support his allegations, Fritsch cited Walther Rathenau's statement: "Three hundred persons, known to each other, control the fate of the world today." [9] Rathenau had made the remark in 1904 in speaking of the economic fate of the world and referring, disparagingly, to the immensely wealthy capitalists who controlled international financial operations. It goes without saying that Rathenau had no specific Jews especially in mind. In the mouths of Fritsch and his henchmen, however, the statement was twisted into a self-incriminating admission of the existence of a Jewish secret society which held the fate of the world in its hands, for good or for evil. An allusion of this nature even made its way into the *Historisch-politische Blaetter*. According to the author of an article in this Catholic journal, the Freemasons were aided in their plotting to corrupt the world by a partner: the Stock Exchange.[10] Thus world Jewry and international Freemasonry were placed side-by-side.

If such mental combinations already showed signs that the joint indictment of Jews and Freemasons was beginning to crystallize, another circle in Germany had striven to create such an impression all along. This group was the Verband gegen die Überhebung des Judentums in Berlin (Charlottenburg) with its official organ, the monthly *Auf Vorposten*. This Society against Jewish Domination was founded in 1912 by writers, professors, and public figures who were members or sympathizers of the Alldeutscher Verband.[11] Most prominent among its members were the political publicists Fritz Bley, Count Ernst Reventlow, and Ludwig Müller von Hausen. The last-named was the editor of the *Vorposten,* and several of the founders were active in the leadership of the Alldeutscher Verband.[12] This nationalistic movement, which had functioned since 1890, consisted of tens of thousands of members and exerted broad influence on outside circles. At first, the Alldeutscher Verband had abstained from taking any stand on the Jewish problem. Later, its anti-Semitic tendencies became stronger, and finally, in 1912, the decision was made that it identify itself with racist principles, although the resolution was given no publicity at the time.[13] The leadership apparently had not deemed the present opportune for engaging in a public campaign to promote anti-Semitism. The founders of the Verband gegen die Überhebung des Judentums felt otherwise. They openly proclaimed their desire to wage war on the Jews both in public and in private. The supporters and sympathizers, among them the readers of the *Vorposten,* were undoubtedly drawn from the Alldeutschen.

In its activities and its periodical the *Verband* was mainly preoccupied with the Jews. But as the war continued attention turned toward the Freemasons as well. Müller also first drew from Catholic sources [14] and, according to his own testimony, he began to interest himself in the relevant French literature,[15] including most recent publications, the nature of which we shall presently consider. Here, too, his early allegations were hurled only against the Italian and French Masons, but he soon ceased making distinctions; all Masons were accused of conspiring against the monarchy in collusion with, or as being essentially identical with, the Jews.[16]

The periodicals from which this joint indictment of Jews and Freemasons radiated commanded no large circulation or effective influence.[17] Loud reverberations only made themselves heard for the first time when Prince Otto Salm-Horstmar included it in his address in the Upper House (Herrenhaus) of the Prussian Parliament on July 19, 1918. An active participant in the affairs of the Alldeutschen movement, he had apparently been a supporter of the Society against Jewish Domination. On the day in question his remarks were focused on the struggle taking place between the two rival *Weltanschauungen:* the Jewish democratic and the German aristocratic. Such terms as *patria* and *Vaterland* were alien to international Jewry who were assisting the Freemasons in secretly fomenting revolution. In proof of his assertion he cited the fact that the Russian revolutionaries Trotsky and Lenin were both Jews and at the same time members of the French Masonic movement. These remarks were culled from the pages of *Auf Vorposten,* but they reached a large audience and evoked wide response on account of the forum from which they had been pronounced. Immediately after he had spoken, two members took the floor and reprimanded the Prince for sowing dissension among German citizens by hurling wholesale accusations against entire groups. The government spokesman, "State Secretary" Dernburg (incidentally, an apostate descendant of a distinguished Jewish family) declared that there were no grounds for assuming the German nation to be divided into two camps carrying different banners. Yet the Prince's remarks did not on that account fall into oblivion. They were extensively quoted and discussed in the press.[18] To many ears, the Jewish-Masonic combination was a surprise and a shock. Maximilian Harden devoted an entire article to the subject in his weekly, *Die Zukunft.*[19]

He derided the chauvinistic aristocrat for his desire to join Jews and Freemasons together and make them the scapegoat for the frustration of the Prussian Junkers' grandiose dreams. Harden and others like him, however, failed to dampen the ardor of Müller von Hausen and his henchmen. They continued to disseminate hate and received increased support from day to day.

With the collapse of the German political and military establishment, the populace became inclined to lend their ears to each and every rationalization of their defeat and the events that led up to it. Innumerable books and articles rained down upon the public between 1919 and 1920, and kept reiterating the accusations against the Jews and the Freemasons. Friedrich Wichtl's *Weltmaurerei, Weltrevolution, Weltrepublik* achieved wide publicity. It came off the press in March 1919 and was reprinted several times in less than a year.[20] His main arguments and proofs were directed at the international, Judaized Freemasonry—but he was careful to include German Freemasonry in his allegations.[21] He was the master of a brilliant, polemic style, and his influence is discernible in succeeding literature. One of the most popular anti-Semitic tracts of the time was the *Judas Schuldbuch* by Paul Bang, a leader of the Alldeutschen, published in 1919.[22] In the first edition (March 1919), the Freemasons were not mentioned at all. In later editions, Bang, following in Wichtl's footsteps, included them in his accusations, although he did seek to exclude the "Christian" Masons from his charges.[23] His colleague Fritz Bley, also a member of the Alldeutschen, testified that he had formerly regarded the Masons as an essentially patriotic movement, but now—in 1919—he tended to accept the view that behind their ranks lurked secret Jewish leadership. Bley, too, had in the interim made the acquaintance, among others, of Wichtl's work.[24] A second-rank anti-Semite, Dr. Ludwig Langemann, a member of the Göttingen Alldeutschen, took the same position. In 1919 he published a collection of articles, written during the war years and revolutionary days, in which he spewed his venom against the Jews, whom he held responsible for all the tribulations suffered by the German people during its difficult years.[25] At that time the Freemasons did not enter into the picture at all. In April of the same year, a new edition appeared which contained a special chapter devoted to "World Masonry, the World War, and the Jews."[26] He too, had managed to read Wichtl between one edition and the other.

The Alldeutschen propagandists were now reinforced by the new rightist groups which were destined to constitute the nucleus of the Nazi movement. At the beginning of 1919 a newspaper named *Auf gut deutsch* began to appear in Munich. The editor was Dietrich Eckhart, and associated with him was Alfred Rosenberg. Close attention was concentrated upon the Freemasons to whom the newspaper was implacably hostile. To the two of them, the fact that Jews and Freemasons were identical was self-evident and they found constant support for their "convictions" in Wichtl's work.[27]

As the large number of tracts devoted to the issue clearly proved, belief in the common guilt of the Jews and Freemasons had gained wide currency.

Ludwig Müller von Hausen's *Geheimnisse der Weisen von Zion* was just one more example of this type of writing. Only 75 of the book's 250 pages were occupied by the actual *Protocols of the Elders of Zion*. the rest consisted of an introduction to the *Protocols* and a conglomeration of diatribes against Jewish organizations and their crimes and machinations. It ended with a proposal for the enactment of a law, set down with all its clauses, restricting the rights of Jews in the state. After he had published his articles in *Auf Vorposten* on the links between the Jews and the Freemasons, the author stated in his introduction, Russian acquaintances had advised him that he should now publish the *Protocols* as the complement to his articles. Having procured a copy, he was now issuing it in German translation. Were the *Protocols* true? "Our Russian brothers, who are quite reliable, do not know of any attempt by Jews or Freemasons to cast aspersions on the truth of the *Protocols*. Apparently, in their tried and tested manner, they have considered it wiser to minimize the danger by keeping silent, getting hold of the books and destroying them." [28]

In describing historical events, we have been warned, one should never reason from later to earlier events. The fact that the *Protocols* evoked enthusiastic acclaim and achieved world-wide circulation once they had been translated into German cannot provide any clue to the motives of the editor or editors. Their intentions can only be deduced from what is known of their activities prior to the publication of the work.

There were several participants in its publication, and each had his own particular motives. The original was brought to the West

179

by Russian émigrés. Wishing to provide its publication with a romantic halo, Müller von Hausen later related that his copy was carried out of Russia by an emissary who, together with the Imperial German Diplomatic Mission, boarded the last train to leave Russia on the outbreak of the Revolution.[29] He contradicted his own story when he published the German version. Then he asserted that he had received the original from Russians fleeing from the Bolshevik Revolution.[30] White Russians had, indeed, used the *Protocols* to incite Ukrainian peasants against Jews and inflame passions against the Bolshevik regime.[31] The document purported to prove that the revolutionaries—who, it insinuated, were Jews—were undermining Christian monarchies and endeavoring to replace them by a world communist government. To the White Russians, who were trying to court the West to gain sympathy and help for the cause, the *Protocols* seemed to offer a convenient tool. That such was their intention is indicated by the fact that the work was published, as we shall see, in England and Germany simultaneously. It is also well known that the manuscript was submitted by Russian agents to various individuals in the United States in 1918. There was even an attempt by the Russians to extort money from Jewish organizations in exchange for suppressing the *Protocols*.[32] Whether all those engaged in distributing the work were part of any organized group or whether each individual was acting on his own is not known. At all events, once the *Protocols* had fallen into the hands of interested parties, there was no hesitation in publishing them.

No one was more interested in disseminating the *Protocols* in Germany than Müller von Hausen and his colleagues. For them, this document only reiterated and reaffirmed what they had asserted long ago, that the Freemasons had become the accessories of the Jews in trying to subvert the foundations of the existing order. That Müller was anxious to reinforce his own thesis by the *Protocols* is clearly proved by his tampering with the original text. In the Russian version, the Freemasons were mentioned a few times only; the German translation, on the other hand, refers "to the Masonic lodges on every second page." [33] As editor, Müller inserted subheadings over the various sections and incorporated the Freemasons in the headings whether sections of the work referred to them or not. While the text speaks only of Jewish deeds, the subheadings combine Jews and Freemasons together.

Die Unueberwindlichkeit der juedischen Freimaurerschaft (The invincibility of Jewish Freemasonry); Grundsaetze der juedischen Freimaurerloge (The principles of the Jewish Freemason lodge); Die Grundlagen des Unterrichtes an den kuenftigen Volksschulen der Freimaurer (The basis of instruction in the future primary schools of the Freemasons). These headings appear over the various sections of the first chapters, while the text there does not mention the Freemasons even once.

We are even aware of what Müller and his group precisely were out to achieve by spreading their anti-Semitic propaganda at the time. Part of a royalist group that had remained loyal to the House of Hohenzollern even after Wilhelm II had fled to Holland, they hoped to bring order to the confusion following the proclamation of the Weimar Republic by restoring the monarchy. The same political aspirations were nurtured by the Alldeutscher Verband.[34] A letter written by Prince Salm-Horstmar is still extant, addressed to the former chairman of the conservative party in the Prussian Herrenhaus and dated July 1919, the very time when the *Protocols* had gone to press. Describing what he considered important in the publication, Salm-Horstmar appealed to his compeer to help defray the cost of the printing. "In my opinion, this endeavor, which has as its purpose to enlighten people on the war waged by Jewry for decades against the monarchy and the Fatherland will also assist our struggle on behalf of the Royal House and the conservative point of view." [35] The book itself throws some light on its goals. It is dedicated to the Princes of Europe. At its end it contains a portrait of the great Elector, founder of the House of Hohenzollern, with the Latin caption: *Exoriare aliquis nostris ex ossibus ultor* (May an avenger arise from our bones), and the German translation.[36] When critics pointed to the royalist intent of the book, a cause that was far from popular in the Germany of the time, the author freely admitted that he was, even then, loyal to the monarchy and was striving for its restoration.[37] To promote the infiltration of anti-Semitism into German society seemed to him and his coworkers the most effective means for achieving their goals.

We have no idea of the extent of the expectations of the publishers in their indulging in this type of propaganda. All indications are that the editors could never in their wildest dreams have imagined that the *Protocols* would attain so vast a circulation in so

181

short a time. At first there were no signs of any significant success whatsoever. The view, generally accepted by historians, that the *Protocols* aroused world-wide reaction immediately upon their appearance in Germany is utterly false. We must establish the exact chronological order of events and in this way determine what factors produced its sensational circulation and influence.

Müller's edition—published under an assumed name, Gottfried zur Beek—bears the date 1919. Actually the work only reached the book market in the beginning of January 1920.[38] And yet, despite careful and elaborate publicity—prior notice in the *Vorposten* and the distribution of tear sheets—the book elicited no real interest during the first months following its appearance. The anti-Semitic press praised it and Jewish periodicals, constantly on the watch for all anti-Semitic publications, branded it as some new type of dementia.[39] The public at large, the Freemasons among them, were totally unaware that it existed. Dietrich Bischoff, a leader of the liberally minded Masons, compiled a pamphlet in defense of the Masons in the spring of 1920.[40] For the most part, his work was a rebuttal of the charges Wichtl had leveled in an address delivered in Leipzig on February 10, 1920. Bischoff made no mention at all of the *Protocols;* he obviously did not know of their existence. No wonder, since the general press, too, ignored the work until the middle of May! [41] A five-month silence on a book specifically written to provoke a furor normally indicates a total failure.[42] In this instance, however, the defeat became transformed overnight into a dazzling victory. An impulse, triggered in England, effected an entire transformation.

The English version of the *Protocols* came off the press a month after the German.[43] In England the Russian promoters were able to rally some support among certain reactionary circles which had banded together round the *Morning Post.* During July the paper devoted a series of articles to the *Protocols,* which were subsequently collected and published in book form both in England and the United States.[44] The publicity gained did cause a flurry of interest. In Parliament, already at the end of March, the Home Secretary was asked whether he was aware of the nature of the book and whether legal steps should not be taken to have it banned.[45] The answer was negative. No stop was put to the circulation of the book and it was reprinted several times during the following few months. There was no dearth of reviews. On May 8, *The Times* (London) carried an article on the *Protocols* and its allegations against Jews. The reviewer pointed out that the charges were not new, but believed that recent events, the Bolshevik revolution in particular, had shown the allegations to possess more than a grain of truth. Could it be possible that Jews had gathered together in some secret hideout to plot the wars and revolutions that rob nations of their tranquillity? If so, England also would fall, unaware, into the hands of the Jews. The country had with difficulty managed to escape the *Pax Germanica;* all the effort would be in vain, if instead, the country would fall victim to the *Pax Judaica.* The reviewer therefore called for a public inquiry into the truth of the *Protocols* and the validity of their charges.[46]

Who wrote the article and how it slipped past the editorial eye we do not know.[47] A contemporary, the author Lucien Wolf, suspected that German anti-Semites had perpetrated the act, since they stood to gain most from giving publicity to the *Protocols* in England.[48] This assumption of the existence of collusion is an unproved conjecture, and the course of events can be explained without resorting to any such supposition. England, too, had circles that had been shocked by current events—the bloodletting of the war and the subsequent revolutions—and who were ready to clutch at any explanation, no matter how farfetched it might be.[49] And so the *Protocols* succeeded in gaining some attention, to the extent that even the staid *Times* suffered a similar, temporary seizure.

This was the golden opportunity the German promoters of the *Protocols* needed. They hastened to give all possible publicity to the review. Appropriating the expression of the *Times,* Graf Reventlow called his article on the subject, *Pax Judaica.*[50] He exploited the German feeling of inferiority as compared with the English, as well as the prodigious prestige of the London daily. If the *Times* itself had treated the book with respect, then doubt of its veracity could no longer be entertained.

With the publication of Reventlow's article, on May 17, the *Protocol* bandwagon was set in motion. "Things really began to move," Müller noted with satisfaction soon afterward.[51] From then on the matter received extensive coverage in the press, and the *Protocols* became the propaganda material of the rightist parties for whom anti-Semitism was daily bread. We have contemporaneous evidence

183

of the key role played by the *Protocols* in molding public opinion at the time. "Side by side with Dinter's vulgar novel, *The Sin against the Blood,* the *Protocols* today constitute the spiritual fare of the anti-Semites in their halls, at their meetings, and around their group tables [*Stammtische*]," wrote Otto Friedrich of Lübeck in September 1920.[52] Benjamin Segel described the Berlin election climate of the same year.[53] Everywhere, the *Protocols* was the chief topic of conversation. By quoting from its pages, political demagogues inflamed audiences with their portrayal of the Jews as the archconspirators responsible for all the people's sufferings.

This calculated propaganda campaign achieved its goals. Yet it could never have produced such an astounding success had the slogan been out of tune with the times. We must accordingly assume the *Protocols* to have possessed some singular attraction for the generation which had emerged from the ravages of the war only to fall prey to turbulent revolution, political frustration, and economic insecurity.[54] Alfred Rosenberg describes the effects of the *Protocols* on its readers (for himself, he needed no proof of Jewish and Masonic guilt) thus: "Millions suddenly found in it the answer to so many otherwise unintelligible phenomena of the present—which suddenly ceased to appear . . . as chance occurrences but as the result of joint action . . . of the leaders of classes, parties, and nations which to the visible eye seemed to be fighting each other." [55] The author of the *Morning Post* articles, which had been collected in *The Cause of World Unrest* and had made the *Protocols* famous in England and the United States described the effects similarly.[56]

Against this blind faith in the *Protocols,* the proofs of their being a literary hoax could make little headway. That the work was a blatant fraud had already been demonstrated by Otto Friedrich and others as early as in 1920. They pointed out its resemblance to the discussion of the tribal representatives in the Prague cemetery in Goedsche's novel.[57] This story had been time and again reproduced by anti-Semites and was known to every one who followed the progress of their propaganda efforts.[58] Friedrich even conjectured that there was another, unknown source, besides Goedsche's novel, for the *Protocols.*[59] This source, finally discovered by Philip D. Graves, the *Times's* Istanbul correspondent, was the *Dialogue between Machiavelli and Montesquieu.* A Russian acquaintance had handed Graves Joly's book and drawn his attention to the similarities between passages in it and the *Protocols*. In its issues of August 16, 17, and 18 the *Times* published the correspondent's reports with the clear intention of atoning for its previous error.[60] All that exposed the *Protocols* as a forgery and its contents as absurd was summarized by Benjamin Segel in 1924.[61] Yet, if he thought that he had thereby disposed of the accusers and their arguments, he was mistaken.[62] Rational discussion, with its insistence on fact and logic, was out of the question for those who believed in the authenticity of the *Protocols*.

Anyone with even the most minimal critical faculties could instantly see through the *Protocols*. He would need no recourse to literary analysis. Its forgery was, after all, patent. This critical sense was not altogether dormant even among the anti-Semites. Theodor Fritsch reacted coldly to the *Protocols* when they first appeared [63] —and not out of personal animosity as Müller von Hausen sought to explain.[64] Fritsch admitted some time later that, "on first making the acquaintance of these documents, I cast grave doubts on their authenticity, especially since the first German edition . . . had gained in irrationality by the defective translation." He himself arranged for a new translation and argued that his mind was now at rest since he had become convinced of the truth of the work. So he stated in the introduction to the new version which he himself published in 1924. Yet he was once again constrained to question its truth, and it is most obvious that his doubts had been suppressed but by no means allayed altogether. After beating about the bush by declaring that no Aryan mind could have conceived of so base an idea as that contained in the *Protocols,* and so on, he concluded with this statement: "Even if it were to be assumed that these documents never emanated from a Jewish hand, they still constitute a masterpiece in describing the Jewish mind and its plots." [65]

Fritsch was an inveterate anti-Semite. He had already published books in the 1880's,[66] even before it had become fashionable in Germany to argue that the Freemasons were agents of the Jews. Yet this hardened anti-Semite was always ready to learn and, at the end of World War I, fell in with the new attitude. Once the neo-anti-Semitic circles made the *Protocols* the focal point for their thesis, Fritsch followed them. He laid any doubts gnawing at his heart to rest by his "even if" argument.

I have cited Alfred Rosenberg's exuberant hailing of the *Proto-*

185

cols as offering the masses the solution to the otherwise inexplicable riddle of historical events. He had committed his observations to writing in 1923, just three years after the *Protocols* first appeared in Germany and at the time when their world-wide distribution had revealed their latent utility. Yet, although he had dealt extensively with the same topic, Rosenberg at first ignored the book completely. He himself had published two works on the same theme in 1920 and 1921, and he concluded that "at the head of present world politics and behind their scenes stand the Jews and the Freemasons." [67] Rosenberg held himself out as a philosopher who sought to substantiate by profound reflection what others had tried to establish by study and penetration to the facts. He therefore relied extensively on his predecessors, and cited Wichtl by way of example. Going beyond Wichtl, he repudiated every distinction between the German Freemasons and those of the rest of the Western countries. In this spirit he published an article in the *Völkischer Beobachter* in March and April 1921.[68] In all these writings he followed the same line as the *Protocols,* which he could have cited as an authority substantiating his opinions. Yet nowhere was there any reference to the *Protocols,* and only in 1923 did he make open use of them by publishing extracts which, as it were, he illuminated with his philosophic explanations. It may reasonably be assumed that Rosenberg hesitated at first to place his weight on a support which could later prove to be a broken reed. Even afterward he made no pretense of believing in the truth of the book. In his introduction to it he dismissed the problem of its authenticity with the assertion that no Jewish attempt to prove the *Protocols* a forgery had ever met with any success. Nevertheless, he added that, "in the present circumstances it is impossible either to adduce decisive legal evidence either of their absolute authenticity or of their being a forgery." [69] When it became clear that even the most convincing proofs to the contrary could not shake the faith of the believers in the truth of the *Protocols,* he was able to place complete reliance on them without fear of their being exposed as a forgery. Their utility having been convincingly demonstrated, all doubts of their truth disappeared.

Like Rosenberg, Adolf Hitler grasped the immense possibilities of the *Protocols* in winning adherents to his cause. Any question as to his belief in them is meaningless since, for him, the facts were always subordinate to his designs, needs, and frenzies. At all events, he ignored the problem completely. " 'They are an obvious forgery,' the *Frankfurter Zeitung* keeps groaning over and over again in the ears of the world; and this is the best proof that they are true." Here the problem is cynically shelved. So, to cover this up, Hitler immediately diverts the discussion to the contents. "What many Jews perhaps do unconsciously is here clearly presented as conscious." Who had presented this? To Hitler the only question was which Jew had written the work—and thus the problem had been approached by Rosenberg—not whether the author was a Jew or a Jew-hater. "It makes no difference from which Jewish head these revelations have emerged"; the main point was that the revelations fitted the nature and ultimate purposes of the Jews. "Anyone reviewing the historical developments of the past hundred years from the standpoint of this book will immediately understand the howls of the Jewish press; at the hour when this book will become the public property of a certain people, the Jewish threat can be regarded as having been averted." [70] The merest glance at this excerpt reveals its fallacious logic. It begs the question. Yet the cunning with which the author leads the reader to his suggested, desired conclusions is just as clearly revealed.

Hitler himself had studied the *Protocols* so well that it was argued that he had derived his strategy for world domination from its contents.[71] Whether such a contention has any foundation is beyond the scope of this book. For our purposes, it is sufficient to see how superbly he put the main thesis of the *Protocols,* the alliance of the Jews and Freemasons, to use. "The Jew fought on with all his characteristic tenacity for religious toleration. In Freemasonry which is so completely subservient to him, he found an excellent tool for the advancement and penetration of his purposes." [72] This is a succinct and telling summary of the *Protocols.* Hitler had no love for Freemasonry. In his conversations with Hermann Rauschning he gave vent to his animosity against the entire movement. He regarded the association as a social framework which led its members to spiritual ends by a dependence on rationally inexplicable signs and symbols. In this respect the lodges and the churches were in the same category. Both were serious rivals to the new order sponsored by his party, to which he wished to reserve the sole right to bind adherents by means of nonrational connections.[73] Since he

187

denied the right of the Freemasons to exist, he was happy to see the movement identified as the tool of the Jews and so to prepare public opinion for its future elimination.

The scales became heavily weighted in favor of accepting the *Protocols* as authentic through Eric Ludendorff who, as German general in World War I, had covered himself with glory. He had gone into politics after the war and participated in the Hitler Putsch of 1923. Thereafter he remained the spokesman for the extreme right. An exponent of racist and cultural anti-Semitism, he was also critical of international Freemasonry. Although he had achieved fame in the past, he now revealed himself as unreflecting and intemperate in his public appearances, his deeds and utterances approaching pathological proportions. It is not at all surprising that he upheld the validity of the *Protocols* as unimpeachable. He had relied upon them in his book *Kriegsführung und Politik,* written in 1922.[74] Together with his wife, Mathilde, he began publishing special tracts in 1927 denouncing Jews, Freemasons, and all other open and secret enemies of mankind.[75] Even though these books are nothing but a conglomeration of wild fantasies, the measure of their influence cannot be underrated. In the eyes of the masses, Ludendorff's name was a sufficient guarantee of the veracity of any slogan, and it was at these masses that the anti-Jewish and anti-Masonic propaganda was directed at the time.

188

Both Jews and Freemasons had become inured to this type of slander. Nevertheless, the flaming hatred fanned by this propaganda toward the end of the war and soon afterward took them aback. To such absolute denigration of their nature and existence, even Jews had not been accustomed—certainly not the Freemasons. It does not fall within our present discussion to describe how Jews responded to this stream of venom; it is the reaction of the Freemasons which henceforth largely determined the real relations between them and the Jews, that does concern us.

The anti-Masonic attacks called forth an entire apologetic literature, consisting in part of books and articles produced by individual authors on their own initiative and in part of manifestoes issued by the Grand and affiliated lodges. In addition, a number of writings were sponsored by the Verein deutscher Freimaurer. This society, consisting of about 18,000 members, had for a long period of time occupied itself with the study of the history and ideology of Freemasonry and it now took up arms to ward off the attacks of its detractors.[76]

Two trends became marked in the Masonic defense against the nationalist groups. One took pains to prove that Freemasonry, especially its conservative wing, was almost of the same mind as its critics in respect to their aspirations. All the allegations against Masonry were the result of a misunderstanding stemming from a lack of discrimination between some Masons and others. This was the approach adopted by the Prussian lodges. They apparently could refer to their past, to their consistent loyalty to Christian principles. What grounds could there be for alleging that they were dependent upon Jewry when they had always refused to permit Jews to enter their lodges? [77] As for the Royal York, which had lowered its barriers against Jews for a short while, it had replaced those same bars in 1924.[78] The Prussian lodges gave demonstrative emphasis to the difference between them and the other lodges. Since 1872 all German Grand Lodges had been united in the Deutscher Grosslogenbund. The three Prussian lodges served notice on April 12, 1922, that they were resigning from the Grosslogenbund, and accorded wide publicity to their decision.[79] Their transparent intention was to draw a line of demarcation between themselves and the rest of the Masons. The Prussian lodges were prepared to admit the truth of some of the charges against the others pervading the German atmosphere at the time.

The liberal lodges were in a predicament. They could not very well claim that the presence of Jews in their ranks was incidental, a temporary expedient; it was a matter of principle in their Order. They could only set the record straight by pointing to the true state of affairs. The number of Jews in their lodges had never reached more than modest dimensions. Hence the accusation that Freemasonry was the tool of the Jews was absurd. This line of defence was taken up by Dietrich Bischoff in his abovementioned,[80] apologetic work, published in 1920, as well as in an article in the Masons' journal *Latomia,* by another author, which had appeared a year before.[81] At a later stage of the developments, the apologists cited actual statistics. In 1928 the Verein deutscher Freimaurer released the following figures: The Prussian lodges numbered 57,000 members, not one of whom was a Jew; the humanistic lodges had 24,000 members,

189

and of these less than 3,000 were Jews.[82] By 1930 the number of Jews had shrunk even more. Rudolf Mülhausen, head of the Leipzig Minerva lodge, declared that Jews constituted less than 4 percent of the liberal lodges,[83] only one-third of the estimate made two years before.

Let us for the time being set aside the question of the accuracy of these figures. Their compilers intended at all events to prove that Jews played an insignificant part in all German Freemason groupings. The apologists were completely on the defensive. The humanistically disposed no longer dared to demand of the Prussian lodges that they rescind restrictive clauses barring the admission of Jews. Their very defence of their own lodges' admission of Jews was extremely weak. Bischoff praised the level of Masonic achievement reached by some Jews, but did not challenge the general opinion that they were not as fit for membership in the Freemasons as were the members of the German race.[84] In 1928, the Verein deutscher Freimaurer issued a brochure which, in its entirety, was a refutation of the allegations against the Masons and their organizations. Yet when these apologists took up the question of the Jewish presence in their lodges, their voice faltered.[85] Mülhausen did better. He claimed, not without pride, that in his lodge, which had once fought to uphold the principle of universalism, there was not a single Jew left.[86]

There can be no doubt that the Jews were gradually being driven out of the German Masonic movement during the Weimar Republic. The smallness of their numbers is not the criterion. If we accept the Verein's figures, there were 3,000 Jews out of a total of 81,000 Masons in Germany in 1928, that is, about 4 percent or four times the proportion of Jews to the general population, though not to the intelligent, middle class from which the Freemasons were drawn. This number apparently kept declining as anti-Semitism kept on increasing in the years immediately prior to the Nazi seizure of power.[87] Nevertheless, neither the absolute nor the relative figures are as significant as the fact that the majority of the Masons now turned even against the Jews who still remained within the liberal lodges.

By right, Jews who had retained their membership in the Freemasons were entitled to admission in all, including the Prussian, lodges. Yet in the light of the prevailing mood, it is difficult to conceive that Jews were accorded the brotherly welcome to which they had looked forward. They were regarded as innately so inferior that spiritual and social contact with the members of the German race was withheld from them.[88] Even converts from Judaism were, on these grounds, often discriminated against in the Prussian lodges.[89] The Prussian Freemason movement still continued to consider itself Christian, but its concept of Christianity was defined in terms of an individual's background rather than the dogmas and beliefs he subscribed to. Jews were still required to convert to Christianity to belong to a Prussian lodge, yet, even if a Jew took that step, he would not thereby rid himself of his inferiority.[90]

The liberal Masons refused to accept the racist doctrine that assigned the hidden traits of the collective to each individual. But this does not mean that all the members in their ranks were uninfluenced by such ideas. We have the personal testimony of August Horneffer, one of the most prominent Masons of the time, who wrote his memoirs after World War II. He declared that he, too, was attracted to the Christian-racist (*völkisch*) ideology. As a result, he exchanged his participation in humanistic Masonry for a leading office in the Royal York. He was not the only one. A veritable flood of members poured from one camp to the other,[91] and Horneffer merely went along with it. Nor did the racist enthusiasts need to transfer their membership to gain their ends. They could quite easily vote down all Jewish applicants, and constrain the Jews already in the lodge to leave and thereby make the lodge *judenrein*. Here is the reason why, although thousands of Jews clung tenaciously to their Masonic membership until the Nazi rule, their numbers were not distributed evenly among the lodges. Some, like the Minerva of Leipzig, had no Jewish members at all; others had a substantial number.[92] Some lodges resisted the pressure of public opinion—but most yielded and clearly indicated their opposition to Jews.

If the Masons expected to appease their adversaries by yielding, they were mistaken. Once the propagandists had begun to attack Jews and Freemasons in the same breath, the patriotism of the Freemasons was no longer taken for granted. While the Freemasons dissociated themselves from the Jews, other circles sought to dissociate themselves from the Freemasons. Formerly many prominent figures of the nobility and the standing army had been Freemasons. This was especially common in the Prussian lodges. In the Weimar Re-

191

public the status of the army had been lowered; yet many former officers still continued to band together in groups among themselves. The Prussian Freemason movement endeavored to derive strength from these groups, but suffered a bitter disappointment in 1924, when the National Society of German Officers declared that membership in the Freemasons was incompatible with membership in their own union.[93] Having been a former officer, Ludwig Müller von Hausen was then active in the union, and it was he who brought about this decision. Its implication was that the loyalty of the Masons to the German people was now to be placed in doubt. The Prussian lodges were gravely offended. They issued a vehement protest especially in the name of their many members who had served in, or were still on active duty with, the armed forces.[94] Yet this protest only threw into bolder relief the fact that the Masons could no longer look upon themselves as part of the elite who stood above all criticism.

Nevertheless, the objections raised by the officers against membership in the Masons still bore the nature of an internal quarrel confined within the circles of the elite, who retained their privileged state or prestige from Imperial days. But the criticism was not contained within these circles. In consequence of the anti-Semitic and anti-Masonic propaganda campaign, the criticism seeped down to the broad masses. We have already seen how the Nazis snatched the hate-slogan from the hands of royalists and used it for their own ends. The debate on the Masons passed from the upper ranks to the public domain. Now the Masons were exposed to public gaze as an exclusive and arrogant minority, which, like the Jews, did not acknowledge the slightest brotherly obligation to any but their own. The agitators endeavored to elicit the mass response that it was not worthwhile to allow either of these minorities to exist. We have already noted Hitler's definition of the Freemasons as a group whose existence was irreconcilable with the Nazi party, since to that party alone the functions of the elite, of leadership, belonged in the new totalitarian state.

Despite the open, savage incitement marking the years of the Nazi rise to power, the Freemasons, like the Jews, had no inkling of the fate in store for them. Yet a few months of actual Nazi rule sufficed to show that it was bent on the total liquidation of all Masonic lodges. Some Masons tried to save themselves at the expense of their principles. At one stage it might still have seemed possible to operate the lodges in the Third Reich on condition of their acceptance of the Aryan clause, which required the expulsion of all Jews and all of Jewish descent. The Jewish members took the hint and left. They were thanked by one of the heads of the liberal lodges: "For this gesture of generous self-sacrifice on behalf of the general good, the lodges extend their deep gratitude." This noble Jewish sacrifice and the Masons' readiness to accept it were to no avail. One week after the compromise proposal of April 18, 1933, Goering intimated to the representative of the Christian Masons in Berlin that there was no place in the Nazi state for Freemasonry. The lodges, therefore, decided to disband.[95]

Nevertheless, the lodges did try to maintain some sort of existence under the guise of an open Christian society. Only two years later an end was put to this practice as well. In the summer of 1935 the doors of the last lodges in all of Germany were finally closed.[96]

I have given due prominence to the part played by the slogan "Jews and Freemasons" in preparing the ground for the Nazi rise to power. Clearly this slogan could only operate successfully against the background of other auxiliary factors. The decisive influence of political and social conditions as against pure ideology will come to the fore when we compare events in Germany with what occurred in other countries where the slogan had penetrated. Its most effective promoter was, after all, the *Protocols,* which entered upon a new literary career with the appearance of its German and English translations. These versions served as the vehicles for translations into other languages, for the most part European, but even Arabic and Chinese.[97] The extent of the *Protocols'* circulation and of its influence on the readers of other languages belongs to the province of the study of anti-Semitism and anti-Freemasonry in each respective country. Here we must content ourselves with a few observations.

There was some similarity between the effects in Germany and in Poland, Rumania, and Hungary where fascist anti-Semitic movements flourished. The translation of the *Protocols* into the respective languages of those countries certainly contributed to the rise of the anti-Jewish movements.[98] Furthermore, the book gained a wide circulation and evoked considerable reaction in the United States through the active sponsorship of Henry Ford who, between 1920 and 1927, made himself the trumpet of extreme anti-Semitic opinions.[99] In England, interest in the *Protocols* soon waned and it is doubtful whether the work left behind any trace whatsoever in the public mind.

France of course merits special attention. There the *Protocols* had been translated twice, the first time as early as in 1921 on the initiative of several groups. One version was published through the inspiration of the Action française [100] which had inherited its anti-Semitic and anti-Masonic ideology from Edouard Drumont. Led by French intellectuals, this movement was nationalistic in character and not very different in its structure and goals from the German Alldeutschen. In the eyes of these Frenchmen the *Protocols* were no more than a confirmation of what they had long believed. Hence, even after the London *Times* had exposed the spurious nature of the document and its French model, the Action française did not cease to put the ideas contained in the work to use. Books and periodicals still continued to warn of the danger posed by the Jewish-Masonic alliance with the same urgency as when they had raised the alarm before the first appearance of the *Protocols*.[101]

The second French translation was prepared by a Catholic, Ernest Jouin,[102] who since 1912 had been the editor of the *Revue Internationale des Sociétés Secrètes*. According to his personal testimony, he had become convinced that the decline of the Catholic religion had been caused by the influence of the Freemasons on the French masses. He had therefore taken upon himself the task of issuing a monthly organ to explain the destructive nature of Freemasonry and at the same time to draw attention to the part played by the Jews in this destructive process.[103] Jouin prepared his periodical methodically, making full use of his erudition and his familiarity with Masonic and Jewish history. Copies of his monthly even came into the hands of Müller von Hausen, and the two established contact after the War.[104]

Jouin suspended his activities during World War I, but resumed them immediately after the cessation of hostilities. One of his first acts was to publish a new edition of the *Protocols*. For him the work contained nothing very new. He was reminded of Drumont's, Lémann's, Goedsche's, and Gougenot de Mousseaux's works, all of which had been issued prior to the publication of the *Protocols* and had exposed the Jewish-Masonic conspiracy, each in its own way.[105] Were it not for his ingrained prejudices he could quite easily have

194

discovered the primary sources from which the *Protocols* had been drawn. Yet, in his eyes, the striking similarities between these works and the *Protocols* were only a confirmation of their veracity. The *Protocols* reinforced Jouin's convictions, inspiring him, as he himself admitted, to coin a new term: *Judéomaçonnerie*.[106] If, until now, Jews and Freemasons had appeared as collaborating in one area or another, they now seemed to him to be a single hydra-headed body.

Despite the striking similarity between the arguments of Jouin in France and Müller von Hausen in Germany, the influences they attained cannot be compared. The *Revue Internationale* remained the central literary organ for French opposition to Freemasonry. It was a bulky publication, containing prolix articles burdened with quotations and dialectic. Jouin went on to found a Ligue anti-judéomaçonique, but the remarks with which he opened the founding meeting in 1928 were far from having any popular appeal.[107] They were suited to a closed society of a chosen few joined together for the promotion of social goals. Furthermore, Jouin was a professing Catholic, and his mode of speech could only influence those who had assented to the dogmas of the Catholic Church.

Such limitations did not affect the spokesmen of the Action française. They were not particularly devout Catholics; they were only interested in introducing Catholic traditional symbols into their nationalistic conceptions. The Church's attitude toward them was ambivalent. In 1926 differences between the two almost caused an open clash.[108] Prior to that date the influence of the Action française was limited to circles professing adherence to Catholicism, and in the ensuing years its influence had been reduced almost to a minimum. Only in the thirties did the movement gather strength once more, when Hitler's successes in Germany aroused rightist circles in France to exploit his propaganda methods for their own ends. From then on the cry "Jews and Freemasons" began to make itself heard. With the occupation of France in 1940 the slogan became the weapon of collaborators eager to carry out Nazi directives in French society. The propaganda pamphlets issued in France at the time resembled—in content and even in format—the publications appearing simultaneously in Germany.[109]

Anti-Jewish and anti-Masonic literature did not cease proliferating in Germany even after the demise of the targets of the incitement. If there was no longer any need for continuing agitation against the adversary, it was still necessary to find justification for the fate of the victim. To this end, a so-called study was undertaken of the history of the Jews and the Freemasons,[110] to lend, as it were, "scientific" support for the views of the conquerors. All that time the public was covered by an avalanche of information bulletins on Jews and Freemasons, presenting them as the ills and enemies of mankind.[111] The Nazi regime intended not only to determine the fates of its victims but also to pronounce the verdict of history on their nature. We shall conclude our historical account with the description of one event where this inhuman arrogance was arrested.

During the thirties the Nazi movement began to infiltrate into Switzerland. Its sponsors, actively aided and abetted by the German Nazi movement, set the usual propaganda machinery in motion. Here, too, the targets of their agitation and slander were the Jews and the Freemasons. Among the materials openly circulated was the *Protocols of the Elders of Zion*. Determined to fight back, the Jews turned to the courts. In 1934, the League of the Swiss Jewish Communities together with the Berne Jewish community instituted proceedings against the distributors of the *Protocols* for willful and malicious slander, which constituted an open incitement against Jewish citizens.[112] The Court had to consider the question of the authenticity of the *Protocols* and so called for the expression of the learned opinions of experts. For the plaintiffs, there appeared Professor A. Baumgarten of the University of Basle; for the defendants, Ulrich Fleischhauer, a German anti-Semitic writer, and C. A. Loosli, a Swiss author, was appointed by the Court.[113] All the well-known arguments and counterarguments were presented by the representatives of both sides, but this time the claims had to be submitted to a third party, a neutral expert acting in the presence of a presiding judge who had to decide between plaintiffs and defendants. The neutral expert unhesitatingly sustained the plea of the plaintiffs, and the judge found for them. The *Protocols* were branded as a literary forgery and the alleged Jewish-Masonic conspiracy declared the figment of a hostile and malicious imagination. The judge summed up in a sentence which was much repeated later. The day would come, he declared, when people would wonder why it was necessary to deliberate for a whole fortnight to prove the spurious nature of a document which was so patently false.[114]

196

Historical Significance

In this account of the sequence of events, I have traced the concatenation of Jewish-Masonic relations as they extended over a period of two hundred years in those European countries where the problem became acute, especially Germany.

These two centuries are usually regarded as constituting an epoch completely separate and distinct from the preceding period in the histories of the Western peoples. Their distinguishing feature is the breakdown of traditional patterns in most areas of life. Obsolete methods of commercial production were discarded, new forms of state government and organization introduced, and social classes reconstituted and set off against each other in such a manner as could never have been conceived of by earlier generations. Cracks began to appear in the traditional structures of the various religions. The institutions of organized religion lost much of their authority, and individual commitment to systems of belief and modes of worship became weakened.

Most of these changes did not develop slowly and proceed unnoticed by the generations involved in them, as normally occurred in the transformations undergone by human society in most times and places. Many of the present changes were deliberately forced through so as to conform to definite and explicit principles, among which the most important were the concepts of rationalism and universalism. The former granted supreme authority to human reason in regulating human affairs in theory and in practice, in respect to both man's dominion over nature and his relations to whatever transcended nature. The principle of universalism held each individual person to possess the same worth and equal rights, irrespective of his origin or adherence to any group or class.

No new society, however, was created through the implementation of these principles. Their effect was to fuse together—in varying proportions in each area—what had been accepted and handed down from the past and was now judged right and wise in the light of reason. Only in terms of the clash between these conflicting elements and the repeated efforts to effect compromises between them can episodes of greater and lesser importance in modern history be explained. One of these episodes was the rapid spread of the Masonic lodges which subscribed to the principle of absolute universality; another, the entry of Jews into European society and their absorption into its community of citizens. Had they not been propelled by the universalist ideal, the two could never have occurred. Yet, attempts made to fulfill this abstract ideal always encountered vestiges of past conceptions which obstructed its transformation into the guiding principle for the future.

Nowhere is the problem of translating the principle into practice so clearly exemplified as in the clashes that arose where the two events impinged on each other. Had the universalist principle operated without impediment in both areas—the lodges and society—Jewish admission into the Masonic movement would have proceeded swiftly and smoothly. Yet the first twelve chapters of this book are replete with evidence of the difficulties encountered in this area—though not in equal measure and in all locations and at all times. Let us recapitulate the causes of the difficulties as they increased or decreased prospects for the fulfillment of the ideal.

The universalist principle was included in Anderson's first constitution compiled in 1723. It narrowed the qualifications for entrance into the lodges to obedience to the moral law. Only atheists were barred; and these were regarded as having automatically excluded themselves from the community, so that the command to regard all men as brothers did not apply to them. The author of the constitutions was fully aware of the distinctions in dogma and ritual that split mankind apart, but laid down that within the community of the Masons these differences were to be ignored. At first no declaration seems more expressly universalist than this, as long as the formulation is judged by its pure, logical denotation. Yet the objective meanings of and the subjective intentions behind the words do not always coincide.

Any Christian author writing in the early eighteenth century about conflicts in religious customs and principles can be presumed to have had the differences between the various Christian denominations in mind. European, and especially Anglo, Jewry only existed on the fringes of a society which was essentially Christian. The presence of Jews was an established and well-known fact, but their affairs were not taken into account in matters affecting the totality

of society. Even such generalities as were presumed to have universal application were not held to apply to Jews, unless this was specifically mentioned. It would follow, therefore, that Anderson may
not have intended to include Jews at all among those worthy and
ready to mix in Masonic company; his intentions and his verbal ar-
ticulations being separate and distinct. Yet, according to its implication, his definition did include Jews, and anyone desiring to have
Jews permitted to join the Freemasons could derive support from
Anderson's constitution. His first paragraph was quoted time and
again as positive proof that Freemasonry made no distinctions between members of different religions, Jewish or Christian.

Yet, as we have learned, determining the true meaning of Anderson's text was not the only, and by no means the most powerful, factor in the solution of the Jewish problem as it manifested itself in
the Masonic lodges. Even after it was formally decided that Jews be
allowed to enter the lodges, they were still hampered by difficulties
which refused to disappear, the hindrances coming from the involvement of Freemasonry in the Christian tradition. The speculative lodges, the subject of our discussion, began their activities in
the early eighteenth century. They were not creations *ex nihilo,* but
came into existence through the transformation of the nature of the
lodges, which were originally composed of actual construction work-
ers, masons in the literal sense. Heretofore the lodges had been the
organizational cells for the protection of craftsmen's common interests, for maintaining proper standards of workmanship, and for
providing mutual assistance when and wherever needed. To
strengthen their cohesion in their social group, the masons cultivated a common tradition among other things of partly esoteric doctrines, legends, songs, and slogans which were handed down from
one generation to another through the medium of more or less emo-
tionally charged ceremonies. The induction of any candidate was
also effected by solemn ceremony. When knocking on the door for
admission, the initiate would have to disrobe or else don some special ceremonial dress,[1] and so indicate that he had undergone a certain rebirth as he rose from the lower level of the ordinary human
being to the higher status of the Freemason. Similar ceremonies
marked the transition from one degree to the next.

These traditions and ceremonial patterns became crystallized
from pure Masonic elements, but not in complete detachment from

199

the stores of concepts and thought complexes predominating in society as a whole. Even though masonic rites resemble no Church ceremonies and the doctrines included in the Masonic tradition are not those of any of the known Christian denominations, all of them did draw from Christian culture and are not devoid of recognizable Christian elements. References to Christian principles and especially to the belief in the Trinity were included in the prayers and hymns which normally formed part of the work of the lodges. When the place of the operative masons was taken by the speculative Masons, those who merely sought social gratification, and the lodges were robbed of their professional functions, the Masonic tradition became the link binding the former and latter generations together. The first speculative Masons were no less enclosed in Christian surroundings in their lodges than the craftsmen had been in their trade union.

The situation changed apparently with the adoption of Anderson's constitution in 1723. It affected a certain indifference to the substance of any positive religion. Yet the change was significant in principle rather than in practice. The pronouncement did not lead to the purge of any positive, Christian elements from lodge activities. This was unnecessary; every lodge member, after all, was a professing Christian. True, it may be surmised that there was an increase, in the third decade of the eighteenth century, in the number of Masons subscribing to deism; its influence is apparent in Anderson's constitution. Yet the acceptance of this philosophy did not entail the repudiation of Christianity. Many choices lay open to the deist, enabling him to retain the verbal formulations of Christianity while mentally reconciling them by reinterpretation with the truths of his deistic doctrines. It is a known fact that the acknowledgment of the ideal of deism and loyalty to the main tenets of the Presbyterian faith coexisted peacefully in Anderson's mind.

For the Jew entering a Masonic lodge, the situation was entirely different. He came upon neutral symbols such as the compass and angle-bar, craftsmen's work tools interpreted allegorically by the Masons. He even discovered items of his own cultural and religious heritage. King Solomon was designated as the founder of the Order in Masonic legends, and his Temple was the structure symbolizing the perfection which Masons were striving to attain.[2] Other Biblical heroes—Noah, Abraham, Boaz, and David—occupied specific positions of honor in the Masonic tradition,[3] and these figures were near to the heart of the Jew. Yet the trouble was that these were not the only figures. There were in addition personalities of the New Testament. John the Baptist and John the Evangelist had always been regarded as patrons of the Masons and their feast days, June 24 and December 27, were observed as Masonic festivals and memorial days. The Bible, with the New Testament included, was laid open on the lodge table while sessions were in progress, thus showing that the book constituted a Masonic symbol. Furthermore, even the name of Jesus was expressly pronounced in the lodges during the recitations of prayers and singing of hymns.

The Jewish Mason's predicament was a reflection of his status problem in the surrounding society at the time when gates were being opened and he longed to enter. From the beginning of the Middle Ages, when the Jew had been thrust among Christians, he had existed on the fringes of their society, isolated both in respect of his institutions and his values. He rejected the Christian faith and abhorred its symbols. In his consciousness they had become transformed into a negatively charged taboo,[4] which the common origins of Judaism and Christianity could in no way dispel. On the contrary, the fact that Christianity considered itself the legitimate heir of ancient Judaism only intensified the antagonism of the Jews, since they had never acknowledged its claims and looked upon them as spiritual thievery, the stealing of the Biblical poor man's sheep.

Historical development created a blatant incongruency in the relations between the two religions. Christianity rejected the Jewish view of its heritage; it contended that Jews failed to penetrate to the true significance of their own Bible. These books had not been repudiated by the Church. On the contrary, they had been included —after some hesitation—in the Church canon, and given a Christian interpretation. The Church adopted a different attitude toward post-Biblical Jewish religious literature. These works were certainly not acknowledged as divinely inspired, and many Christians condemned them, especially the Talmud, as worthless weeds harmful enough to be burnt. Nevertheless, these writings were not completely rejected or banned. When any Christian studied Talmudic literature in the hope of discovering traces of some true revelation or prophecy, no protests were raised against him. Indeed, it is

201

known that not a few Christian theologians—especially converts—
quoted Talmudic passages in proof of the truth of Christian doctrines. To the Cabala the Christian attitude was especially magnan-
imous. From these sources entire sects drew nourishment, and
they regarded such works as having genuine Christological tendencies.[5] Even among the Freemasons there were factions which
helped themselves as liberally to Cabalistic doctrines as they held
necessary, and felt no compunction at thereby appearing to defile
their Christian heritage.

The history of Judaism has no analogy to such an adaptation of
the doctrines of the other side. If Christian sources had any effect at
all on Judaism in the Middle Ages, if certain customs and attitudes
were carried over, the affected were unaware of the existence of any
such influence. Such customs and attitudes were absorbed without
any attention being paid to their source. They were swallowed up,
and left no trace of their former state. Consciously to take sacred
Christian writings and to Judaize them for one's own needs would
have been absolutely inconceivable. The taboo imposed on every
Christian religious article and idea prevented any access to them
whatsoever. This categorical rejection of Christianity was the result
of historical experiences, the outcome of the initial rejection of
Christianity as a dissident sect that had mutilated Judaism. Once
the Jews had become the oppressed minority in Christian countries,
they were naturally forced to take up permanent defensive positions
and this reinforced their resolution to eschew whatever bore the
label of Christianity.

Whatever the historical explanation of this Jewish attitude to
Christian content and symbols may be, the fact remains that the
eighteenth-century Jew, emerging from his ghetto and attempting
to enter European society, bore with him this burden of utter withdrawal from any and all manifestations of Christianity. Many Jews
actually regarded this tradition as irksome and well worth abandoning. Indeed, we know of enlightened Jews of the period who attended Church services either out of curiosity or else to enjoy the
appealing Christian sermon,[6] an act which their forefathers would
have refused to perform even at the peril of their lives. It is no wonder, then, that Jews could henceforth be met in the Freemason
lodges, who would not even recoil from the Christian constituent

in the Masonic rites. The first Jewish Masons should be conceived as educated individuals endeavoring to lighten the oppressiveness of their Judaism and to mitigate the feeling of isolation that had over-taken them, once the revulsion against intimate contact with their Christian environment became mitigated. This type of Jew reap-pears later, at times under the cover of an ideology justifying the disregarding of religious difference and at others of nullifying the problem and significance of all religion.

Yet, common as this type of Jew had become, they were not the only individuals eyeing the Freemasons. At their side appeared the Jew, faithful to his religion, who hoped that the lodges would draw the proper logical conclusions from their avowed principles and banish all Christian concepts and symbols from their Order. Para-doxically, it was most difficult to effect such a change precisely in England, the home of the first declaration of tolerance. There the lodges had emerged as a gradual, historical outgrowth and they re-tained the elements of their lengthy tradition, which contained an admixture of Christian ideas and symbols. Their declaration of ab-solute tolerance was conditioned by this ancient tradition, which concealed, but by no means removed, the drawbacks a Jew was likely to encounter. The satisfactory solution for such Jewish Ma-sons as were consistent in their Jewishness was the institution of sep-arate practices when they were involved, at least on the occasion of the recitation of prayers, and so forth.

A less complicated situation existed on the continent. There the lodges had been established in conformity with the 1723 and 1736 versions of the English constitution, and it had been possible to or-ganize them, from their very inception, on the foundations of toler-ance and keep them free of any involvement in one or other of the positive religions. Undoubtedly the rapid spread of the lodges through central and western Europe resulted from the longing of the various social classes and Church denominations to escape from the narrow confinement of their traditional groups. It could have been expected that such lodges would base themselves on the pure, rationalistic principles and on the universalist religion clearly im-plied in the English constitution, the charter of the entire move-ment.

That the historical development of the Masonic movement did not proceed along lines consistent with abstract logic is evident

203

from our account of its history. Almost from their very inception, French and German lodges introduced restrictions, and the exclusion of Jews was more rigidly enforced in these countries than in England. Certainly the phenomenon needs explanation, and this can be offered in terms of two parallel considerations. First, Jews on the continent were held to be outside the pale of human society as a matter of course, even where neutrality in respect of religion was accepted as self-understood. In England, and perhaps also in France (outside of Alsace), the Jews, when their entrance to the Masonic Lodges began, was so few in number that they attracted no attention. In Germany, Jews were separated from their neighbors by so wide a cultural gap, that it may be assumed that they would have never been considered for membership, when the English constitution was published in its German version in 1741, even if an explicit clause disqualifying them had never been included. We have seen how the exclusion clause in France was formulated and became incorporated in the official constitution of the German Masons. This adaptation was not accidental; it expressed the reaction of the Freemasons to a situation into which circumstances had thrust them.

204

The novelty of Freemasonry was that it offered diverse sects and classes the opportunity to meet in neutral territory. The leaders of the movement could believe or make believe that this constituted no transgression of the boundaries of their accepted value systems. Yet their claims were not universally sustained and the vigilant guards of traditional values and old institutions sensed the significance, from their point of view, of the change. Even though the Freemason movement did not come to replace any older organizational units or to negate the validity of the accepted religions, it nevertheless threatened to arrogate some of their functions to itself and so to challenge their complete authority. It was not out of mere fanaticism that the Catholic Church was adamantly opposed to the Freemasons. That establishment which regarded itself solely responsible for the cultivation of the religious spirit of its flock, for the salvation of the souls of its faithful, as it called them, could not very well share its functions with any rival who sought to gain the same ends by different means. Nor did opposition emanate from Catholic quarters only. We have learned of the misgivings of the representatives of Jewish conservatism toward Freemasonry. Their reason, too, was fear lest Jews break out from the enclosure which ensured complete commitment to the Jewish religion. The anxiety that religious functions might be usurped by the new spiritual societies fell upon the adherents of all religions. A German Protestant writer expressed his concern almost at the time when the first lodges were being inaugurated: "It is tantamount to the denial of Jesus or of the Christian religion to seek peace of soul, not through Christianity or the word of the Redeemer, his teachings, and his acts, but by relinquishing him and choosing other means." [7] This verdict was rendered in a pamphlet written in 1742 by an Egidus Günther Hellmund of Wiesbaden, whose purpose it was to have the new society investigated. Here Freemasonry was not disqualified on account of any detail of its actions or principles but because it claimed the right to provide its members with spiritual elevation, a right which until now had remained strictly within the province of the accepted institutions of religion.

The Freemasons were, almost from the inception of their movement, forced on the defensive. True, their association had come into being in consequence of class structure's becoming weaker and the cooling of the individual's ardor for religious institutions and doctrines. By joining the lodges the members sought out some new social and spiritual environment beyond the boundaries of their class and the control of their Church. Yet they had no intention of erecting any competing social structure. Nor did they seek to become the means for undermining the existing order. Such aggressive designs were only professed by the adherents of one or two trends in Freemasonry, the Illuminati in Bavaria and perhaps the Martinists in France—both during the years immediately prior to the French Revolution.[8] Generally the lodges were regarded as rallying points for the peaceful, who might have been inclined toward novelty but had discovered how to satisfy their longings without courting danger. The lodges included the highest echelons of government, even heads of states, in the eighteenth century. The Freemason constitution specified that the lodges were not to become involved in politics, and the members usually obeyed the injunction. Accordingly, even though they were semi-secret, closed societies, the lodges existed with the full knowledge of the governments, as in Prussia, or else through being deliberately ignored by the governments, as in

205

France and Austria. Actions to proscribe them were only undertaken in countries where the Catholic Church exercised a controlling influence over government action, such as Spain, Portugal, and Italy.

At all events, the open or veiled patronage of governments could not protect the lodges against attacks by extremists—the fanatical guardians of the welfare of the state and the authority of religion. Their contentions that, by its very existence, Freemasonry was undermining the stability of state and Church could not be silenced. Spokesmen for the Masons had to keep reiterating their replies to these charges over and over again. Only the rebuttals of the religious accusations fall within the purview of this study. And these replies always included the declaration that Freemasonry remained faithful to the Christian religion, upheld its principles, and did not contradict its doctrines. As we have seen, the substantiation of this argument always consisted in asserting that, actually, no member of any other religion, be he pagan, Moslem, or Jew, was acceptable in the Masonic lodges. The fact of Jewish exclusion was exploited to validate the Christian character of Freemasonry. Once the exclusion of Jews was given explicit formulation, it in turn reinforced the tendency to maintain the exclusion in practice.

Even though the need for apologetic statements helped strengthen the tendency toward exclusion, we cannot attribute the existence and persistence of the restriction to that need. The principle of universality expressed in the first paragraph of the Anderson constitution, and ensuring the opening of the lodges to candidates regardless of their adherence to any particular religious denomination, could never have been implemented within the structure of the old order. This would have entailed not only the abrogation of Church dogma but also the development of an entirely new system of belief which would provide a basis for deistic principles and humanistic ethics. The Masonic lodges needed to infuse an intellectual content into their activities and symbolic, ceremonial patterns. To provide such an ideological content with all its attendant principles would obviously have been no easy task. And the Masons made no effort to achieve this goal. Instead, they took from what was already available—namely, Church traditions—while at the same time purging what they took of its ecclesiastical elements. In this respect there was no difference between the lodges in England, the land where Masonry was born, and those in the countries to which Masonry had spread as a new social movement. On the contrary, since there was no binding local tradition in the other countries, it was relatively simple to adopt ideas and symbols from any source that appealed to the mood and fancy of the members of each particular lodge, and among them were those predisposed to mystic and mystifying doctrines. This type certainly did not abjure any Christian concepts and symbols but even presumed to lead the Masons, in the higher degrees, to the revelation of profound Christian mysteries.

From such rites, the Scottish, for instance, Jews were automatically barred. But even in the lower degrees, the lodges still clung to the specific Christian elements—such as taking the oath on the Gospel of Saint John. No Jew could ever feel at home in any lodge maintaining such practices, unless he diverted his attention from what was transpiring among the Christian members, and they in turn diverted their attention from his Jewishness. Certainly the presence of the few Jews in the lodges during this period can only be understood as the outcome of compromising and accepting on both sides. This tolerance was an expedient. It was not the consistent fulfillment, on principle, of the great universalist rule which the first paragraph of the Masonic constitution had solemnly proclaimed.

207

XIV Real Relations

The integration of Jews into European society only became a public problem from the 1780s on, from the time when the writings of Christian Wilhelm Dohm in Germany, Count Mirabeau and Father Grégoire in France, and others like them brought the question into the limelight.[1] From now on, what occupied the attention of politicians was not the maintenance of order and supervision of the Jewish communities, but what new position and status to accord to Jews in society and state. The first step in this direction was the Edict of Toleration, promulgated in 1781–82 by the Austrian Emperor, Joseph II. If not expressly, then implicitly, he gave recognition to the Jews of Austria as subjects with the right of residence in their existing localities. Yet bringing the Jewish problem to the fore was not achieved solely by these writers' labors. It was the result of changes and transformations in state and political life that made the relegation of Jews to the status of an alien group seem an intolerable anomaly. The Jews themselves were caught in the stream of change, and, although the new attitude toward them was not brought about by their initiative or intervention, were not oblivious to its presence. Once they discerned the change, or at least its symptoms, they began to contribute their share toward hastening the transformation.

The efforts to compel changes in the Masonic lodges ran parallel to this social and political process. The establishment of the Asiatic Covenant and the attempts of the founders to obtain unqualified approval for Jews to join the Freemasons were significant symptoms of this process, despite the doubtful characters and actions of the persons involved. When that Order and the other unauthorized lodges, mentioned before, were founded, there appeared in Germany not only isolated individuals but entire Jewish circles which desired to join organizations consisting of non-Jews. As for the gentiles, the number of those welcoming such aspirations was not at all negligible. As these phenomena occurred almost simultaneously with the public discussions of the Jewish problem and the first benefits conferred on Jews, they can, and must, be regarded as complementary aspects of the same general historical process. The 1780s were years of awakening. It was widely felt, not only in France but in Germany as well, that the existing social and political situation could not endure much longer. No one of course could foresee at the time what character the changes would assume or where they would lead. When they took the form of the French Revolution, the nature of the future transformations was once and for all determined, for good or for evil.

Through the Revolution the lot of the Jews who were under French rule, or came under French hegemony during those twenty years, was separate and distinct from that of the rest of European Jewry. The former acquired full citizenship rights almost immediately and lived to see a temporary retrogression only at the end of Napoleon's reign. The latter were compelled to battle for their rights for decades, painfully wresting each gain, and frequently forced into retreat.[2] Many phenomena in the history of these two section of Jews are illuminated by this background of difference, and there is a clear parallel to their divergent courses in the history of the Freemasons. The French Republic had severed itself completely from all connections with the institutions of the Christian religion. The French Freemasons did the same. In their lodges all obstacles to Jewish entry were removed. Following the example of the state, French Freemasonry became a secular organization. Even though to turn their back on their Christian heritage was by no means easy, the lodges laid down that the vestiges of past symbols were not to constitute a bar to the entry of non-Christians.

The situation in Germany was radically different. Even such states as had granted Jews citizenship had done so without giving up their attachment to Christianity. The states did not abolish the use of religious symbols to justify their rule and even presumed, with greater or lesser sincerity, to embody a religious system of values. Social groups, too, chief among which were the Masons, acted similarly. Jews were excluded from such circles, since their Christian spokesmen claimed that their *raison d'être* could only be justified by their adherence to Christian values. Other arguments were also put forward, it being at times alleged that Jews were unfit to mix in Masonic company. The first and ultimate justification for the exclusion of Jews, however, was the commitment to Christian principles. And the same reservation was responsible for delaying political emancipation where it had not yet been attained and whittling it down where it had been conferred.

This commitment to Christian values was not allowed to go unchallenged, either in the state or among the Freemasons. During the thirties and forties the liberal movement aimed at cutting the state free from all connection with religion and constructing it upon universal, secular principles. The example set by the French Revolution continued to exert influence even after its course had taken unexpected turns. Yet, since the principle of the separation of Church and state had not been carried into practice, the emancipation of the Jews was not successfully accomplished. The German states refrained from enacting edicts of emancipation all at once. Only gradually, under the pressure of political and social conditions, through compromise and concession, without any goodwill on the part of the givers or complete satisfaction on the part of the receivers, was emancipation finally achieved.

A similar process operated among the Freemasons. The liberally minded brethren sought to find in the Masonic movement the ideal, universalist society. They pointed out the blatant contradiction between the broad-minded and generous definition of the first constitution and the Christian exclusiveness enforced in contemporary lodges. The Jewish Masons seized upon this argument and reinforced it by reference to the examples of lodges in other countries: England, France, and Holland. They themselves belonged to lodges in those lands or else to the "Jewish" lodges (in Frankfurt) which existed, by virtue of the universalist principle, under the auspices of lodges outside of Germany. To protest this travesty of the principles of their Order and this contempt for their legitimate rights, Jews pressed their struggle within the Masonic association with all the means of persuasion at their command.

Here in microcosm is the story of the Jewish community's struggle for full emancipation, a struggle which reverberated through all the German states for more than two generations. During that time the significance of the Masonic struggle changed from what it had been in the early stages, when a few Jews attempted to become part of an elite composed of members of diverse estates. Clearly the social composition of the lodges was no longer the same as it had been before the Revolution. Then the barriers between the estates had been maintained by force of law; now the barriers between the opposing classes were maintained by social forces. Transition from one class to another had become possible, since the contacts between them were no longer formally restricted. Nevertheless, the members of each class continued to confine their social intercourse to their own group. This they did by inclination and without any feeling of being compelled or coerced. The Masonic lodges were now deprived of one of their functions—the mitigation of the feeling of isolation of those held down in their social groove. The lodges continued to exist, but henceforth only those belonging to one specific class were by and large concentrated there, namely, the middle class, in the broader sense of the term. Even though no precise studies of the existing situation are available, the signs give unmistakeable indications that, in the nineteenth century—after some semblance of equilibrium had been restored—the lodges were in the main composed of financially and culturally independent persons, and no longer included the ruling and intellectual cadres. Most of the Masons were respected dignitaries in their communities. If we find no important political rulers or great creative thinkers in their midst, neither do we find among them the social adventurer, so common in the eighteenth century. The nineteenth-century Masons, at least in the countries dealt with here, could no longer be suspected of harboring designs for change and revolution except by persons endowed with especially morbid imaginations. At this time the main function of the lodges consisted in providing peaceful citizens with the opportunity to cultivate social and spiritual values in retreats far removed from the surrounding reality. If Masonic membership in the eighteenth century was a sign of marginal status in one's original social class or else of a leading position in the general society—of a straggler or a pioneer—it gave evidence in the nineteenth century of a secure and recognized status in the group constituting the central pillar of society as a whole.

211

Here is the key to an understanding of why Jews flocked so eagerly to the Freemasons in the nineteenth century, and why they felt deprived and disappointed when this privilege was denied to them. Jews naturally desired to become integrated in the surrounding society, to become part of that group to which they would most likely have belonged, had no social discrimination stood in their way. In the eighteenth century, only a few, mostly intellectual or social adventurers, tried to breach the barriers and join groups outside the Jewish community. By the first half of the nineteenth century, however, there was a marked increase in the number of middle-class Jews who had acquired some education and financial independence, and whose achievements could bear comparison with the corresponding level in gentile society. These Jews sought appreciation and recognition of their achievements in accordance with the criteria accepted in their environment. Since membership in the Masonic lodges had become a badge of the social elite, to bar the entry of Jews into that organization was to deny them a benefit they considered themselves fully entitled to receive. Only prejudices inherited from the past could, as far as the Jew was concerned, account for his being rejected by the group to which he rightfully should belong. Hence the resentment and outcry with which the Jews conducted their struggle.

Anti-Jewish Masons often argued that in their efforts to join the Masons, Jews were more deeply motivated by a craving for social prestige than were gentile candidates. It is difficult to substantiate or refute such claims; yet, if they do have some foundation, they can readily be explained. Acceptance in the Masonic fold had a twofold significance for the Jew: a sense of personal accomplishment, and the overcoming of the social barrier blocking his group. Since such powerful forces were driving him forward, it is no wonder that, for him, the social overshadowed the spiritual significance of the achievement.

The German liberal movement failed to reach most of its goals. Its failure is rightly regarded as the turning point in German history.[3] The movement essayed to channel developments in Germany in the same direction taken in the western countries. Since these efforts did not succeed, Germany retained its own individual character, its state and society developing along their own separate paths. This does not mean that the country was completely impervious to any influence of the new currents in practical and intellectual life —in technology and economics, in philosophy and religion, and so on; on the contrary, Germany was as much affected as other countries. In contrast to them, however, in Germany these new ideas did not produce adequate political and social patterns but were forced into old forms, and an awkward and distorted adjustment was produced by mutual adaption.

Our particular topic—the status of Jews in Freemasonry as an example of their position in state and society—reflects this process and allows one to glance behind the scenes and discern the factors controlling it.

Granting equal rights to Jews would have been the logical consequence of the application of the universalist principle, according to which the state merely acts as the structure for protecting the freedom of the individual by providing him with legal and police protection. Subgroups in society were, of course, free to organize according to the rules and regulations that appealed to their members. The status of the Jew in society, then, his entry into or exclusion from any circle, should have been left to the free interplay of social trends. The thought complexes from which the ideas of universalism had emanated were no less prevalent in Germany than in the rest of the western countries. The new social forces also exerted pressure and the introduction of new methods of economic production required that the social order be reconstructed to conform to the new reality. As I have said, the liberal movement fought for the implementation of the universalist principle—but failed to achieve its final goals. While in France, Holland, and, needless to say, the United States, equal rights for Jews became an accomplished fact, and in England only the right to stand for Parliament was still denied to Jews, the Germans still continued to debate whether Jews should legally be considered aliens and whether the rights granted to them during the Napoleonic era should not be revoked. A similar situation obtained among the Freemasons. In other countries of western Europe, Jewish fitness for candidacy in the lodges was universally acknowledged; in Germany, Jews still had to fight in most lodges even for the right to participate as visitors.

The lag in Germany resulted largely from prejudices inherited from much earlier generations. There apparently the residue of the past carried much more weight than in the other countries. Yet the influence of the past is not the only reason for the difference. Conservative forces still possessed considerable strength in Germany and cherished the hope of arresting the social transformations and even of turning the clock back. Integrating Jews into state and society would symbolize the relinquishing of their old privilege. Moreover, in practice it would entail the discarding of those symbols which they had carried over from their Christian heritage. It is no wonder,

213

then, that the conservatives made a determined effort to block the Jewish infiltration, if not from hatred of the Jew then from love for the old order and its values. One obvious example of this effort is the attempt of the old guard, with the Hohenzollerns at their head, to prevent Jews from joining the Prussian Freemason brotherhood. The resulting intervention of outside bodies caused the conservatives much trouble and embarrassment but failed to deter them. To them, the preservation of old patterns and ideas was worthwhile at any price.

In a historical evaluation, all this conservative action appears as the congealing of social patterns by the application of political pressure. The lodges had always contained elements opposed to the admittance of Jews. Yet, had it not been for political interference, the liberally minded would have pursued their course of action and the process would have ended in some balance between the opposing forces. As a result of the political intervention, the conservative forces outweighed the liberals and no equilibrium reflecting the relative strengths of the social forces could be established.

214   That the halt to the absorption of Jews in society and state was artificial at this stage is evident from the fact that it did not endure. Even those who at first were adamantly opposed later had to become reconciled to granting full civil rights to Jews in the northern states and afterward in the Empire as a whole. This change of attitude is demonstrated in Bismarck's contradictory behavior. In 1847 he had taken his stand in the Prussian Landtag against the broadening of Jewish rights; yet in 1866 and again in 1871 he included, in the constitutions of the states which he headed, the principle of unqualified and unrestricted emancipation for all. Any country wanting to compete with its neighbors in the economic, technological, or scientific fields, could hardly afford to deny those principles which constituted the very basis for development and progress. One of these principles was the universalist ideal of equality for all citizens under the law. As someone once remarked, Jews were granted emancipation not out of any love for them, but because the concept of a modern state had forced those in power to be consistent.

The irresistible force of the universalist idea during this period is even more clearly discernible in the social sphere, here again exemplified by events in the Masonic lodges. As a voluntary social organ-

ization, the Freemasons had every right to band together in accordance with the rules they saw fit to set themselves. Each group could
impose such regulations even if others disapproved. As we have
seen, no pressure exerted by other lodges in Germany and elsewhere
could compel the Prussians to accept Jews or even to allow them to
attend meetings as visitors. Yet, what outside pressure was unable to
force through was brought about by the penetration of new ideas.
One of the Prussian Mother Lodges repealed the restrictive clause
outright in 1872, and the other two made far-reaching concessions
in allowing Jews to participate in their activities. Since it was a political factor which prevented the opening of the doors to Jews during the liberal era, it is pertinent to try to discover what eliminated
this factor once the Reich was established.

The sequence of events portrayed in this book reveals, it seems to
me, that the enlargement of the political unit, first through the con-
federation of the northern provinces and afterward through the unification of the Empire, broadened the basis of allegiance upon
which the security of the House of Hohenzollern rested. As before,
the conservative Prussian elite groups, among them the Freemasons,
continued to constitute central pillars for the Northern Confedera-
tion and the Reich, but they were not the only groups the Empire
had to reckon with. In Freemasonry itself, several groupings which
had long been opposed to Christian exclusiveness had now come
under Prussian guardianship. If the House of Hohenzollern wished
to assure itself of the loyalty of these circles, it would obviously have
to refrain from forcing them to acquiesce in a practice which ran
counter to their convictions. So a compromise was arranged. Each
group was allowed to retain its own accepted regulations, while the
House of Hohenzollern was to spread its patronage over all of
them. In effect, this spelled the abandonment of the principle of
Christian exclusiveness. Henceforth, even in the Prussian lodges the
liberals could raise their heads. In this way it became possible to repeal the restrictive clause in the Royal York and its affiliated lodges
and to circumvent the clause in the other Prussian lodges by granting permission to Jews to enter as visitors.

Breaking or outflanking the defences of the Prussian lodges was
the limit of Jewish achievement in German Freemasonry. Soon afterward the wheels of progress were reversed and lodges which had

accepted Jews expelled them. Until that time Freemasonry had been regarded as one of the routes leading to social integration, or at least as the arena where the battle for integration could be engaged. The late 1870s marked the beginning of a new chapter in the history of the Jews in Europe—and especially in France, Austria-Hungary, and Germany. A counterreaction to emancipation set in. The attitudes of the Freemasons toward Jews were also altered. In the next chapter we shall study the character of this new relationship but, before passing on to that stage, we shall revert to the period under discussion and direct our attention upon it from a standpoint not previously adopted in this summing up.

Undoubtedly in contemporaneous Jewish eyes the chief importance of Freemasonry lay in its opening a path for Jewish integration into the social environment. Yet relatively few Jews succeeded in gaining access to the lodges. The question may well be raised whether Masonic membership only had significance for those who belonged to the brotherhood or whether, through them, an influence was brought to bear on the Jewish community as a whole.

In the course of our historical account we did come across some positive evidence of that influence, but without any indication of its extent or intensity. Certainly the individual Jewish Masons were affected by their membership in the brotherhood, and not only in the conduct of their personal lives. They carried over their inspiration to the intellectual and communal activities of their own community. The line of persons bearing that influence begins with Sigismund Geisenheimer and ends with the philosopher Samuel Hirsch. These and many others were known from their active participation in Masonic affairs as well as in the activities of the Jewish community. Quite often the similarity between their activities in both groups is clearly manifested. The Jewish community at that time was undergoing a metamorphosis—shedding one form and assuming another. The trend was toward abandoning the specifically Jewish tradition for a universal value-system which they could display before all men. Yet this process encountered resistance, from both within and without. The innovators had to overcome the tenacious adherence of their community to its ancient heritage, which beside its religious function also served as the means of identification for the individual and the group. Even those who were disposed to seek innovations contented themselves with the adaptation of their tradi-

216

tion to new forms and needs, but recoiled from uprooting their entire past.

Possibly this hesitation might more easily have been overcome had Jews been convinced that the universalist principle, in the name of which the axe had been raised over ancient Judaism, was in truth destined to become the basis for the new society which would include both Jews and gentiles without distinction. Perhaps the Jewish Freemasons were able to see themselves banded together with their non-Jewish brethren in conformity with the universalist principle, and could more easily believe in the force of this ideal than the ordinary Jew who confined his private life within the boundaries of his own community. Almost all the Jewish Masons whose attitudes toward religious innovations are known to us belonged to the radical wing of the Reform movement. (The converse, however, does not hold true; there were radical reformers who derived their views through other channels.) One cannot logically look upon this as a chance occurrence. On the contrary, we have the clearest evidence in the case of the Frankfurt community. Here the reference is not to isolated individuals but to an entire group, distinguished both by the number and caliber of its members. The Reformist activities of the Masons were undoubtedly conditioned by their Masonic ideology, just as their social cohesion resulted from their contacts with one another in the intimate atmosphere of the lodge. Even though the Frankfurt brethren were forced to fight for recognition by the Christian Masons, they were not on that account prevented from introducing the universalist principle into their own Jewish community. Here they gave demonstrative affirmation of their own absolute faith in the Masonic principle. And this faith was not without any basis; although their proximate Masonic environment ignored them for the time being, they had, after all, been upheld by famous lodges abroad.

The Frankfurt Mason—like his lesser-known brothers in Wesel, Berlin, and elsewhere—looked upon himself as a member of a gigantic brotherhood spread over the entire world and embodying pure, universal humanism. No wonder that he felt himself the representative of this body even when he took his stand upon the question of religious reform in his own community. The Jewish Masons were most confident that theirs was the right way. Like other enlightened Jews, they found support for their views in the opinions

217

of learned and wise men; but they also found, in their own experience, the uniting force of their humanistic faith. And, though their numbers were not as large as those of the Frankfurt community, the influence of Jewish Masons of other cities should not be assessed in terms of numbers but of the force of their ideas and convictions as these influenced their activities and conduct in their own communities.

Imaginary Relations

The close of the historical account has dealt not with the real position of the Jews in the Masonic movement, but with the connections imagined to exist between the two—a belief which spread further and further abroad and produced a mass hate-slogan. Even if the rise of a slogan was deliberately promoted by interested parties, its securing of ready support requires elucidation. And the rapid spread of this particular slogan requires explanation in two respects: first, because it seemed to grow as if by itself, and, second, because it continued to spread even where its validity was flatly contradicted by the existing reality. In Germany the slogan received assent, not when Jews had almost succeeded in gaining access to all lodges, but at the very time when most of the lodges appeared as hotbeds of anti-Semitism.

The meaning of the cry "Jews and Freemasons" is obvious: two bodies, Jews and Freemasons, had combined in an attempt to dominate the world. The accusation that each of these bodies separately had such aspirations had evoked sympathy and backing in wide circles even before the two had become associated in a single slogan. Rumors that "secret elders" controlled and exploited the rank and file of the Freemasons for their own ends had been circulated almost from the very inception of the movement. Belief in this allegation gained wider and firmer currency after the French Revolution, when many of its antagonists blamed the Masons for organizing it. The best-known literary exposition of this view is the work of a Jesuit, Augustin Barruel, *Mémoires pour servir à l'histoire du Jacobinisme*. Its five volumes came off the press between 1797 and 1798, were reprinted several times, and were translated into a number of languages. From then on, the innocent and those to whose benefit it was to appear naive did not cease expressing their belief that some Masonic conspiracy lurked behind the scenes of world events.

As for the Jews, the allegation that they craved for world power was fed by a deeper historical source. This was the Jewish belief in a messiah who would restore the Jewish people to their ancient homeland, and, according to the popular conception, establish Jewish hegemony over the nations of the world. Jewish messianism had attracted the attention of the Christian world from ancient times, when the two religions split on this issue of whether the messiah had already come or was to appear in the future. Antagonists assailed the Jews for persisting in their folly of conjuring up visions of a glorious future, which had no prospects of ever coming true. It will suffice to mention Johann Andreas Eisenmenger's *Entdecktes Judenthum,* published in 1700, which devoted entire chapters (part II, chapters XIII–XV) to the Jewish belief in the glory they would attain in the messianic era—a belief which in his eyes was nothing but a delusion harbored by those who stubbornly refused to acknowledge the Christian redeemer. From the time of the publication of the book, it became an unfailing source of reference from which anti-Semites could draw their charges. Through it and other channels, information on the Jewish messianic belief was spread about, and with that information contempt for those who presumptuously dared to hope that the day would dawn when the tables would be turned, when the scattered and lowly among nations would ascend ever higher and become the rulers of the world. Once Jews had begun to escape from the ghetto and many of them, after becoming citizens in their lands of residence, even gained influence, especially in the economic sphere, the accusation was altered to fit the new conditions. Not in the future but here and now were Jews aspiring to rise to power. They had begun, as it were, on their own accord to translate their messianic dreams into a present reality.

It need occasion no wonder, then, that, once the charge had been leveled that the Freemasons constituted an international society controlling the destiny of the world, there were some who recalled that the allegation had been directed at an earlier target: the Jews. In later anti-Masonic literature there appeared a letter by an Italian army officer, dated 1806 and addressed to Barruel, the "expert" on the Masonic conspiracy. The officer informed Barruel of Jewish designs for world rule and maintained that this plot constituted a graver threat than anything the Masons were able to pose.[1] It may be recalled, too, that in his Frankfurt writings of 1816, Dr. Ehrmann had accused Jewry of infiltrating the Masonic lodges so as to seize control by this means over the entire world.

Such mental associations rise and become stale. The exclusion of the Jews from the Masonic lodges in the early years of their existence prevented this association from becoming a permanently ingrained thought-complex. In the course of time, however, conditions came about which removed the impediments to such thinking. On the contrary, events now lent support to the mental association of Jews and Freemasons to the extent that, finally, there was an almost complete identification of the two.

Some grounds for the claim of Judaization were provided by the Freemasons themselves, to their increased use of symbols taken from the Bible and even more their later absorption of Cabalistic concepts and doctrines.[2] True, these elements were hidden beneath a heavy layer of concepts and symbols of a distinctly Christian character. In the eyes of the ordinary Mason these items were thereby infused with Christian meaning, as long of course as the entire complex of concepts and symbols was not given a universalist deistic interpretation. Jewish Masons, on the other hand, were just as free to seize upon the Jewish sources of Masonic doctrine and interpret the Christian accretions to suit themselves. Gotthold Salomon did so, as we have seen. This Reform rabbi argued that Freemasonry was more Jewish than Christian. His intention was to praise Masonry, to see in it, as did others not all of whom were Jews, a tradition antecedent to Christianity, and to trace the descent of the movement to Jewish rather than Christian ancestry.

The tendency to seek out a Jewish genealogy for the Order was, nevertheless, the desire of only a small minority of Masons. Of the two main groupings in Masonry, one assigned the movement to neutral ground, beyond the reach of any positive religion, while the other planted it by Christian waters. Definitions of Masonry, however, were supplied not only by its own members but by its enemies as well. We shall return later and summarize the causes for their antagonism. For the present we are dealing with the reasons advanced for their opposition, ones which reflected the point of view, even as it changed, of each opponent. Here our interest focuses on a type of individual who combined within himself the negative attitudes toward both groups. For him, the identification of Freemasonry with Jewry was the most simple and efficient expedient. He could address himself to an audience which was already antagonistic or negatively disposed toward Jews and needed to offer no justification for this attitude. Were an agitator of this type to create the impression that Jews and Freemasons were identical, he would have attained his objective. He could attach to Freemasonry those labels which his audience already associated with Judaism. Nor did he have to seek far to find the means for establishing such an identity. It sufficed for him to consult Masonic literature, to extract the excerpts suiting his purpose. That King Solomon's Temple was a central symbol in Masonry, that Hebrew terminology was resorted to, and other such facts were regularly exploited in anti-Masonic and anti-Semitic writings. As self-incriminatory evidence, the agitator could even cite the statements of those Masons who believed the genuine source of their order to lie in Judaism. Gotthold Salomon's pronouncements were repeatedly quoted in such contexts by all the agitators, beginning with the anonymous publisher of the inflammatory sheets in Berlin in 1848 and continuing down to Müller von Hausen [3] during the Weimar Republic. That exuberant Reform rabbi, who devoutly believed that Freemasonry was close to Judaism, could not in his furthest imagination have foreseen for whom his remarks would furnish ammunition.

The Jewish content in the Masonic tradition certainly facilitated, though it was not the primary cause of, the association of Freemasonry with Judaism. Nor can the decisive factor be found in the realm of ideology. It is to be sought, instead, in the social forces behind the ideas. First to be taken into account is the existence of antipathy and hostility toward both the Jews and Freemasons, which stemmed originally from diverse sources. A tradition of hatred extending over hundreds of years had been built up against the Jews. Freemasons aroused resentment because they had introduced an innovation which broke down the fences erected by past ages. For this reason, during the first generations of Freemasonry's existence the two camps opposing Jews and Freemasons could not combine forces. On the contrary, the Masonic lodges themselves not only entertained serious reservations against Jews but even gave vent to expressions of contempt for Jews and to the systematic exposition of anti-Semitic ideas.

This situation persisted as long as the structure and composition of society retained its resemblance to the old order. Soon, however, as a result of political revolutions and economic progress, a shift took place. By the middle of the nineteenth century a new social structure had arisen, different from the accepted one of the past.

Only vestiges were left of the estates of the old order. The corporate authority of the Jewish community had been dissolved; it was reduced to a religious community only. The state now derived its support from the direct connection with all its citizens through its institutions and symbols. In theory at least, all citizens shared equally in the obligations toward the state, and the arrogation of higher status or privilege by any individual or subgroup was considered reprehensible.

Against this altered background, those opposing Jews and Freemasons had to adopt new tactics. Opponents of the former now hurled the accusation that Jewish abandonment of communal autonomy was only for appearance's sake; Jews actually continued to preserve the advantage of an organized minority at the expense of the population at large. A similar antagonism was aroused against the Freemasons. They had admitted that their goal was the creation of a brotherhood of all belonging to their Order and they never denied that this bond of brotherhood entailed mutual aid and assistance for all of them. To the accusers, such solidarity could only damage the interests of those kept outside the circle of the organized group.

At times such arguments were advanced by devotees of universal equality, who regarded any concentration in a limited group a defilement of their sacred ideal. But the same claims were made in the name of members of other organized groups—the nobility, who had preserved their inherited privilege, and clericals, like the Jesuits, as well as their spokesmen, eager to preserve their honor and status. Both groups branded Jews and Freemasons as "a state within a state." [4] This term had been coined in the seventeenth century to define the position of the Huguenots in France, who had reserved certain rights for themselves in their own districts. Subsequently, in the second half of the eighteenth century, when emphasis was given to the sovereignty of the state, the formula was directed against any corporate body which assumed such authority for itself as, according to the prevailing political climate of opinion, belonged exclusively to the all-embracing state. The Jesuits, the Freemasons, and—once the possibility of their integration in society was seriously entertained—the Jews were all alleged to be organizations of this type. The label was most frequently attached to the Jews and the Freemasons, and it expressed the reason for the opposition to both.

The fact that other bodies, like the Church, the nobility, and the army, still retained their internal organization did not mitigate the gravity of the accusation against the Freemasons and the Jews. These other bodies had received the approbation of the past history of each and every nation. Not so the Freemasons. They constituted an elite which had no roots in the popular, historical consciousness. Their presumption of distinction was considered a usurpation. Against the Jewish internal cohesion, the reverse reasoning was used for condemnation. Their involvement in the history of nations had been entirely negative. They bore on their shoulders the burden of the prejudice of many generations. What was considered permissible or even right for honored institutions like the army and the Church could not be condoned in the upstart Masons and certainly not in Jews, who were stamped from the past with the inferiority of pariahs.

The tendency to mention Jews and Freemasons in the same breath became marked, as we have seen, among conservative and Catholic writers in Germany during the fifties and sixties. The desire to defend the old, accepted social order against all who would tear it down impelled these authors to suspect Jews and Freemasons of complicity in a plot to subvert the foundations of society and its religious institutions. These critics of both bodies were merely isolated individuals. In that period hostility to the Masons grew more intense, but the antagonism to Jews declined, although it did not disappear. The attitudes toward both took different lines for an obvious reason: the Masons themselves were held to be antagonistic to Jews, as was shown by the restrictive clause in the Prussian lodges, the greatest in number and rank of all the Masonic associations in Germany.

A different situation obtained in France. The process of secularization produced two apparently unrelated effects: the complete formal emancipation of Jews, and the re-establishment of the Masonic movement on completely secular foundations. The connection between these two phenomena was demonstrated in the fact that Jews could now enter the lodges freely and ascend to the highest degrees without any obstacles hindering them. Yet, as is known, the entire process of secularization met with the approval of only a part of French society. The rest accepted the verdict under the pressure of prevailing circumstances. These, the conservative elements in French society, even though split into diverse factions by social and political colorings, found common ground in their opposition to institutions which had cast off the religious authority of the Christian tradition in general and of the Catholic Church in particular. The deep cleavage in French society clearly and obviously placed Jews and Freemasons on the same side—in the secularist camp.

There was no lack of attacks against them. Anti-Masonic writings flourished in France. Conservative writers had for long blamed the outbreak of the French Revolution and all subsequent tribulations on Masonic (and Protestant [5]) activity. Jews could hardly have been held responsible for the Revolution—they played no active part in French public life at the time. Yet from the 1840s onward, many Jews, and the Rothschilds most prominently among them, had aided the emergence of a modern French capitalist economy with its industry, railroads, and so on. In the transition to the reconstituted economy the affected strata of society suffered considerable hardship. Besides, to the conservatives, every step toward modernization was repugnant, and in this regard, they could point to the Jewish capitalists as the culprits. The hostility against Jews on the social and political plane intermingled with the old theological resentment, engendered by the prevailing Christian tradition of Catholic France against the Jewish aspiration to world domination in the messianic era.[6]

If it was still premature during the 1850s to speak of an anti-Masonic movement in France and even more so of an organized anti-Semitic movement, there was at all events a literary whispering campaign carried on with considerable acrimony. From the point of view of the old guard the Jews and the Freemasons were one by virtue of their secular posture. As the number of Jews in the lodges increased and as it became clear that many of them had been appointed to key functions, the two groups did overlap to some extent. Only a small effort was required to link them together mentally—to regard their social proximity, not as brought about by fortuitous circumstance, but as the expression of their historical and ideological similarity. Once German anti-Semitic literature began casting about quotations identifying Judaism with Masonry, the seeds fell on fertile ground; they soon took root and produced better fruit than they could have in the land of their origin. Toward

225

the end of the seventies, Jews and Freemasons were linked together systematically, and in the eighties the slogan "Freemasons and Jews" saw the light. We have previously described the spread and effect of the slogan [7] which can now be explained against the background of the similar positions of Jews and Freemasons in the French social structure.

That, in gaining currency, ideas and slogans are dependent upon contemporaneous social realities is most effectively exemplified by the fate of this slogan in the first stages of its dissemination. It landed on fertile soil in countries such as Hungary and Russia, which maintained cultural connections with France, and fulfilled some specific function over there. It failed to cross into neighboring Germany, even when all of France resounded with it during the Dreyfus trial, and the whole world listened with rapt attention to the raging controversy—the Germans, for well-known reasons, with even more interest than anyone else. German immunity was not produced by any lack of anti-Semitism, since, at the time when the slogan was spreading through France, from the seventies onward, political anti-Semitism was on the rise in Germany. The reason lies instead in the very flourishing of anti-Semitism, in its once again permeating the Masonic lodges. If, in the sixties, during the period of tranquillity, isolated agitators could conjure up pictures of Jews advancing to conquer the lodges and so link the Jews and the Freemasons in their imagination, now with the anti-Semites preponderating in Freemasonry itself, such a combination was self-contradictory.

The reverberations of the catch phrase were not heard in Germany until the end of World War I. Then the slogan infiltrated through various channels. To my great surprise I found traces of direct French influence even during the war. In France the use of the slogan did not disappear altogether, although its intensity did decline in comparison with the stormy days of the Dreyfus trial. Second, this mental association gained closer attention because of internal developments in Germany during the war. There was an outpouring of hatred against all minorities regarded as aliens or as having connections with foreigners; it overflowed all boundaries and its streams carelessly intermingled with one another. Since Jews constituted a group scattered over diverse lands and the Freemasons an organization with world-wide ramifications, both aroused the suspicion of collaborating to achieve their international goals. Third, further stimulation was provided by the source of defilement —the Russian émigrés who brought with them the *Protocols of the Elders of Zion,* the Russian version of this anti-Semitic and anti-Masonic concoction modeled on the French pattern. The slogan had been drawn from all manner of channels and its influence now penetrated more deeply and widely than anywhere else. Yet the multiplicity of sources is not a sufficient explanation; even the most abundant source can yield no results unless there is some receptacle ready to receive its contents.

German anti-Semitism had begun to assert itself forcefully during the war years, and it is no wonder that people were ready to believe any accusation against Jews. Moreover, the world had not only just succeeded in extricating itself from a war which had sapped the vitality of the European nations but had also been violently shaken by revolutions in Russia, Hungary, and Germany itself, revolutions which had destroyed or attempted to destroy the social and political order that had provided the security of generation after generation. If, in reference to the war, anti-Semites claimed that Jews had not suffered its ravages to the same extent as the rest of the population, in reference to the revolutions they alleged that Jews were the chief instigators. And here they had concrete evidence to seize on since among the leading revolutionaries were those of Jewish extraction: Trotsky in Russia, Bela Kun in Hungary, Rosa Luxembourg in Germany, and their less prominent subordinates. Possibly this extraordinary political activity by Jews, and especially their leadership of the revolutionary groups, contributed toward strengthening the conviction that there was a world Jewish conspiracy, as the central thesis of the *Protocols* had alleged.

227

Nevertheless, such an explanation ignores the other party mentioned in the slogan; the blame was after all heaped on both Jews and Freemasons. We must ask how the point was reached where Germany, too, became ready to link the two groups together, when the Freemasons themselves were presumed to have rejected Jews rather than form alliances with them. No change had affected the attitude of the Freemasons in the interim. On the contrary, many Freemasons were carried along by the rising tide of nationalism. They sought demonstratively to give expression to their dissociation

from Jews and so clear themselves of all suspicion. This time nothing helped. The repudiation of the Freemasons became as accepted
and widespread a practice as the ostracism of Jews.

To explain this phenomenon, we need to understand the radical
alteration in the position of the Freemasons as a result of the transformation of the social order. Under the monarchy the Freemasons,
especially in Prussia, constituted one of the main royalist pillars. Although the personal connections of the last Kaiser to the Masonic
Order had become rather tenuous, during his reign the Order still
preserved its status as a conservative elite. The Freemasons were
conservatives, but their character and reputation as a closed society
forced them to shun extremes. By contrast, there had always been
fanatical conservatives and Church circles which had never approved of the privileged status of the Masons, yet were unable to
oust them from their position. As long as the monarchy placed its
reliance on middle-of-the-road forces, it continued to enjoy the support of the Freemasons, and their organization in turn was strengthened by its support of the royal house. Yet, as a result of the war
and its aftermath, tensions between the extremes in the state became sharper and the two sides prepared for the final showdown.
The extreme right held its function and destiny to lie, not only in
crushing the left, but also in forcing out the moderates as well. The
activities of Müller von Hausen's circle should be viewed against
this background. They wanted the monarchy to be based on extrem-
ist nationalism. Even after the fall of the Kaiser, this group deluded itself into believing that the rise in nationalistic tension
would restore the deposed ruler to his throne. Jews and Freemasons
were linked together in the propaganda of this group. They were
condemned, not only for what they were, but because this condemnation served as the rallying point for those who would restore the
House of Hohenzollern—and all that it entailed in the minds of
the ultraconservatives—to its former glory.

Müller von Hausen's group had succeeded better than they could
have foreseen. Ostracizing Jews and Freemasons was discovered to
be the most effective weapon for rousing sympathy and gaining political strength. Yet the means did not serve the ends for which they
had been fashioned. The slogan was snatched away by other hands
belonging to groups anxious to consolidate their political power,
but not at all interested in restoring the regime of the Kaiser. These

228

groups strove to establish an entirely new government by crushing the elite guards of the right and the left. The slogan "Jews and Freemasons," seized from the rightist groups, was made to serve the propaganda purposes of the new populist Hitler movement. And here the cry gained a concrete significance vastly greater than ever imagined by those who first coined and disseminated it. In Hitler's hands the slogan constituted the means of persuasion for the liquidation of the Freemasons and the physical extermination of the Jews.

With this we reach the terminus of the history of the slogan. It was like some magic formula which had fallen into the possession of a demon, revealed the immense proportions of its destructive powers, and then exploded before the eyes of the terror-stricken and horrified spectators.

Notes

Chapter I. The Problem and Its Background

1. These facts will be substantiated and interpreted later in the book.

2. See Jacob Katz, *Tradition and Crisis: Jewish Society at the End of the Middle Ages* (Glencoe, Ill., 1961), pp. 245–259.

3. The contribution that the study of Masonry can offer to the understanding of modern Jewish history is dwelt on in my address to the Fourth World Congress of Jewish Studies, which was published in *Molad* (Jerusalem, 1966), pp. 399–405.

4. Гессен, Юлий Исидорович. *Евреи в масонстве.* (J. Hessen, *Jews among the Freemasons*), (St. Petersburg, 1903).

5. August Wolfstieg, *Bibliographie der freimaurerischen Literatur,* vols. I–III (Leipzig, 1923).

6. In the course of discussion I shall refer to many works compiled by Nazis. Their free access to the Masonic archives allowed them a distinct advantage in the establishment of certain facts in which they happened to be interested.

7. In their letter dated November 2, 1965, the United Grand Lodge of England denied me permission to use their archives—their excuse being their desire to keep their affairs away from public controversy.

8. The lodge was named Quatuor Coronati, its quarterly entitled *Ars Quatuor Coronatorum.*

9. A bibliography of the Kloss collection has appeared in print: *Beschrijving der Verzamelingen van het Groot-Oosten der Nederlanden, Handschriften der Klossiansche Bibliotheek* (The Hague, 1888), hereafter referred to as HKB.

Chapter II. Early Encounters

1. On Masonic history too, there is an immense literature, and the works are listed in the bibliographies I have referred to. I shall, however, refer specifically to the writings on certain topics with which this book is concerned.

2. See D. Knopp and G. P. Jones, *The Genesis of Freemasonry* (Manchester, 1947), pp. 129–185. Among the older works, these should be mentioned: Georg Kloss, *Geschichte der Freimaurerei in England, Irland und Schottland* (Leipzig, 1847); Wilhelm Begemann, *Vorgeschichte und Anfänge der Freimaurerei in England,* 2 vols. (Berlin, 1909–10).

3. From the very inception of the Masonic brotherhood, John the Evangelist, too, occupied a prominent place in the pattern of its ideas

and symbols, and the two personalities are often confused. See Kloss, *Geschichte in England,* p. 20.

4. [James Anderson], *The Constitutions of the Free-masons* (London, 1723), p. 50.

5. To what extent the author of the constitutions had really been imbued with rationalistic and deistic ideas is not altogether clear. See D. Knopp and G. P. Jones, "Freemasonry and the Idea of Natural Religion," *Ars Quatuor Coronatorum,* 56 (1946), 38–43. I am indebted to Harry Carr, the editor of the *Ars Quatuor Coronatorum* in London, for his clarification of many points.

6. [James Anderson], *The Book of Constitutions* (London, 1738), pp. 143–144.

7. Karl Christian Friedrich Krause in *Die drei ältesten Kunsturkunden der Freimaurerbrüderschaft* (Dresden, 1891), II, 333, had already pointed in his time to John Selden as the possible source of influence on the Constitutions. The same assertion was repeated by Ernst Wilhelm von Hengstenberg, *Die Freimaurerei und das evangelische Pfarramt* (Berlin, 1854), p. 32. The subject was extensively dealt with by Friedrich Nielsen, *Freimaurertum und Christentum,* 2d. ed. (Leipzig, 1882), pp. 26–28. All three sought to prove that Freemasonry was not, fundamentally, a Christian institution, the proof being the deistic basis of the Constitutions. Nielsen pointed out that the number "three"—rather than "seven"—mentioned in the Constitutions had been culled from Selden who identified the Noachide commandments with the three principles of the *jus natura* as defined by Ambrose, one of the Church Fathers: (1) belief in and adoration of God; (2) to live the moral life; and (3) to set an example to others by this conduct.

8. See Jacob Katz, "The Vicissitudes of Three Apologetic Passages" (Hebrew), *Zion* (Jerusalem, 1958), nos. 23–24, pp. 172–176.

9. The description of the incident in the Masonic literature is culled from newspaper reports. The matter is thoroughly treated in M. Levy's article, "Jews as Freemasons," *The Jewish Chronicle* (Sept. 16, 1898), p. 11.

10. The information was given to me by Harry Carr in his letter of November 12, 1964.

11. *Annalen der Loge zur Einigkeit . . . Frankfurt am Main, 1742–1811* (Frankfurt am Main, 1842), p. 5.

12. Levy, "Jews as Freemasons," p. 11.

13. Laurence Dermott, *Ahiman Rezon* (London, 1756).

14. The reference is to a passage in the Babylonian Talmud (Eruvin 54b): "What was the order of instruction? Moses learned it from God. Aaron entered and Moses taught him his . . ." The passage is quoted in an explanatory note on the prayers (*Ahiman Rezon,* pp. 43–44).

15. According to Levy, "Jews as Freemasons," the Joppa lodge was founded after 1799 and was a "Jewish" lodge; see Tychsen's remarks quoted below in note 19.

16. Friedrich Münter, who was thoroughly familiar with Masonic af

fairs, stated so unequivocally in his work, *Authentische Nachricht von den Rittern und Brüder-Eingeweihten aus Asien* (Copenhagen, 1787), p. 3; Erich Servati [Heinrich Sautier], *Bruchstücke zur Geschichte der Deutschen Freymaurerey* (Basle, 1787), pp. 148–149.

17. That exclusively Jewish lodges existed in Holland is reported in Johann August Freiherr von Starck, *Ueber die alten und neuen Mysterien* (Berlin, 1782), p. 308, and also by Servati, [Sautier] *Bruchstücke*, pp. 148–149. On the other hand, August Siegfried Goué confirms the fact that Jews were being accepted by the Dutch lodges, but states that he had never heard of separate Jewish lodges; see his *Bemerkungen über Saint-Nicaise und anti-Saint-Nicaise* (Leipzig, 1788), p. 37.

18. See above, notes 10, 12.

19. *Bützowische Nebenstunden,* part 5 (1769), pp. 75–77.

20. For the cultural levels of both communities, see Cecil Roth, *A History of the Jews in England* (Oxford, 1964), pp. 197–212; Thomas W. Perry, *Public Opinion, Propaganda, and Politics in Eighteenth-Century England: A Study of the Jew Bill of 1753* (Cambridge, Mass., 1962), pp. 5–12; Eljakiem Menachem Bolle, "De opheffing van de Autonomie der Kehilloth (Joodse gemeenten) in Nederland 1796," diss. (Amsterdam, 1960), pp. 50–54, 62–66.

21. The social functions of the Freemasons are analyzed in Bernard Fay, *La Franc-Maçonnerie et la revolution intellectuelle du XVIII siècle* (Paris, 1942), pp. 123–126. Reinhart Koselleck's *Kritik und Krise, Ein Beitrag zur Pathogenese der bürgerlichen Welt* (Freiburg and Munich, 1959), attempts to view the Masonic fraternity as an expression of the civil community's resistance to the absolute state (see especially pp. 49–81). His conclusions are reached by way of philosophical generalizations rather than deduced from material evidence.

22. *Milestones in the Records of the Lodge of Tranquillity,* no. 185, p. 11. This reference was supplied by Harry Carr. According to him, he had been able to ascertain from the lodge minutes themselves that this was not the only instance.

23. This complaint appears in a French pamphlet (with no title) by Antoine Dailly, dated "The Seventh Year of the Republic" (that is, 1801). It is addressed to Citizen Holtrop, the head of the Amsterdam lodge. M. H. Gans of Amsterdam kindly allowed me to photograph his copy.

24. See Georg Kloss, *Geschichte der Freimaurerei in Frankreich* (Darmstadt, 1852), I, 18–19, 30–32; Albert Lantoine, *Histoire de la Franc-Maçonnerie Française* (Paris, 1935), pp. 3–21.

25. The author of the book has not been definitely identified. See Wolfstieg, *Bibliographie,* no. 23736.

26. *Apologie pour l'Ordre des francs-maçons* (The Hague, 1742), pp. 14–15.

27. Kloss, *Geschichte in Frankreich,* p. 79. The other laws, too, show that, as Kloss remarks (p. 82), the order was intended for Christians participating in Catholic worship.

28. The bull was reprinted time and again. It is quoted here from [August Siegfried Goué], *Notuma, nicht Ex-Jesuit über das Ganze der Maurerei* (Leipzig, 1788), p. 48, "contenti honestatis naturali specie."

29. Theodore Henri Baron de Tschoudy, *L'Etoile flamboyante ou la société des franc-maçons* . . . (Frankfort and Paris, 1766), II, 199; translated into German as, *Der Flammende Stern oder die Gesellschaft der Freimaurer* (Berlin, 1779), p. 141.

30. See Katz, *Tradition and Crisis*, pp. 45–59; and Jacob Katz, *Die Entstehung der Judenassimilation in Deutschland und deren Ideologie* (Frankfurt am Main, 1935), pp. 32–46. As against the date I have designated as marking the beginning of the change, Azriel Shohet in *The Beginnings of the Haskalah among German Jewry* (Hebrew) (Jerusalem, 1961), has propounded a thesis which predates the change to the beginning of the century. Jacob Toury, *Bulletin des Leo Baeck Instituts* (1961), pp. 55–72, attempted to effect a compromise between the two views. In his address to the Fourth Congress of Jewish Studies (see *Molad*, 1966, pp. 330 ff.), Shohet came nearer to my position and designated the sixties as the period when the change began. I believe that the study of Jewish-Masonic relations will contribute greatly to clearing up this point.

31. Karl Wiebe, *Die Grosse Loge von Hamburg und Ihre Vorläufer* (Hamburg, 1905), p. 233.

32. See notes 11 and 18 above.

33. *Annalen der Loge zur Einigkeit,* pp. 58–59.

34. See the quotation above, note 19. Tychsen uses the Hebrew word, *minim*, which he translates as *Ketzer und Profane.*

35. *Nebenstunden*, p. 78. It is appropriate here to adduce the evidence of R. Hayim David Azulai. During his visit to Tunis in 1774, a private inquiry was addressed to him on the permissibility of killing Italian Jews who had come there and were known as "Frankmason." "Tell your father," he replied, "that it is absolutely forbidden to kill them, even as an emergency measure, since we know of no prohibition in this matter, and they declare that it [Freemasonry] is not contrary to the law of Moses and Israel. And this [i.e., Masonry] would seem to be like some kind of comedy, and I admit that even as a comedy it would be forbidden, and certainly this [Masonry]. Yet what do you think, one should persecute them to death, God forbid?" (Chajim Josef David Asulai *Ma'agal-Tob Ha-Shalem* [ed. Aron Freimann, Jerusalem, 1934], p. 64). The question of Freemasonry, then, could not have been new to him, and he regarded membership in the association as one of the signs of the abandonment of religious observance which had just recently begun to affect the Jewish community.

36. Christian Ernst Simonetti, *Sendschreiben an die ehrwürdige Loge der Freymäurer in Berlin* (Berlin and Göttingen, 1744): "Wie sich dieses mit den Sätzen: Der Orden nimmt nur Christen in seine Gemeinschaft auf . . . verbinden lasse, verstehe ich nicht" (p. 65).

37. Franz August von Etzel, *Geschichte der Grossen National-Mutter-loge in den Preussischen Staaten genannt zu den drei Weltkugeln* (Berlin, 1903), pp. 54, 189.

38. The exact text of the minutes was copied at Kloss's request and is in his archives, HKB, XIV, 2. The account of the incident is also included in the printed proceedings of the Royal York lodge, in the minutes of the session held on February 5, 1845. At that time the effort was made to eliminate the restrictive clause and to show that it had never been valid.

39. *Annalen der Loge zur Einigkeit*, p. 58.

40. "Die maurerische Emanzipation der Juden in Hamburg," *Hamburger Circelcorrespondenz*, no. 125 (1847), p. 129 (a handwritten mimeographed circular).

41. *Apologie*, p. 116.

42. Gotthold Ephraim Lessing, *Ernst und Falk, Gespräche für Freimaurer* (Leipzig, 1909), p. 203.

43. The conversation was reproduced by Lessing's brother as he had heard it from Mendelssohn. Karl G. Lessing, *Gotthold Ephraim Lessings Leben* (Leipzig, 1887), p. 171.

44. This note too was transcribed by K. G. Lessing in his letters dated October 28, 1778, to his brother, Gotthold Ephraim: "Was man an den Berlinischen und anderen neueren Theologen tadeln könnte, sagte er, könnte man auch an Deiner Freimaurerey tadeln. Allein die grossen Aussichten, die Du überhaupt den Menschen darin machst, verkennt er dabey nicht" (*Gotthold Ephraim Lessing's sämtliche Schriften* [Leipzig, 1907], XXI, 233).

235

Chapter III. The Order of the Asiatic Brethren

1. The affairs of the Order of the Asiatics receive frequent, though perhaps brief, mention in Masonic historical literature. Many details have been collected in the *Allgemeines Handbuch der Freimaurerei* (Leipzig, 1900), and in *Latomia* (1863), pp. 18–37. Kloss gathered together a large amount of material on the history of the Order from printed books and manuscripts. (HKB, XIV, 1–2) one manuscript being a history of the Order by Franz Josef Molitor in two versions—the shorter version written in 1820 (after the death of Hirschfeld, with whom this chapter will deal at length), and the longer version written in 1824. The shorter version was published by me as an appendix to Katz, "The First Controversy over Accepting Jews as Freemasons," *Zion*, XXV (1965), 204–205. It will be referred to as Molitor (*a*); the second, longer version as Molitor (*b*).

2. Ecker gives the date as 1780 in his book (see below, note 76), *Abfertigung an den ungenannten Verfasser*, p. 89. In the *Allgemeines Handbuch der Freimaurerei*, I, 49, doubt is cast on the correctness of this and

1782 is given instead. (See Gershom Scholem in *Yearbook VII of the Leo Baeck Institute* [1962], pp. 259–260, who accepts the date given by the *Handbuch*.) For myself, I see no reason to doubt the earlier date. In a manuscript document (HKB, XIV, 7a, 99b), Ecker mentioned 1781 as the year when a conflict broke out in Vienna in connection with the founding of the Order. In 1782–83 he was living in Innsbruck. The Order underwent several transformations, and the various dates might be referring to successive stages in its development.

3. [Hans Heinrich von Ecker und Eckhoffen], *Der Rosenkreuzer in seiner Blösse* (Amsterdam [Nuremberg], 1781).

4. Besides being mentioned in both of Molitor's versions, Justus, known in the Order as *Ish Zaddik* (righteous man), is also referred to in Hirschfeld's account compiled in 1787 during his visit to Frankfurt (HKB, XIV, 19h). Hirschfeld claimed to have known Justus personally and to have received instruction from him over a period of five years. Justus is also referred to in Ecker *Abfertigung*, pp. 85–86, as one no longer living, and this corroborates Molitor's testimony that he had died shortly before Hirschfeld left Vienna. Baron Schoenfeld (see below) mentions the late *Ish Zaddik* as having shared in Hirschfeld's education (HKB, XIV 7c, 163).

5. The main facts on Azariah are given by Molitor—especially in (*b*) —and he received his information directly from Hirschfeld. See Katz, "The First Controversy," 182, note 47.

6. As early as 1778, Ignaz de Luca devoted an article in his work, *Das gelehrte Oesterreich. Ein Versuch* (Vienna, 1776–1778), II, 105–107, to Schoenfeld. Further details on him appear in Constant von Wurzbach, *Biographisches Lexikon des Kaiserthums Oesterreich* (Vienna, 1856–1891), XXXI, 151–152.

7. The *Allgemeines Handbuch der Freimaurerei* I, 50, mentions a Schoenfeld among the active members of the Order, and Scholem has identified him as Baron Thomas von Schoenfeld (see Gershom Scholem, "Ein verschollener juedischer Mystiker der Aufklaerungszeit, E. J. Hirschfeld," *Yearbook VII of the Leo Baeck Institute* [1962], pp. 247–278).

8. Wurzbach, *Biographisches Lexikon*, XXXI, 151–152.

9. So in Molitor (*a*); in Molitor (*b*) no connection with R. Jonathan Eybeschütz is mentioned.

10. See M. Brunner, "Geschichte der Juden in Brünn," Hugo Gold, ed., *Die Juden und Judengemeinden Maehrens in Vergangenheit und Gegenwart* (Brünn, 1929), p. 150. As to R. Jonathan Eybeschütz's relatives by marriage, see Gutman Klemperer, *R. Jonathan Eybeschütz* (Prague, 1858), pp. 143–145; B. Brilling, "Die Nachkommen des R.J.E.," *Hebrew Union College Annual*, XXXV (1964), 255–273. Nowhere is any allusion made to connections with the Dobruschka family.

11. V. Žáček, "Zwei Beitraege zur Geschichte des Frankismus in den boehmischen Laendern," *Jahrbuch der Gesellschaft fuer Geschichte der Juden in der tschechoslowakischen Republik*, IX (1938), 362.

12. *Der Rosenkreuzer*, pp. 102–104.

13. W[öllner] *Signatstern* (Berlin, 1803), vols. I–II, where the writings of the *Ritter* are published.

14. Friedrich Kneisner, *Landgraf Carl zu Hessen und seine Wirksamkeit in der deutschen Freimaurerei* (Berlin, 1917).

15. Testimony to this fact is contained in the letter of one of the Landgrave's aides, dated February 7, 1787. It is quoted by G. van Rijnberk, *Épisodes de la vie ésotérique, 1780–1824* (Lyons, 1946), p. 104.

16. The letters exchanged between the Berlin Lodge and Ferdinand of Brunswick are preserved in the Kloss collection (HKB, XIV, 2).

17. [Friedrich Münter], *Authentische Nachricht von den Ritter—und Brüder—Eingeweihten aus Asien* ([Copenhagen], 1787), p. 1.

18. On the residence of Ecker and his wife in Innsbruck during 1782–83, we have the testimony of one of the inhabitants of that city, as well as of inhabitants of Vienna (HKB, XIV, 7a, 56, 66). In his letter from Vienna, dated February 3, 1784, Ecker himself mentioned that he would soon have his personal effects and writings transferred to that city (HKB, XIV, 5).

19. See HKB, XIV, 7a, 50. In this document written by Ecker in 1790, while the trial instituted against him by Hirschfeld in Schleswig was in progress, Ecker related the history of their acquaintance. Hirschfeld gave his own version of their relations (HKB, XIV, 59). Both accounts are reproduced in the documents pertaining to the trial, and from these sources the incident can be reasonably well reconstructed.

20. The Uffenheimers were a prominent Tyrolian Jewish family. See Aron Taenzer, *Geschichte der Juden in Tirol und Vorarlberg* (Meran, 1905), the relevant sections indicated in the table of contents. Götz Gabriel Uffenheimer moved to Vienna. About him, see Bernhard Wachstein, *Die Inschriften des alten Judenfriedhofes in Wien* (Vienna, 1917), II, 426.

21. I have presented the details that follow in Jacob Katz, "Mendelssohn und E. J. Hirschfeld," *Bulletin des Leo Baeck Instituts,* Year VII (1964), 295–311.

22. This letter of recommendation and also Itzig's testimony on Hirschfeld's sojourn in Berlin were printed in *ibid.*

23. Molitor (a). Hirschfeld claimed in 1789 to have been in Ecker's service for the past seven years (HKB, XIV, 7a, 51).

24. In his letter dated February 3, 1784, Ecker referred to Hirschfeld as his *compagnon de voyage* on his travels to Vienna (HKB, XIV, 7a, 3). While in Frankfurt in 1787, Hirschfeld related that he had received instruction from Justus over a period of five years. This assertion cannot be sustained unless Hirschfeld had met Justus while he was still in Innsbruck.

25. A letter of recommendation written and signed by Count Kinigel on April 25, 1785, was received by Hirschfeld prior to his departure from Innsbruck (HKB, XIV, 7a, 6).

26. In J. B. P. von Hartenfels' letter of March 3, 1788. At that time the tension between Hirschfeld and Ecker had become quite evident, and

237

Hartenfels, who was friendly with both of them, warned that they would ruin each other, "und es waere doch schade um so ein Paar Originale" (HKB, XIV, 7a, 32).

27. Molitor (*b*).

28. The names appear in "Die Asiatischen Brüder in Berlin und Wien," *Latomia, Freimaurerische Vierteljahrsschrift,* XXII (Leipzig, 1863), 29. This article was constructed from the account of a past member of the Order. Its documentary value lies, as the author of the article observed (p. 18), in its being personal reminiscences which faithfully reflect the atmosphere surrounding the activities of the Order.

29. The first six signed, with their titles appended, a letter of testimony on behalf of Ecker, sent from Vienna to Schleswig, during his trial with Hirschfeld (HKB, XIV, 7a, 65). The first signatory, Hartenfels, is known from his letters to Hirschfeld (see above, note 26), and he represents himself as a member of the Order. Undoubtedly, the others were too. The last-named, Fr. von Ost, is mentioned as a Vienna member of the Order in Hirschfeld's long letter to Ecker dated September 4, 1789 (HKB, XIV, 7a, 51).

30. (HKB, XIV, 7a, 59b). This was Nathan Adam Arnstein (1748–1813), brother-in-law of Isaac Daniel Itzig of Berlin, who, in his letter to Carl von Hessen in 1790 (HKB, XIV, 7b, 99b), mentions Arnstein as being in touch with Hirschfeld. Bernhard Eskeles was a brother-in-law of both Arnstein and Itzig. (On these last two, see Salo Baron, *Die Judenfrage auf dem Wiener Kongress* [Vienna and Berlin, 1920], pp. 118–123.) The Hönigs were a prominent Viennese family; see Alfred Francis Pribram, *Urkunden und Akten zur Geschichte der Juden in Wien* (Vienna, 1918), the relevant passages indicated in the table of contents.

31. HKB, XIV, 7a.

32. The accusation (HKB, XIV, 7a, 61b) was corroborated in Itzig's testimony (*ibid.,* 7b, 99b).

33. Molitor (*b*).

34. An instructional manual (ms.) of this type is in the Kloss collection (HKB, XIV, 1022).

35. See the report compiled in Frankfurt in 1787 (HKB, XIV, 19h).

36. E. J. and P. Hirschfeld, *Biblisches Organon* (Offenbach, 1796). The contents of the book have been critically analyzed by Scholem in "Ein verschollener Mystiker," pp. 247–254; see also Katz, "Mendelssohn und E. J. Hirschfeld," p. 303.

37. Pascal Hirschfeld has lived, prior to this, in Maastricht. In a letter addressed to him there on February 3, 1784 (HKB, XIV, 7a, 3), Ecker predicted a great future for Pascal's brother if the latter would join him in Vienna. Molitor (*b*) testifies to Pascal's Jewish scholarship.

38. Several of Pascal's letters to various persons have been preserved and afford an insight into his character (HKB, XIV, 7a, 30b, 44).

39. There is no consistency in the use of bynames. Kneisner (*Landgraf Carl zu Hessen,* p. 59) mentions other bynames by which the Ecker brothers were addressed; according to him, Schoenfeld was called "Scharia."

40. Scholem, "Ein verschollener Mystiker, p. 262.

41. Münter, *Authentische Nachrichten*, pp. 20–22. See Chapter II, note 6.

42. In a document dated about 1789, Ecker himself wrote: "Mr. Arnsteiner, voyant que j'emploiais tous les ressorts—toutes mes facultés possibles pour procurer à sa nation une liaison maçonnique en Allemagne" (HKB, XII, 7a, 59b). So the author (about whom see note 112,.below) of *Der Asiate in seiner Blösse* testified: "Auch bemühten sich die Vaeter (der Asiaten) den Israeliten Eingang in die Johannis Logen zu verschaffen. Doch damit wollte es nicht fort" (p. 22).

43. Münter, *Authentische Nachrichten*, p. 2.

44. Scholem, "Ein verschollener Mystiker," pp. 263–273. His critical analysis is based on the writings of the Order collected together in *Die Brüder St. Johannis des Evangelisten aus Asien in Europa* . . . (Berlin, 1803). According to Molitor (end of *b*), this book was compiled from copies in Itzig's literary remains in Berlin.

45. See *Die Brüder St. Johannis*, pp. 37–38, and also Scholem, "Ein verschollener Mystiker," pp. 265–266.

46. *Die Brüder St. Johannis*, p. 38; "Ein verschollener Mystiker," p. 266.

47. Heinrich Graetz, *Geschichte der Juden* (Leipzig, 1900), 141–156; Salo Baron, *Die Judenfrage auf dem Wiener Kongress*, pp. 117–145; Henry Brunschwig, *La crise de l'État prussien à la fin du XVIIIe siècle et la genèse de la mentalité romantique* (Paris, 1947), pp. 36–46; Jacob Katz, *Die Entstehung der Judenassimilation;* Katz, *Tradition and Crisis*, pp. 245–254; Hilde Spiel, *Fanny von Arnstein oder die Emanzipation, ein Frauenleben an der Zeitwende 1758–1818* (Frankfurt am Main, 1962). This last work is not scientifically critical, but it is based upon the examination of first-hand sources and succeeds in reconstructing the atmosphere of the period. The fusing of Sabbatian and Enlightenment influences in the Order of the Asiatics rouses some interest in how the two could be related. The question was first raised, as is known, by G. Scholem in his article (Hebrew) "Mitzvah Habaah Ba'averah" (The fulfillment of a Divine precept by sinning), *Knesset*, II (1937), but the subject has not been sufficiently examined until now.

48. The structure of the lodge is delineated in the constitution quoted by Münter in *Authentische Nachrichten*, pp. 8, 12–24, and in *Die Brüder St. Johannis*, pp. 1–20. The constitution provides for a Sanhedrin composed of seventy members, but this is a fiction, as the description itself proves. Molitor (*b*) explicitly stated that seven real members represented the seventy imaginary ones.

49. The constitution expressly stated that the permission to establish a new lodge should only be denied in exceptional circumstances (Münter, *Authentische Nachrichten*, pp. 18–19).

50. In Molitor (*b*) the Order is stated to have been widespread in Prague. Several local names are mentioned: for instance, Japhet (HKB, XIV, 7a, 37), and Ismael (HKB, XIV, 7b, 99)—the latter, however, is a

lodge name, and the former might be one too. The importance of the center in Prague is attested to by Hirschfeld's remaining there for several months during his tour in the interests of the Order.

51. Hirschfeld was first employed there in transcribing Masonic material for this group (HKB, XIV, 7a, 59c). Several of the members afterward testified against him (HKB, XIV, 7a, 66–67).

52. Molitor (b) refers to him as *ehemaliger asiatischer Obermeister*. In his letter to Carl von Hessen (HKB, XIV, 7b, 99b) he speaks in the name of the whole Berlin group. According to him, too, the wealthy Berlin Jews were pillars of the organization.

53. Kneisner, *Landgraf Carl zu Hessen*, p. 58; *Latomia: Freimaurerische Vierteljahrsschrift*, XXII (1863), 23–24.

54. HKB, XIV, 19h.

55. "Hans Carl Ecker von Eckhoffen," HKB, XIV, 2, a manuscript written by a contemporary acquainted with the man and his affairs. Many details are confirmed by other sources. The history of the Hamburg group is also related by Manfred Steffens, *Freimaurer in Deutschland, Bilanz eines Vierteljahrtausendes* (Flensburg, 1964), pp. 478–479. This book does not give the sources for any of its details. The author was unaware of, or else deliberately ignored, the connection existing between the Hamburg group and the Order of Asiatics.

56. HKB, XIV, 2.

57. HKB, XIV, 7a, 1.

58. On Wolf, see Salomon Wininger, *Grosse Jüdische Nationalbiographie* (Černauti, 1925–36), VI, 304. The anonymous historian (see above, note 55) of the group, observes: "Wer erstaunt nicht in dem Verzeichnis den Superintendanten von Luebeck, unter einigen gar nicht gebildeten Juden zu finden."

59. Steffens, in *Freimaurer in Deutschland*, reproduces an excerpt from the minutes of the remarks of Jacob Götz, delivered when the Jewish members were forced to resign (see below): "Dass die Israeliten, Mitglieder keiner anderen Loge sein wollen, als einer solchen, welche aus christlichen und juedischen Mitgliedern bestaende.—Dass Jud' mit Jude in Gesellschaft zu sein nicht begehre."

60. *Unpartheiische und gründliche Nachricht von der Freymäurerloge der Juden und anderen geheimen Gesellschaften in Hamburg* (Hamburg, 1786), pp. 3, 4. This pamphlet and the reply to it (see note 63, below) are not listed in Wolfstieg's bibliography. I found both in The Hague library and have photostats in my possession. Actually, unauthorized lodges did admit Jews here and there, as was noted at the end of the previous chapter.

61. *Ibid.*, p. 7. There is a slight disparity between the date, December 7, 1785, given by the anonymous author (note 55 above) and the "beginning of the year," that is, 1786, given by this author for the initiation of the lodge. The number of members participating in the ceremonies was according to the latter, nine Jews and four Christians (p. 5). The list in

my possession gives the names of nine members (among them five Jews) who had been admitted as early as 1785, and four (among them one Jew) who were admitted in 1786–87. The author states that the number of registered members exceeded thirty that year, yet some had already become disappointed and had left (p. 7). The 1787 list is only comprised of those who had remained in the Order, and so the dates of the two sources agree.

62. *Ibid.*, pp. 5, 8.

63. *Ein Wort zum Nachdenken über die sogenannte Unpartheiische und gründliche Nachricht von der Freimaurer-Loge der Juden und anderen geheimen Gesellschaften in Hamburg* (Altona, 1876), pp. 9, 12–13. See above, note 60.

64. The source mentioned in note 55.

65. Molitor (*b*) gives an unrealistic description of the reasons for the departure of the Asiatics from Vienna. According to him, Hirschfeld had access to the Emperor, and political circumstances alone had put an end to that influence. This is a figment of Hirschfeld's imagination (and Molitor got the information from him) and reveals his true nature. Ecker himself (HKB, XIV, 7a, 59b) speaks of a plot against him by Dietrichstein and other Viennese Masonic leaders. Another source (*Latomia* [1862], pp. 20–21) attributes the forcing of the Asiatics to leave Vienna to the same reason. See also the account of Kuess-Scheichelbauer, *200 Jahre Freimaurerei in Oesterreich* (Vienna, 1959), pp. 65–71.

66. There is not enough information available to establish an exact chronology. In his letter of August 8, 1821, Prince Carl gave the date as December 30, but he did not remember whether he had been head of the Order in 1786 or 1787 (HKB, XIV, 2). According to my reckoning, it appears that his acceptance should be dated as early as the end of 1785. Van Rijnberk, in his *Episodes de la vie ésotérique,* p. 104, gives the year as 1786 (without adducing any support for this assertion). It is possible that, when the Hamburg controversy erupted, the Duke was not yet head of the Order, but that his name was already used since the Order had already been in contact with him.

67. Here, too, Molitor's account (*b*) is not precise. According to him, both Hirschfeld brothers had left for Vienna together, yet Pascal's letters from Vienna which have been preserved continue till 1787 (HKB, XIV, 7a, 30–31).

68. The source is given in note 55.

69. The criticism against the Order, about which we shall hear later, was indeed the work of a single author, but the succeeding events indicate that it reflected, to my mind, the view of the Masonic lodges.

70. This is how the author of the last pamphlet, the one closing the controversy (see note 112 below), explained his ability to know what had transpired in the lodge.

71. See Wolfstieg, *Bibliographie,* no. 42967. It was printed in Copenhagen. On Münter, see Ø. Andreasen, *Aus den Tagebuechern Friedrich*

241

Münters (Copenhagen and Leipzig, 1937); and, by the same author, *Aus dem Briefwechsel Friedrich Münters* (Copenhagen and Leipzig, 1944). It is not clear where Wolfstieg obtained the information on Münter's authorship.

72. Münter, *Authentische Nachricht,* pp. ix, xxii–xxiii.

73. *Ibid.,* pp. 1–4.

74. *Hirschfeld im Asiaten-Orden,* no. 157, HKB, XIV, 2.

75. Münter, *Authentische Nachricht,* p. xxiv. It is apparent that Münter was familiar with the affairs of the Asiatics, and his attack came as a reaction to the removal of the center of the Order to the vicinity of Copenhagen.

76. Hans Heinrich Freyherr von Ecker und Eckhoffen, *Abfertigung an den ungenannten Verfasser der verbreiteten sogenannten: Authentischen Nachrichten von den Rittern und Brueder-Eingeweihten aus Asien* (Hamburg, 1788).

77. (Carl Ferdinand von Boscamp gen. Laspolski [Hans Carl von Ecker]), *Werden und koennen Israeliten zu Freymaurern aufgenommen werden* (Hamburg, 1788).

78. *Abfertigung,* pp. 59, 77; see also p. 39.

79. *Ibid.,* pp. 53, 56, 57. The three names are Wolf Hoenig of Vienna, who had been admitted in Paris; Habakuck Barocy of Gibraltar; and Jacob Baruch Sclow of Minsk, who had been admitted in England.

80. Von Ecker, *Werden und koennen,* pp. 17–18.

81. *Ibid.,* pp. 32–35.

82. See *ibid.,* pp. 22–24. Ecker quotes the German version which mentions the concept "sons of Noah"; *ibid.,* pp. 39–40.

83. *Ibid.,* pp. 43–46.

84. *Ibid.,* pp. 46–49.

85. See J. Katz, "The Term 'Jewish Emancipation': its Origin and Historical Impact," in A. Altmann, ed., *Studies in Nineteenth-Century Jewish Intellectual History* (Cambridge, Mass., 1964), pp. 12–14. A similar ambivalence between revulsion and rational contemplation was found in Goethe's famous remarks on the Judengasse in Frankfurt by E. Simon "Frankfurt on the Main" (Hebrew), (*Knesset,* VIII [1943–1944], 134–135).

86. Von Ecker, *Werden und koennen,* pp. 41, 51, 52.

87. *Ibid.,* p. 44.

88. This tour is mentioned on several occasions in documents. Hirschfeld also described his itinerary (HKB, XIV, 7b, 90).

89. In his letter to Hirschfeld, dated August 31, 1789, Heinrich von Ecker referred to the former's intention to marry in Hamburg (HKB, XIV, 7a, 50). In another source, his betrothed's family name is explicitly given as Gerson (H. Ecker to Hirschfeld, October 19, 1791; HKB, XIV, 7c, 147). A letter (no year stated) addressed by Heinrich von Ecker's wife to Hirschfeld, c/o Bravo, in Altona, has been found (HKB, XIV, 7a, 29) Hirschfeld wrote to Ecker from Hamburg in September 1789 (*ibid.,* 51)

90. Pascal Hirschfeld wrote Heinrich von Ecker on October 26, 1787, that his brother was indeed endeavoring to acquire the necessary books, but the person who stored his knowledge in his mind was incomparably superior to the one who had need of papers (HKB, XIV, 7a, 30b).

91. Molitor (*b*). According to this source, a conflict over the acceptance of a Jew provoked the controversy between Ecker and Hirschfeld. Documents reflecting the course of the argument, however, mention no such occurrence. Nevertheless, the assertion should not be dismissed as a fabrication. It can readily be assumed that the rejection of a Jew had occurred earlier, and in Hirschfeld's account, or in Molitor's report of his remarks, the events may have become confused.

92. Steffens, *Freimaurer,* as in notes 55 and 59 above.

93. He later took the same position in his attitude to the Frankfurt Jewish Lodge, with which the next chapter deals.

94. We can deduce his attitude from Hirschfeld's replies to him in this matter.

95. In his letter of September 4, 1789, Hirschfeld reproved Ecker for his behavior (HKB, XIV, 7a, 51).

96. [Johann Christian Ehrmann], *Das Judenthum in der M[aurere]y* (Frankfurt am Main, 1816), pp. 9–10. Ehrmann accused Hirschfeld of having smuggled Judaism disguised as Christianity into his *Biblisches Organon.* In a polemical tract which appeared in Frankfurt in 1825 (*Darstellung der Gruende welche die . . . Grossbeamten veranlasst haben . . . ,* p. 3), Hirschfeld was branded as an apostate Jew.

97. In the document he submitted to the court, Ecker accused Hirschfeld of having posed as a Christian (HKB, XIV, 7a, 75).

98. After his brother's death, Carl von Ecker accused Hirschfeld of not understanding that the two could not have been of equal status in Schleswig (HKB, XIV, 7c, 147). Hirschfeld himself, in his letter of September 4, 1790 (HKB, XIV, 7a, 51), had stated that his education was the equivalent in status of Ecker's lineage.

99. The documents are for the most part contained in HKB, XIV, 7b.

100. The course of events is described in several of the documents referred to in the previous note. The best account is given in the letter of the Landgerichtsadvocat, Jacob Hennich Medelburg, dated August 16, 1790, addressed to Itzig in Berlin, (HKB, XIV, 7b, 99).

101. The circular is listed in Wolfstieg, *Bibliographie,* no. 42996, where the date inscribed is December 28, (1749) 1789. I have not seen the circular, but excerpts quoted in Hirschfeld's reply will be referred to below.

102. HKB, XIV, 7a, 59b.

103. HKB, XIV, 7a, 62, 66, 67. The letters were written in March 1790. Leopold Graf von Kinigel, who had written an official letter of recommendation for Hirschfeld when the latter left Innsbruck (*ibid.,* p. 6), now stated: "Der Jude Hirschel hat sich meines Wissens nur einmal bey mir eingefunden wie ich denn vermoege meiner Charge niemanden den Zutritt in Geschaeften versagen konnte. Sollte sich selber hingegen einer

243

Vertraulichkeit von was immer einer Art zu ruehmen erkuehnen, so muesste ich dieser dreisten Unwahrheit auf das Feierlichste widersprechen mit dem Beisatze, dass er es in Innsbruck schwerlich gewagt haben wuerde wider einen Freyherrn von Eckhoffen aufzutreten."

104. HKB, 7c, 151.

105. "Da aber auch nur in den Grundsaetzen der wahren Cabbalistic die einzige reine wahre und allgemeine Religion liegt, so ist auch nichts Natuerlicher, als dass sich hier (im Orden) all nur moegliche Religionsverwandte vereinigen. Der orthodoxe Jude, Mohametan und der Christ lernten z.B. hier das heilige *drei-eins* und den wahren Glauben der unverfaelschten *Lehre Christi* kennen, von den die beiden ersten nichts wissen duerfen und der dritte glatterdings nichts weiss, oder wenigstens davon so viel weiss wie er im Grunde von den uebrigen heiligen Sacramenten z.B. von der H. Taufe oder vom H. Abendmahle ausser dem O[rden] je wissen kann."

106. This was his final, definite position, as I have shown in Katz, "Mendelssohn und Hirschfeld."

107. Medelburg's letter referred to above in note 100 was written through the agency of Hirschfeld.

108. HKB, XIV, 7b, 99b

109. I published an excerpt from this letter in Katz, "Mendelssohn und Hirschfeld."

110. Itzig ascribed this announcement to the two brothers and was most likely correct in his assumption.

111. In the letter dated August 26, 1790, Ecker is mentioned as having died shortly before (HKB, XIV, 102). Lenning's *Encyclopädie* gives the date as the 14th of the month.

112. Wolfstieg, *Bibliographie,* no. 42969, gives Leipzig as the place of publication, but notes that Kloss in his bibliography, no. 2711, gives Bremen. Since the book was needed in a hurry in Schleswig, it is reasonable to assume that it was printed somewhere nearby.

113. Pp. 20–24.

114. The author refers to Hirschfeld and Ecker by their lodge names— Hirschfeld as Marcus ben Binah, Ecker as Abraham (pp. 76, 77). Other members as well, like Carl von Ecker, were referred to by their lodge names and the author threatened to expose their true identities if they did not mend their ways.

115. HKB, XIV, 7c, 150, 160. According to Molitor (*b*), it was agreed that Hirschfeld withdraw from all Masonic activities.

116. HKB, XIV, 7c, 125, 126, 128. No. 130 is apparently the draft of a reply, but it is only two pages long.

117. He explained his wanting to go to Frankfurt or its vicinity, by the fact that the cost of living was cheaper there (HKB, XIV, 7c, 152), but it is doubtful that this was the true reason.

118. The course of the events is summed up in the letter of Meier (one of the Landgrave's officials) to Hirschfeld dated February 18, 1792 (HKB,

XIV, 7c, 160), where Hirschfeld's forthcoming journey to Schleswig is referred to, also from Hirschfeld's letter dated June 14, 1792 (*ibid.*, 161), to Carl von Hessen and I. ben Jos.'s letter of the same date (*ibid.*, 163).

119. Molitor (*a–b*). According to the second version, Hirschfeld escorted Schoenfeld, before he left for France, to Darmstadt "zu den Prinzen Friedrich und Christian." There Schoenfeld performed an experiment in magic in their presence. Chronologically it is quite possible for this journey to have taken place.

120. L. Kahn, *Les Juifs de Paris pendant la Revolution* (Paris, 1898), pp. 249–250. In the middle of May, Schoenfeld announced that he had "now for four months been living in the land of freedom."

121. See his letter (mentioned in note 118) to Hirschfeld (HKB, XIV, 7c, 162).

122. Kahn, *Les Juifs de Paris*, pp. 250–252. Kahn thought that all had traveled together, but my sources reveal that Schoenfeld traveled alone, his family, apparently, by a different route.

123. In his letter to Carl von Hessen, Hirschfeld had written that I. ben Jos., alias Schoenfeld, had left Strasbourg for Switzerland. It was not convenient, apparently, to reveal that he had gone to Paris.

124. Molitor (*a–b*).

125. Kahn, *Les Juifs de Paris*, pp. 261–266. In *Major Trends in Jewish Mysticism* (New York, 1954), p. 421, G. Scholem notes that a monograph of Schoenfeld would be a desideratum. My account is a contribution toward such a monograph.

126. In 1790 the Toleranzloge was founded in Berlin with the active participation of Itzig, as we shall see in the next chapter. It appears that this lodge, which openly advocated the admission of Jews, came to take the place of the Order of the Asiatics.

127. Carl's continuing connection with the Asiatics may be deduced from the excerpts from his letters of the 1820's collected by Kloss (HKB, XIV, 2—*Hirschfeld in Asiaten Orden*).

128. Kneisner, *Landgraf Carl zu Hessen*, pp. 110–114.

129. Molitor testifies to his connection with the Frankist movement.

130. See Katz "Mendelssohn und Hirschfeld."

Chapter IV. The Frankfurt Judenloge

1. The history of this lodge is given in "Geist der Maurerei nach Aktenstücken nebst einer ausführlichen Geschichte der Toleranzloge in Berlin, gestiftet durch die hochwürdigen Brüder von Hirschfeld und Catter," *Maurerisches Taschenbuch* (Berlin, 1802–3), pp. 204–245.

2. *Ibid.*, especially p. 223. A brief account of the history of the lodge is also contained in the pamphlet *Bekenntnis zur Loge der Toleranz* (Berlin, 1790).

3. "Geist der Maurerei," pp. 240, 241. Such an appraisal is not far from

245

the truth. Reflecting that the enlightened Christianity then prevalent in Berlin might be acceptable to Jews, David Friedlander later made his famous proposal to Provost Teller. Already in 1782, however, a Jewish doctor reported that Berlin Jews would have been prepared to undergo conversion to Christianity, were the Church to forego the requirement of belief in the Trinity. See Jacob Katz: "To Whom was Mendelssohn Replying in his 'Jerusalem'?" (Hebrew), *Zion*, XXIX (1964), 117–118. The Levy referred to here was apparently David Samuel Levy, mentioned by Josef Meisl in his *Protokollbuch der juedischen Gemeinde Berlin* (Jerusalem, 1964), p. 481. The Herz is obviously Marcus Herz; and the Itzig brothers, Daniel Isaac and his three brothers. See Jakob Jacobson, *Die Judenbürgerbücher der Stadt Berlin, 1809–1815* (Berlin: W. de Gruyter, 1962), pp. 51–52.

4. See Chapter III. There is a clearly anti-Asiatic overtone in the remark of the *Geist der Maurerei* that Jews and gentiles should be united in a single lodge of St. John and not in Melchizedek lodges, the Asiatic invention.

5. *Ibid.,* pp. 242, 244.

6. The information on this lodge is provided by *Kurze Geschichte des Buches Sarsena,* published by Z. Funk (Bamberg, 1838). I have not seen the actual book, but I found an excerpt from it in a manuscript in the Kloss collection.

7. Carl von Ecker is mentioned as the person who worked to obtain the London authorization. A Jewish-Christian lodge, founded in Hamburg after the dissolution of the Asiatic Order, is also described in Wilhelm von Schütz, *Freie Bekenntnisse eines Veteranen der Maurerei und anderer geheimen Gesellschaften* (Leipzig, 1824), pp. 39–49.

8. The manuscript is in HKB, XIV, 2. The letters of Geisenheimer's and Dr. Baruch's names as they appear in the title are transposed, but are corrected in the margin.

9. On Geisenheimer see H. Bier, "Sigismund Geisenheimer," *Jahrbuch des Nützlichen und Unterhaltenden für Israeliten,* ed. K. Klein (Frankfurt am Main, 1857), pp. 105–112.

10. I have found no mention of a resolution expressly rescinding the restriction against Jews. That the change did occur is evident from the subsequent course of events; see Georg Kloss, *Geschichte der Freimaurerei in Frankreich (1725–1830),* (Darmstadt, 1852).

11. Heinrich Gürtler, *Deutsche Freimaurerei im Dienste Napoleonischer Politik, Die Freimaurerei im Königreich Westfalen* (Berlin, 1942). The book is written from the Nazi point of view, but its facts, derived from lodge archives, are reliable.

12. On the occasion of its centenary, the history of the lodge was committed to writing by Adolf Brüll, *Geschichte der Loge zur aufgehenden Morgenröthe in Frankfurt am Main* (Frankfurt am Main, 1907). This book was mimeographed by the lodge in 1960 and two copies were given

to me, one for myself and one for the Hebrew University and National Library in Jerusalem, by the Master of the Lodge, Dr. Robert Beisinger. I take pleasure in thanking him for his kindness. The references to the quotations follow the mimeographed edition. A list of the founders appears on pp. 1–3; a membership list appears in *Tableau des FF.'.composant la R .'. L .'. de St. Jean sous le titre distinctif de l'Aurore naissante, régulièrement constitué par le G.'.O.'.de France à la date du . . . 5807 a l'O.'.de Francfort sur Mein, Frankfurt a/M.* The Frankfurt City Library was gracious enough to send me the book on international loan.

13. Bier, "Sigismund Geisenheimer," p. 109.

14. *Festgaben dargebracht von Brüdern der Loge zur aufgehenden Morgenröthe im Orient zu Frankfurt a/M Zur Feier ihres 25 jährigen Jubiläums* (Frankfurt am Main, 1833), p. 36.

15. Karl Paul, *Annalen des Eklektischen Freimaurerbundes zu Frankfurt a/M. 1766–1883* (Frankfort, 1883), referred to hereafter as *Annalen*, p. 58.

16. Brüll, *Geschichte*, p. 5.

17. *Planche de travaux de l'institution de la R .'. L.'. de St. Jean sous le titre distinctif de l'aurore naissante a l'O.'. de Frankfort sur le Mein* (Mayence, 1808), pp. 4–5. The Frankfurt lodge was la Loge de l'Union which is otherwise not known to me, and which was, presumably, founded by French soldiers stationed there.

18. *Ibid.*, pp. 84, 85. One of the speakers was Ernst; his language, French, the other, Roussvele de Chamseru; the lodge, Francs chevaliers.

19. Concerning Molitor, see Carl Frankenstein, *Molitors metaphysische Geschichtsphilosophie* (Berlin, 1928), pp. 106–117. Molitor was born in 1779 and came to Frankfurt before 1804 (*ibid.*, p. 109). Prior to his joining the Masons, he held a position in the Philanthropin. See Hermann Baerwald, *Einladungsschrift zu der . . . öffentlichen Prüfung der Real- und Volksschule der israel. Gemeinde* (Frankfurt am Main, 1869), p. 12.

20. *Planche de travaux*, pp. 60, 62, 65–66. Molitor delivered his address in German. The importance ascribed to it is evident from the fact that it was translated into French (*ibid.*, pp. 67–80).

21. Brüll, *Geschichte*, p. 17; *Annalen*, p. 58.

22. The L'aurore Naissante file, nos. 29–30, 34–39. Bibliothèque Nationale, Paris.

23. *Circulaire du Grand Orient de France du 19.6. 5811 (1811)*.

24. Information on these discussions is culled from the pamphlet by A. Bailleul, *Lettre adressée au . . . Delahay Officier du G . . . O . . . de France* (n.p., n.d.), 14 pp.

25. See Isidor Kracauer, *Geschichte der Juden in Frankfurt a/M* (Frankfurt am Main, 1927), II, 355–421, especially p. 358.

26. Brüll, *Geschichte*, p. 5.

27. Bier, "Sigismund Geisenheimer," p. 110.

28. It is difficult to believe that the rabbi would have had the audacity to invoke a ban, since this practice had already been prohibited by the authorities of most countries.

29. The *Tableau* referred to in note 12 above.

30. Unless I am mistaken in identifying them, over twenty-five of the Jewish members were born outside of Frankfurt.

31. See the relevant entries in Alexander Dietz, *Stammbuch der Frankfurter Juden* (Frankfurt am Main, 1907).

32. Rothschild had been initiated on June 14, 1809 (Brüll, *Geschichte*, p. 24), and resigned on May 4, 1812 (*ibid.*, p. 35).

33. See Chapter II, note 30.

34. On Michael Hess, see *Festschrift zur Jubileumsfeier der Realschule der israelitischen Gemeinde (Philanthropin) zu Frankfurt a/Main 1804–1904* (Frankfurt am Main, 1904), pp. 91–94.

35. See note 25 above.

36. *Planche de travaux*, p. 36.

37. Brüll, *Geschichte*, pp. 19–21, 24–26, 28–34. Börne's address to the lodge in 1811 is included in all editions of his collected works. See L. Börne, *Gesammelte Schriften* (Nuremberg, 1880), II, 172–179.

38. Brüll, *Geschichte*, p. 26. The author of the proposal and the reasons for its defeat are unknown to me.

39. There is some doubt about a few of them; the number cannot, therefore, be given exactly.

40. *Tableau*, pp. 22–23, 35–44.

41. K. Beaulieu-Marconnay, *Karl von Dalberg und seine Zeit*, 2 vols. (Weimar, 1879).

42. This paragraph was quoted repeatedly in subsequent debates on the acceptance of Jews. See Philipp Jacob Cretzschmar, *Religionssysteme und Freimaurerei untersucht in ihren gegenseitigen Beziehungen . . .* (Frankfurt am Main, 1838), p. 56.

43. L. D. P. Rumpy's letter dated April 28, which is included among the documents in the Kloss collection (HKB-A4, 1), "Grossherzogliches Frankfurtisches Verbot der Maurerei, 21. April 1812." Dalberg was exposed to conflicting influences, and for some time the activities of the lodges were suspended (Brüll, *Geschichte*, p. 34). The documents indicate that this action was the result of pressures exerted by the conservative citizens, long-standing members of the lodges.

44. Brüll, *Geschichte*, pp. 37–38.

45. In addition to the addresses delivered at the dedication of the lodge and referred to above collections of speeches delivered and poems recited during the first year of the lodge have been preserved. *Reden gehalten in der gerechten und vollkommenen Loge zur aufgehenden Morgenröthe im Orient von Frankfurt a/Main im Laufe des ersten Jahres ihrer Entstehung* (Frankfurt am Main, 1809). See especially pp. 40, 73–74, 81–86. *Auserlesene Gesänge für die g. u. v. Loge L'Aurore naissante im Orient von Frankfurt a/Main* (Frankfurt am Main, 1808).

46. *Auserlesene Gesänge für die g. u. v. Loge zur aufgehenden Morgen-röthe im Morgen von Frankfurt a/Main* (Frankfurt am Main, 1815). The term *teutsch* occurs repeatedly in the compositions.

47. In *Geschichte* (pp. 38–39), Brüll reported that the lodge had secured a new affiliation, but failed to disclose Hirschfeld's part in the whole affair. My information is drawn from a source hostile to the lodge — [Johann Christian Ehrmann], *Das Judenthum in der M[aurer]y, eine Warnung an alle deutschen Logen* (Frankfurt am Main, 1816), pp. 9–10, about which we shall hear later. Further evidence comes from other sources and there is no reason to doubt Ehrmann on this point.

48. Brüll, in *Geschichte* (p. 52), attempted to prove that Carl was aware of the composition of the lodge membership. Yet the evidence he adduces only applies to the later stages of the negotiations. The enemies of the Frankfurt lodge placed their reliance on a certain letter sent by Carl to his brother, in which he stated that he did not know what was involved. *Darstellung der Gründe welche die unterzeichneten vormaligen Gross-Beamten der hochwürdigen grossen Mutterloge der eklektischen Brüder in Frankfurt a/Main veranlasst haben aus derselben zu treten* (Frankfurt am Main, 1835), p. 3. According to Kneisner, *Landgraf Carl zu Hessen*, p. 115, however, the Landgrave himself claimed, in his letter of July 20, 1817, that he was unaware that Jews belonged to the lodge.

49. I found no reference, during the first period of the lodge's existence, to the text of the oath. Presumably the French custom had been followed and so no problem arose until the second period.

50. Brüll's account (*Geschichte*, p. 44) does not specify the offices. These were given, however, in *Annalen*, p. 58.

51. Brüll, *Geschichte*, p. 43.

52. M. Steffens, *Freimaurer in Deutschland*, p. 479.

53. Brüll, *Geschichte*, pp. 44–46.

54. On Molitor's philosophical conceptions, see Frankenstein, *Molitors metaphysische Geschichtsphilosophie*.

55. Kneisner, *Landgraf Carl zu Hessen*, p. 117, quotes a letter from Molitor.

56. The letter is in the Kloss collection (HKB, XIV, 7c).

57. Molitor (*b*).

58. Ehrmann, *Das Judenthum in der M[aurer]y*, p. 11. The name "Asiatic" was not known to him, and so he referred to the Order as Templars. The information is corroborated in Molitor's account to some anonymous person which was transcribed by Kloss and filed in the section, *Hirschfeld im Asiaten-Orden*.

59. "Er hatte nur zuweilen bedeutende Träume, sprach von einem Lichtschein, den er sonst Nachts beym Erwachen um sein Haupt bemerkt habe, der aber seitdem aufgehört, wo er in der Jüdischen Loge zu Frankfurt öfters Verdriesslichkeiten hatte" (Molitor [*b*], Nachträge).

60. Hirschfeld had written the book published as E. J. u. P. Hirschfeld, *Biblisches Organon* (Offenbach, 1796). Its contents have been critically an-

alyzed by Gershom Scholem in the article referred to in Chapter III, note 2, and in my article referred to in Chapter III, note 21.

61. Ehrmann, *Das Judenthum in der M [aurer]y*, pp. 7–11.

62. The anti-Jewish publications of Friedrich Rühs and Jacob Friedrich Fries belong to that year.

63. So, explicitly, in pp. 7–8, and this is the general spirit of the entire pamphlet.

64. *Auszug Conferenz-Protocolles der Loge zur aufgehenden Morgenröthe in Frankfurt a/Main von 13 August 1816* (Frankfurt am Main, 1816).

65. Brüll, *Geschichte,* p. 45.

66. Actually, Jacob Baruch was elected to the office but, in his absence, it was transferred to Goldschmidt, who was duly installed as Grand Master. Brüll, *Geschichte,* pp. 47–48.

67. Brüll's account (*Geschichte,* pp. 49–50) fails to point out the causal connection between the two events. It is, however, brought out in *Annalen,* p. 58, and by E. Wenz, *Geschichte der Loge Carl zum aufgehenden Licht im Orient* (Frankfurt am Main, 1891), p. 3.

68. Brüll, *Geschichte,* pp. 50–52. Here, too, Brüll's account suffers from vagueness. The events, however, speak for themselves.

69. Brüll, *Geschichte,* pp. 53–54; *Annalen,* pp. 59–61.

70. It is undated. *Annalen,* however, gives the date when it was sent out as November 14, 1823.

71. So Brüll, *Geschichte,* p. 58.

72. Wenz, *Geschichte der Loge Carl,* p. 4; Brüll, *Geschichte,* p. 57.

73. Membership lists were published from time to time and are deposited in the Hague library.

74. *Auszug aus dem Protokolle der . . . Loge zur aufgehenden Morgenröthe (N 684) . . . Sitzung von 24 Juni 1820* (Frankfurt am Main, 1820), Anlage A, pp. 7–9.

75. Brüll, *Geschichte,* pp. 58–60.

76. *Statuten des von der . . . Loge zur aufgehenden Morgenröthe in Frankfurt a/M. errichteten Sustentations-Fonds 1819,* especially pars. 3, 4, 22. Such mutual aid societies were founded as adjuncts to many lodges during those times.

77. George Heer, *Die ältesten Urkunden zur Geschichte der allgemeinen deutschen Burschenschaft* (Heidelberg, 1932), pp. 68–70; see also Shlomo Avineri, "Hegel's Views on Jewish Emancipation," *Jewish Social Studies,* XXV (1963), 145–151.

78. On Frankfurt we have the evidence of Ludwig Börne. He applied for admission to the *Lesegesellschaft* on November 12, 1818, but was refused. Karl Gutzkow, "Börne's Leben," *Gesammelte Werke* (Frankfurt am Main, 1845), VI 99–100. In *Der Ewige Jude,* which he published in 1821, Börne listed names of the Frankfurt societies barred to Jews: Frankfurter-Gelehrten Verein, Frankfurter Museum für Kunst und Wissenschaft, Frankfurter Lesegesellschaft, Frankfurter Gesellschaft für nützliche

Künste, Frankfurter Kasino. Börne, *Gesammelte Schriften* (Nuremberg, 1880), VI, 31–32.

79. The details of the debates will be given in succeeding chapters.

80. In the 1820 minutes (note 74 above), such a public statement coming from one of the Potsdam lodges is noted with approval. *Anlage A,* p. 7.

81. Brüll, *Geschichte,* pp. 60, 64–65. I have not seen the circular, only the excerpts quoted in the supplements to C. Lenning's *Encyclopädie der Freimaurerei* (Leipzig, 1822–1828), III, 745–748.

Chapter V. During Revolution and Reaction

1. [Johan J. Ch. Bode], *Nachtrag zu dem Circular-Brief an die s. e. Freimaurerlogen* ([Weimar], 1790), p. 98.

2. See Reinhold Taute, *Die Juden in den Freimaurerlogen* (Leipzig, 1913), p. 4. The author wanted to base his views on the acceptability of Jews in the movement at that time on historical fact. To this end, he collected information on the attitudes of the various lodges especially during the period 1806–1815. Not in every instance was I able to discover the source he drew on. Taute, however, has a reputation for reliability and exactitude in this work, as in his other dealings with the history of the Masons. The incident here referred to is also recounted by Heinz Gürtler in his *Deutsche Freimaurer im Dienst Napoleonischer Politik* (Berlin, 1942), pp. 51–52.

3. *Juden in Freimaurerlogen,* p. 5.

4. The Mainz Les amis reunis played an active part in the founding of the L'aurore Naissant in Frankfurt (see Chapter IV); some of its members were Jews.

5. *Juden in Freimaurerlogen,* p. 5; *Deutsche Freimaurer im Dienst Napoleonischer Politik,* p. 53.

6. Gürtler, *Deutsche Freimaurer im Dienst Napoleonischer Politik,* p. 5; p..52 (Berlin); p. 54 (Göttingen, Eschwege); Taute, *Die Juden in den Freimaurerlogen,* pp. 4–6 (Berlin).

7. Edmund Meissner and Adolf Wenk, *Geschichte der g. u. v. St. Johannis-Loge Apollo im Orient zu Leipzig* (Leipzig, 1905), p. 31; *Die Freimaurerloge Balduin zur Linde in Leipzig* (Leipzig, 1926), p. 41.

8. Gürtler, *Deutsche Freimaurer im Dienste Napoleonischer Politik,* p. 5 (Hildesheim, Ulm); Taute, *Die Juden in den Freimaurerlogen,* pp. 51–52 (Hildesheim, Heiligenstadt), 55 (Einbeck), 56 (Nordhausen).

9. See note 5 above.

10. See above, note 4.

11. Karl Wiebe, *Die Grosse Loge von Hamburg und ihre Vorläufer* (Hamburg, 1905), pp. 234–235.

12. [Franz August von Etzel], *Geschichte der grossen National-Mutterloge in den preussischen Staaten* (Berlin, 1903), pp. 118–122.

13. Gürtler, *Deutsche Freimaurer im Dienste Napoleonischer Politik*, p. 52; Taute, *Die Juden in den Freimaurerlogen*, p. 4; Etzel, *Geschichte der grossen National-Mutterloge*, p. 190.

14. Ismar Freund, *Die Emanzipation der Juden in Preussen* (Berlin, 1912), I, 118–119.

15. The anonymous author of *Die maurerische Emanzipation der Juden in Hamburg* remarks (p. 120): "Eine interessante Reihe der geistreichen Abhandlungen u. Gutachten über diesen Gegenstand seit 1805 wird im Archive unserer Engbünde aufbewahrt. Es war nämlich die Judenfrage schon lange vorher in diesen Kreisen besprochen, ehe noch ein Wort darüber in die eigentliche Logenliteratur drang."

16. The archives of the Westphalian lodges were accessible to Gürtler (*Deutsche Freimaurer im Dienste Napoleonischer Politik* pp. 50–58), and he quotes the remarks of Jewish and gentile Freemasons reflecting these views.

17. See note 1 above.

18. Bode, *Nachtrag zu dem Circular-Brief*, pp. 98–100.

19. Both quotations are taken from Taute, *Die Juden in den Freimaurerlogen*, p. 26.

20. Gürtler, *Deutsche Freimaurer im Dienste Napoleonischer Politik*, pp. 55, 56.

21. The history of that period is now portrayed in Eleonore Sterling, *Er ist wie du, Aus der Frühgeschichte des Antisemitismus in Deutschland 1815–1850* (Munich, 1956).

22. Taute, *Die Juden in den Freimaurerlogen*, p. 6.

23. Freund, *Die Emanzipation der Juden in Preussen*, I, 230–233.

24. "Die maurerische Emanzipation der Juden in Hamburg," pp. 130–131.

25. Taute, *Die Juden in den Freimaurerlogen*, p. 7.

26. *Ueber die Stellung der Freimaurer jüdischen Glaubens in Preussen und über das, was in dieser Angelegenheit geschehen ist* (Berlin, 1843), p. 5.

27. See note 22.

28. *Die Drei St. Johannisgrade der grossen National-Mutterloge zu den drei Weltkugeln* (Berlin, 1843), pp. 5, 125, 128, 129.

29. Georg von Wedekind, *Das Johannisfest in der Freimaurerei* (Frankfurt am Main, 1818), p. 82.

30. "Briefe über Freimaurerei," *Zeitschrift für Freimaurerei* (Altenburg, 1826), part 1, pp. 18, 20–21.

31. Wedekind, *Das Johannisfest in der Freimaurerei*, p. 88. Similarly, another source has: "so kann man bestimmt annehmen, dass diejenigen, die sich als Freimaurer aufnehmen lassen, einen gewissen Grad von Bildung besitzen, denn dem gewöhnlichen Handelsjuden, der fest an seinem von Rabbinen gelehrten Ceremonialgesetz hängt, wird nie einfallen, sich mit Christen so genau zu verbinden oder wohl gar an Tafellogen und christlichen Speisen und Getränken Theil zu nehmen" (Schütz, *Bekenntnisse*, p. 53).

32. *Zeitschrift für Freimaurerei*, pp. 12–17, 22, 24, 28–31.
33. Lenning, *Encyclopädie der Freimaurerei*, II, 156–163.
34. His *magnum opus* is Krause, *Die drei ältesten Kunsturkunden der Freimaurer brüderschaft*. In addition to studies (not reliable) in the history of the Freemason movement, the work also contains a comprehensive and profound analysis of the nature of the movement. Lenning quotes Krause on the definition of the nature of Freemasonry and the conclusions this formulation entails for Jews.
35. Lenning, *Encyclopädie der Freimaurerei*, pp. 157–159.

Chapter VI. Achievements in the Age of Liberalism

1. The membership list of the Frankfurter Adler was printed, and a copy is in the library at The Hague.
2. Adolf Brüll, *Geschichte der Loge zur aufgehenden Morgenröthe in Frankfurt am Main* (Frankfurt am Main, 1907) p. 72.
3. Eduard Reiss, "Ueber Zulassung der Juden in die Freimaurerlogen," *AZJ* (1838), p. 454.
4. This state of affairs is reflected in an interesting document included in *Protocolle der grossen Mutterloge des eclectischen Freimaurerbundes* . . . (28 January 1839). Von Rochow, the Prussian Minister of the Interior and of Police, addressed a warning to the Berlin Mother lodges against German Masons' extending aid to Polish refugees who had caused disturbances in various German states. The Minister also asked for information on the *Carbonari Vereinen*, mentioning that in 1832 attempts had been made by French Masons to establish contact with German lodges. Had any such attempts been repeated? This document was distributed among the other German lodges, and the *Protocolle* asserts that no information on any French approaches had reached them. The heads of the Eclectic Covenant argued, in 1834, that the very definition of Freemasonry as "eines Weltbürger-Vereins, eines grossen Menschheit-Bundes" was enough to arouse the attention of all German governments (*Darstellung der Gründe welche die unterzeichneten vormaligen Gross-Beamten der hochwürdigen grossen Mutterloge der eklektischen Brüder in Frankfurt a/Main veranlasst haben aus derselben zu treten* [Frankfurt am Main, 1835], p. 21). He also testified that one of the royal governments had regarded mystic Masonry as a smokescreen for "ultraliberalism" (*ibid.*, p. 22). In a statement of opinion of 1837—which was basically positive—on the Jewish Question (see below, note 13), the possible reaction of the South German governments is taken into account.
5. Brüll, *Geschichte*, pp. 3–78.
6. *Annalen der Loge zur Einigkeit . . . Frankfurt a/Main 1742–1811* (Frankfurt, 1842), pp. 71–72.
7. *Darstellung der Gründe . . .* , p. 6.
8. *Ibid.*, p. 21.
9. Heinrich Eberhard Gottlob Paulus, *Die Jüdische Nationalab-*

253

sonderung nach Ursprung, Folgen und Besserungsmitteln (Heidelberg, 1831).

10. This opinion was also expressed in a circular (mentioned in Chapter IV) in which the Eclectic Covenant stated its position on the division of the original lodge into two separate sections. The *Darstellung* is devoted, for the most part, to this controversy.

11. Kloss described the course of developments in his polemical brochure: G. Kloss, *Actenmässige Beleuchtung der Persönlichkeiten und Behauptungen* . . . (Frankfurt am Main, 1844), p. 2. His view is summed up in a long letter to Molitor (*ibid.*, pp. 42–49). Kloss was an important research historian of the Masonic movement, as well as the gatherer of a vast collection of their writings (see above, Chapter I).

12. Cretzschmar, *Religionssysteme und Freimaurerei*, pp. 55–67.

13. *Gutachten der Grossbeamten an die hochwürdigste Mutter-Loge des eclectischen Bundes in Betreff des Gesuches der* . . . *Loge zur aufgehenden Morgenröthe* (ms., 23 October 1837).

14. The entire transactions were summarized in the *Annalen zur Loge der Einigkeit*. The details appear in *Auszug der Protokole der Grossen Mutterloge des eclectischen Freimaurerbundes* . . . (7 June 1839).

15. The *Carl zum aufgehenden Licht* set down its views in a defensive tract, *Actenmässige Entgegnung der Loge Carl* . . . (Frankfurt, 1844). It openly and proudly acknowledged that Freemasonry and positive Christianity were identical. See especially pp. 6–7, 35, 40–42, 44, 47. The Christian principle in Freemasonry is also defended in Johann Jakob Scherbius, *Das Christenthum als Grundlage der eklektischen Freimaurerei* (Frankfurt am Main, 1844).

16. In a personal letter to Kloss (Kloss, *Actenmässige Beleuchtung*, pp. 7–8).

17. *Protokoll der grossen Mutter-Loge des eklektischen Freimaurerbundes* (December 1843), p. 10. Only the initials of the names of the Jewish candidates are given: Rechtspraktikant M—— Dr. Med. H——.

18. In brief in *Annalen*, pp. 99–102. At length in Kloss, *Actenmässige Beleuchtung*, pp. 32–37.

19. *Manifest der Gründe welche die grosse Mutter-Loge des eklektischen Freimaurer-Bundes zu Frankfurt a/M bewogen haben, ihre seitherige Tocher und Bundes-Loge Carl zum aufgehenden Lichte am 21 Juli 1844 aus dem eklektischen Bunde zu entlassen* . . . (Frankfurt am Main, 1844).

20. "Der Streit, welcher sich in unserer nächsten Umgebung über Fragen dieser Art erhoben hat, und bei welchem uns die Rolle des ruhigen Beobachters zugedacht ist, so nahe uns auch dieselben berühren, kann uns daher nur eine willkommene Erscheinung seyn. Denn er muss allen Halbheiten ein Ende machen und den unumstösslichen Ausspruch herbeiführen, dass die Maurerei weder eine positive noch eine negative Glaubensverbrüderung ist . . . sondern die erhabene, nur in manchen deutschen Logen verkannte Bestimmung hat, den verschiedenen Reli-

gionsbekennern einen neutralen Boden und ihren Eingeweihten einen rein menschlichen Vereinigungspunkt zu bieten" (Morgenröthe circular, October 1844).

21. Jakob Weil, "Ueber Maurerische Zeitfragen," *Jahresbericht am Ordensfeste des Maurerjahres 5844 (1844) in der . . . Loge zur aufgehenden Morgenröthe im Orient von Frankfurt am Main*, p. 9.

22. *Freimaurer Zeitung* (Leipzig, 1847), no. 7, pp. 54–56; no. 15, pp. 115–117.

23. The circular of the Frankfurter Adler stated: "Die deutschen Freimaurer werden es doch endlich müde werden, sich von dem profanen Leben, in welchem eine Schranke nach der andern fällt, überflügeln, sich von Sängervereinen und Turnvereinen beschämen zu lassen" (*ibid.*, p. 54). These were not idle words. Two of the societies denounced by Börne for having barred Jews (above, Chapter IV, note 78), removed their barriers in the thirties. J. H. Bender, *Der frühere und jetzige Zustand der Israeliten zu Frankfurt a.M.* (Frankfurt am Main, 1833), p. 40.

24. *Annalen*, p. 118.

25. Brüll, *Geschichte*, pp. 95, 96.

26. *Ibid.*, pp. 99, 116–118. For the circumstances in which this decision was made see Chapter IX.

27. J. Marcus Jost, *Neuere Geschichte der Israeliten, Dritte Abtheilung, Culturgeschichte* (Breslau, 1846), pp. 206–210.

28. H. Bier, "Siegmund Geisenheimer," *Jahrbuch des Nützlichen und Unterhaltenden fuer Israeliten*, K. Klein, ed. (Frankfurt am Main, 1857), p. 109.

29. Kracauer, *Geschichte der Juden in Frankfurt a/M*, II, 383–384, 422.

30. In 1840 a committee of nine was coopted to the Board of the community. Seven of the nine were Morgenröthe members.

31. Bier, "Siegmund Geisenheimer," p. 109.

32. *Gutachten der Grossbeamten* (see above, note 13). The excerpt is also quoted in *Annalen der Loge zur Einigkeit*, p. 82.

33. *Festschrift zur Jahrhundertfeier der Realschule der Israelitischen Gemeinde (Philanthropin) zu Frankfurt a/M 1804–1904* (Frankfurt am Main, 1904), pp. 50–54.

34. Bonaventura Mayer, *Die Juden unserer Zeit, eine gedrängte Darstellung ihrer religiösen und politischen Verhältnisse in den drei alten Erdtheilen* (Regensburg, 1842). The appraisals mentioned below appear on pp. 48, 67, 79. In describing the decline of the Frankfurt lodge, Mayer observes: "Es ist Thatsache, dass einige Hundert von ihnen sich sogar eine eigene Freimaurer-Loge gegründet haben." Jost also, as his remarks show, regarded this development as extraordinary as compared with other communities. Graetz quoted Jost (*Geschichte der Juden*, 11, 509), but although he, too, regarded the lodge as the concentration-point for deviants, he was not aware of what was unusual in this development. On the numerical strength of the reformers as compared with the

conservatives, see J. Toury, " 'Deutsche Juden' im Vormärz," *Bulletin des Leo Baeck Instituts* (1965), pp. 65–82. Toury (p. 79) only quotes the figures for the Orthodox and compares them with the total number of Jews given by other sources. Only Mayer's evaluation of the relative strengths of the two has any meaning.

35. Samson Raphael Hirsch, *"Die Religion im Bunde mit dem Fortschritt"* (1854). *Gesammelte Schriften* (Frankfurt am Main, 1912), III, 512–516. E. Schwarzschild, *Die Gründung der israelitischen Religionsgesellschaft zu Frankfurt a/M und ihre Weiterentwicklung bis zum Jahre 1876* (Frankfurt am Main, 1896).

36. Likewise Ferdinand Hiller the composer, and Jacob Dernburg of Mainz, both converts.

37. The historians of the Frankfurt community paid no attention to the development of the lodge and hardly mentioned it. See the references to Jost and Graetz in note 55 above; see also Kracauer, *Geschichte der Juden*, II, 447.

Chapter VII. The Struggle for Masonic Emancipation in Prussia

1. See Katz, "The Term 'Jewish Emancipation' and its Historical Impact," pp. 21–25.

2. The material in the activities of the Wesel brethren is preserved in the archives of the Grand Lodge of Holland in The Hague. I have published several of the pertinent documents as an Appendix to my article: Jacob Katz, "The Fight for Admission to Masonic Lodges," *Year Book XI of the Leo Baeck Institute* (London, 1966), pp. 129–171.

3. Twelve members signed the two documents mentioned below in note 8. The lodges to which they belonged are enumerated there.

4. In his letter of June 10, 1836, Friedler, apparently the Master of the Wesel lodge, wrote to Jacob Meyer, one of the twelve Jewish Masons: "Es soll uns herzlich freuen, wenn ihre Bemühungen Erfolg haben und es uns gestattet seyn würde Sie an unserem Tempel als Bruder empfangen zu können." Friedler seems to have known of the Jewish brothers' intention to bring their case to public notice.

5. Pp. 4–5 of the circular dated *Johannis 1835,* that is, June 24. It was customary for lodges to send out circulars dealing with topics of the day. This circular was devoted in part to the Jewish problem.

6. "Freilich duerfen wir der Ansicht derjenigen Brueder, welche die Maurerei als identisch mit dem Christenthume bezeichnen, uns nur insofern anschliessen, als beide gleich wohlthuend bei der Pflege der hoechsten und herrlichsten Tugenden zusammentreffen, ein Hauptgrundsatz des Maurerbundes uns aber die Pflicht auferlegt, den verdienstvollen edlen Menschen, ohne Ansehen seines Ranges und Glaubens, als Bruder zu umfangen, und, der Aufgabe des Jahrhunderts gemaess, uns mit den Fortschritten der Zeit zu verstaendigen."

7. The Wesel brethren thanked the members of Leipzig Apollo Lodge in their letter of December 18, 1835, the reply to which, dated January 16, 1836, is extant. In their petition (see the following note) the Wesel brethren referred explicitly to the Leipzig circular as well as to the stated opinions of other German Masons who were displeased by the anti-Jewish discrimination.

8. The petition was dated September 1836, the accompanying German letter, October 1836, and its Dutch version, November 1836. The two German texts were reprinted in the *Neueste Zeitschrift für Freimaurerei 1838*, pp. 168–190. I quote from the original printed versions. I published the letter of request, with some omissions, as Appendix I to Katz, "Fight for Admission."

9. "Wenn Ihnen der Geist aller Religionen die reine Himmelstochter Religion nicht genuegt, wenn Sie verlangen dass sie das Kleid des Christentums trage, um in die Hallen der Wahrheit eingelassen zu werden: dann muessen Sie . . . den Naturphilosophen, den Theisten von den Pforten des Tempels zurueckweisen . . . Sie weisen den braven Mann christlicher Confession nicht ab, wenn er auch nicht glaubt, was er nicht fassen kann. Ist aber der Theist darum ein Christ zu nennen, weil der Akt der Taufe an ihm vollzogen ist?" (*ibid.*, p. 197).

10. The accompanying German letter, p. 2.

11. The letter of request, Katz, "Fight for Admission," p. 196.

12. Letter dated March 5, 1837.

13. Letter of February 3, 1837, signed by the Masters of the Ferdinande Caroline, and also of the Loge St. George, Loge Absalom, Loge Ferdinand zum Felsen, and Loge Emanuel.

14. The letter addressed by the Cologne lodge to the Royal York of Berlin is dated October 22, 1836. The name of the lodge does not appear in the copy, but it is known that Agrippina was the Cologne lodge affiliated with the Royal York. See Wolfstieg, 10980.

15. The letter from Cologne to the Wesel brethren has not been found. Yet the Wesel brothers were undoubtedly aware of their action.

16. The Landesloge letter, dated May 26, 1837, is a reply to the letter from M. Latz and Js. Mayer of March 1 of that year. Appendix II in Katz, "Fight for Admission," p. 200.

17. The Landesloge replied to the Wesel brethren on March 4, 1837, apparently after a second request had been addressed to it, that there was no reason to add anything to the answer given the two brethren Latz and Mayer.

18. So it appears from the reply.

19. All these points appear in the reply. See appendix III, Katz, "Fight for Admission," p. 200. This also constitutes the main content of the open letter published by a member of the Ehrfurt affiliate of the Mutterloge in the *Neueste Zeitschrift für Freimaurerei* (1838), pp. 165–199. See *ibid.*, pp. 316–321, for the abridged version of the replies of the Grand Lodges.

20. The reference is probably to the mutual assistance Masons were obliged by their oath to extend in times of need.

21. The circular dated March 1, 1838. A ms. copy has been preserved. Appendix IV in *Year Book XI, Leo Baeck Institute*, p. 202.

22. The name of the German lodge was Loge Blücher von Wahlstatt, that of the Dutch Lo Loge, Les eufaus de la concorde fortifiée. The facts emerge from the circular, mentioned below, which was published in *Neueste Zeitschrift für Freimaurerei* (1838), pp. 405–432.

23. What took place in the Royal York is recounted in brief in the published minutes of 1845: "Auszug aus den Verhandlungen der Grossen Loge von Preussen, genannt Royal York zur Freundschaft betreffend die Revision der Statuten 1845; verhandelt Berlin am 5ten Februar 1845" (5 unnumbered pages).

24. The minutes are not altogether clear, but the essence of what occurred is given in my account.

25. The Mutterloge letter, dated April 8, 1837, to the Wesel lodge stated, among other things: "Die Verneinung des Zutrittes in unseren . . . Werkstaetten gegen einen fuer Juden erkannten Freymaurer beruht . . . auf einem statuierten Gesetz, und dieses auf ausdruecklichem Uebereinkommen der drey grossen Mutterlogen unseres Vaterlandes. Um davon abgehen zu koennen, waere ein neuer einstimmiger Beschluss darueber von denselben zu nehmen. Es ist aber dazu, fuer gegenwaertig wenigstens, kein Anschein vorhanden."

26. There is a book on the Masonic activities of the Protector (Josef August Fitzner, *Kaiser Wilhelm I. als Freimaurer in Wort und That*, Breslau, 1875) but it is no more than a royal eulogy.

27. The Dutch version of the accompanying letter, pp. 1–2.

28. The reply is dated January 1, 1837.

29. The collection of documents and the memorandum are from this lodge.

30. The account is given somewhat vaguely in pp. 2–3 of the printed record of the Royal York referred to above in note 23.

31. The Landesloge sent its reply on November 11, 1840; the Mutterloge on January 27, 1841. See appendixes V, VI in Katz, "Fight for Admission," pp. 202–205.

32. The minutes of the Royal York, p. 3.

33. See above, note 5.

34. E. Meissner, *Geschichte der g. u. v. St. Johannis-Loge Apollo im Orient Leipzig* (Leipzig, 1905), pp. 33, 34.

35. See above, note 6.

36. Wiebe, *Die grosse Loge von Hamburg*, p. 239. The name of the member was Harry Lipschitz. The vote was 66–20 in favor. The minority presented their arguments to a commission composed of the heads of the five Hamburg lodges, but the commission decided to ignore the minority opinion.

37. HKB, II, 13c, app. 7.

38. [Franz August von Etzel], *Geschichte der Grossen National-Mutterloge des Preussischen Staates genannt zu den Drei Weltkugeln* (Berlin,

1840), pp. 107–112. The Royal York affiliates outside of Prussia are not enumerated by Etzel.

39. The sequence of events is recounted in *Ueber die Stellung der Freimaurer jüdischen Glaubens in Preussen* . . . (Berlin, 1840), p. 112. The pamphlet bears the signatures of all the members of the group, the brothers, Dr. Fr. J. Behrend and Joseph Behrend, signing first. Their residential address appears at the end of the pamphlet (p. 16) as the address to which correspondence is to be directed. In the above mentioned minutes of the Royal York, Dr. Behrend is mentioned as the head of the group.

40. *Ueber die Stellung*, pp. 4–5.

41. The letter is printed *ibid.*, pp. 6–7, and reprinted as appendix VII in Katz, "Fight for Admission," p. 207.

42. *Ueber die Stellung*, p. 8; the letter is reprinted as appendix VIII, in Katz, "Fight for Admission," p. 209. The letter of the brethren was signed on January 23, 1842, and the Prince's reply on April 26, 1843.

43. "Mit der Uebernahme des Protectorats ueber die preussischen Freimaurerlogen ist mir auch die Verpflichtung ueberkommen, den Bund in seinen Fundamentalbestimmungen zu schuetzen, und ihn vor Neuerungen zu wahren, die nur dazu dienen koennen die Erreichung des urspruenglichen Zwecks zu erschweren oder zu vereiteln . . .

Wollte ich versuchen an diesen Fundamentalbestimmungen eine Abaenderung vorzunehmen, so wuerde dies, wie ich im voraus ueberzeugt bin, die Folge haben, Unzufriedenheit bei den, diesen Grundsaetzen treu anhaengenden Gliedern zu erwecken, wodruch dem Zwecke, der Mich allein bestimmen konnte, das Protektorat zu uebernehmen, entgegengewirkt werden wuerde."

44. The following account is based on the minutes of the Royal York (mentioned above) pp. 3–4. Relevant excerpts of the Mutterloge minutes appear in the minutes of Eclectic lodges of Frankfurt of 1843 which have been preserved in the Kloss collection. A short summary is to be found in [Etzel], *Geschichte der grossen National Mutterloge* (Berlin, 1903), pp. 192–193.

45. I have no data on what happened at this stage in the Landesloge, but its position is undoubtedly clear.

46. The date is also given by Etzel, *Geschichte der Grossen National Mutterloge*, p. 192.

47. The Royal York minutes, *ibid.*

48. The Kloss collection also contains press clippings pertaining to the Jewish problem. The February 22 issue of the *Frankfurter Ober-Post-amts-Zeitung* (p. 426) reports on the prospects of a change for the better through the influence of the Prince. This item appeared before he sent his reply to Dr. Behrend. The notice of June 12 was an echo of this letter and was released, apparently, to many newspapers. The denial speaks of "several newspapers" where the notice had appeared.

49. Little is known of the attitude of Wilhelm I toward the Jews. See Otto Joehlinger, *Bismarck und die Juden* (Berlin, 1921), pp. 141–153;

259

Walter Frank, *Hofprediger Adolf Stoecker und die christlich-soziale Bewegung* (Berlin, 1928), pp. 108–130. The evidence cited here completes the picture to a large extent.

50. In the minutes of the Royal York (p. 5), the Protector is quoted as having said: "Die von anderen Grossen Logen zu befuerchtenden Repressalien anlagend, so wuerden sich auch die Mittel finden lassen um eine Ausgleichung herbeizufuehren."

51. The letter of the New York Grand Lodge has been printed in the *Transactions of the Grand Lodge of New York, November 29, 1843 to May 29, 1844.* Kloss copied it from there. A German translation appeared in *Diaskalia* (January 20, 1845).

52. Excerpts of the printed minutes of the Grand Lodge of Hamburg in the Kloss collection.

53. Excerpts from the printed minutes of the Mutterloge of July 24, 1844.

54. Regarding the letter quoted above of the New York lodge, Kloss noted that the later issues of the *Transactions* no longer mentioned the protest to Berlin.

55. *L'Orient, Revue universelle de la Franc-Maconnerie, 1844–1845*, pp. 11–16, 38–39, 112–113, 138–139, 301–302, 329–330, 358–360.

56. The details following are included in a document published in *Bulletin trimestriel du Grand Orient de France, 1846*, pp. 258–268.

57. See Chapter VIII.

58. The description that follows is based on *Die maurerische Emanzipation der Juden in Hamburg*, p. 135. The author gives no date for the visit, but that is known from the Prince's biography; Ludwig Hahn, *Wilhelm, der erste Kaiser des neuen deutschen Reiches* (Berlin, 1888), p. 21. It appears that the description is based on accurate information and includes the names of the persons involved; Brother Tandel being responsible for the protest raised in the discussion on the reception of the Prince, and Brother Hebeler, the representative of the Royal York. The incident was also reported in the Masonic press; see *L'Orient, 1844–1845*, pp. 39, 113.

59. "Nachdem nun die Klagen und Proteste jener 6 israelitischen Bb. v. 19, Aug. 1845 in London bekannt geworden waren. . . ," *Die Maurerische Emanzipation der Juden in Hamburg*, p. 135. I have no idea to whom and what the reference is here. From another source comes the information that the Behrend brothers together with Jewish Masons from abroad decided to put one of the lodges to test. Having been refused, they gave wide publicity to the matter (*L'Orient, 1844–1845*, pp. 301–302).

60. A letter of the Landesloge to the Grand Lodge of Hamburg of February 14, 1847 (*Die maurerische Emanzipation*, p. 144) mentions the Grand Lodge of London as being among those protesting the exclusion of their Jewish members by the Prussian lodges, but which did not make any reprisals.

61. The following details are taken from *Die Maurerische Emanzipation*, pp. 135–140, 144–148, 152–158.

62. The reactions of the other localities have been mentioned above— as for Bayreuth, see Bernard Beyer, *Geschichte der Grossloge "Zur Sonne in Bayreuth"* (Frankfurt am Main, 1954), II, 53–57. The Grand Lodge resolved, on August 31, 1847, to rescind the clause restricting membership to Christians. Affiliated to this Grand lodge were lodges in Bayreuth, Hof, Stuttgart, Mannheim, Fürth, and Frankenstadt. The proposal met with some opposition when the vote was taken. The resolution, which was submitted by Sophian Kolb, Master of the lodge, and which formed the basis of the discussion, was afterward published in the *Freimaurer Zeitung* (September 1848), pp. 289–291.

63. The idea was put forward by the Master of the Loge zu den 3 Zedern of Stuttgart (*Maurerische Emanzipation der Juden in Hamburg*, p. 136).

Chapter VIII. Ideological Standpoints

1. See above, Chapter IV, note 42.

2. J. F. L. Theodor Merzdorf, *Die Symbole, die Gesetze die Geschichte, der Zweck der Masonei schliessen keine Religion von derselben aus* (Leipzig, 1836), pp. 15–19, 22, 37.

3. L. von Orth, *Maurerisches Glaubensbekenntniss* (Stuttgart, 1838), pp. 9, 13–14.

4. In 1842, its name was changed to *Maurerhalle*.

5. Fischer wrote three major articles on the Jewish problem: "Ueber die Zulassung der Juden zum Freimaurerbunde," *Neueste Zeitschrift für Freimaurerei* (1838), pp. 249–269; "Ueber die Judenfrage," *Die Maurerhalle* (1843), pp. 115–143; "Das christliche Element im Freimaurerbunde," *Die Maurerhalle* (1844), pp. 255–293.

6. *Die Maurerhalle* (1844), pp. 263–265, 275–278.

7. *Neueste Zeitschrift* (1838), pp. 258, 264, 266; *Die Maurerhalle* (1843), p. 133.

8. *Neueste Zeitschrift* (1838), p. 268; *Die Maurerhalle* (1843), p. 136; (1844), pp. 282–283, 285–286.

9. Christian A. H. Grapengiesser, "Christenthum und Freimaurerei," *Archiv für Freimaurerei*, III, part 1 (1845), 41, 61. The author had expressed his views on the Jewish problem once before in *Neueste Zeitschrift für Freimaurerei* (1839), I, 350–362.

10. Johann Leutbecher, *Noachismus und Christenthum* (Erlangen, 1844).

11. See above, Chapter II.

12. See above, Chapter V, note 28.

13. See Katz, "Fight for Admission," appendix III.

14. See above, Chapter IV.

15. The Darmstadt Lodge Johannes der Evangelist zur Eintracht was very similar to Molitor's in Frankfurt. The tone and language of its circular dated June 24, 1843, bear close resemblance to those of the anonymous brochure.

261

16. *Der Freimaurerbund seinem philosophischen, religiösen und geschichtlichen Standpunkte nach; nebst Hinblick auf das Verhältniss der Israeliten in demselben* (Darmstadt, 1843), pp. 13, 17–18, 22, 33–35, 37–38.

17. *Ibid.*, pp. 37, 38.

18. Johann Jacob Scherbius, *Das Christenthum als Grundlage der eklektischen Freimaurerei* (Frankfurt am Main, 1844), p. 20; by the same author, *Ueber den Zusammenhang des Christenthums und der Freimaurerei* (Frankfurt am Main, 1844) pp. 6, 10. The first work was occasioned by the events, the second deals with principles.

19. K. Strauss, "Christenthum und Freimaurerei," *Archiv für Freimaurerei,* II, part 4 (1844), 3–31.

20. Ernst Gottfried Adolf Böckel, "Noch einige Worte ueber die Frage: Ob Israeliten als Freimaurer aufgenommen, oder als Besuchende zugelassen weren können," *Archiv fur Freimaurerei,* III, part 2 (1845), 56–65.

21. Wolfstieg, *Bibliographie,* no. 14112.

22. *Festgabe dargebracht von Brüdern der Loge zur aufgehenden Morgenröthe im Orient zu Frankfurt a/M zur Feier ihres 25 jährigen Jubiläums* (1833), pp. 25, 31–35, 89, 115.

23. Weil's remarks, *ibid.,* pp. 31–32.

24. Mishneh Torah, Laws concerning Idolatry, chap. I.

25. Heinrich Schwartzschild's remarks, *Festgabe,* p. 64.

26. Solomon Ibn Gabirol, "The Royal Crown," from *Selected Religious Poems of Solomon Ibn Gabirol,* translated into English verse by Israel Zangwill, (Philadelphia, 1923).

27. Jacob Weil, "Ueber maurerische Zeitfragen," *Jahresbericht am Ordensfeste des Maurerjahres 5844* (1844), p. 51.

28. See his introduction to Menasseh ben Israel's *Hope of Israel* in M. Mendelssohn, *Gesammelte Schriften* (Leipzig, 1843), III, 199. Menasseh ben Israel quoted this verse in support of his view that Judaism intended all nations to embrace its faith (*ibid.,* pp. 236–237). Mendelssohn disagreed (*ibid.,* note on pp. 234–236).

29. See, for example, Meyer Kayserling, *Bibliothek jüdischer Kanzelredner* (Berlin, 1870), p. 373.

30. Cretzschmar, *Religionssysteme,* p. 56.

31. Weil, "Ueber maurerische Zeitfragen," p. 5.

32. Gotthold Salomon, *Stimmen aus Osten, Eine Sammlung Reden und Betrachtungen maurerischen Inhalts* (Hamburg, 1845), pp. 62–70, 87, 106–107.

33. *Bulletin trimestriel du Grand Orient de France* (April 1844), p. 258. I have devoted a special article to the positions of Hirsch and the other Jewish Masons mentioned above on this issue, Jacob Katz, "Samuel Hirsch—Rabbi, Philosopher and Freemason," *Revue des Etudes Juive,* CXXV (1966), 113–126.

34. *Bulletin trimestriel,* p. 258.

35. Hirsch's work was published in 1842, while he was still rabbi in

Dessau. He was called to Luxembourg in 1843 and was admitted to the Masonic lodge that same year. See Katz, "Samuel Hirsch."

36. Hirsch's philosophy has been extensively dealt with in the relevant literature. See especially I. Fleishman, *The Problem of Christianity in Modern Jewish Thought (1770–1929)* (Hebrew), (Jerusalem, 1964), pp. 87–92. Hirsch's membership in the Freemasons and the Masonic influence on his second work have escaped the notice of the critics.

37. See especially Fleishman, *Problem of Christianity.*

38. Samuel Hirsch, *Die Humanität als Religion, in Vorträgen, gehalten in der Loge zu Luxembourg* (Trier, 1854). The contents of the book are analyzed in Katz, "Samuel Hirsch." I have gone beyond time-span covered by this chapter by several years. Yet, as appears from his remarks made in 1844, Hirsch had formed his views much earlier, and the speeches he delivered eleven years later are only the detailed elaboration of his earlier views.

Chapter IX. Partial Emancipation and Subsequent Reaction

1. See Chapter VI.

2. The manifesto was published in pamphlet form in *Zur Aufklärung der grossen Freimaurer-Lüge*, XI (May 1849), 12–14, and in Eduard Emil Eckert, *Der Freimaurer-Orden in seiner wahren Bedeutung* (Dresden, 1852), pp. 270–272.

3. [Etzel], *Geschichte der grossen National-Mutterloge*, pp. 193–195.

4. I have not been able to find any source material describing what transpired in the Royal York at this stage, but it was always ahead of the Mutterloge in its liberalism. It may be assumed that this instance was no exception.

5. Leopold Böhmer, *Geschichte der Freimaurerei in Köln am Rhein von 1815 bis 1872* (Cologne, 1873), pp. 39–46.

6. *Nachrichten von der Grossen National-Mutter-Loge . . . Auszüge aus den Protokollen von 19 October und 7 December 1848*, p. 4.

7. Böhmer, *Freimaurerei in Köln*, pp. 40, 41, 45. See also [Theodor Merzdorf], *Die Freimaurer-Logen und die Annexion* (Oldenburg, 1866), pp. 23–24. At this time the lodge had changed its name to Rhenana. See also Etzel, *Geschichte der Mutterloge*, p. 197.

8. Merzdorf, *Die Freimaurer-Logen und die Annexion*, pp. 24–25, according to the Mother Lodge minutes.

9. Böhmer, *Freimaurerei in Köln*, p. 44.

10. At this juncture, the two lodges had united and become affiliated with the Mutterloge. Etzel, *Geschichte der Mutterloge*, p. 197.

11. Böhmer, *Freimaurerei in Köln*, p. 45.

12. *Freimaurer Zeitung* (1853), p. 183.

13. The newspaper bore the name *Freimüthige Sachsen Zeitung*. Eckert himself had labeled his paper *"antirevolutionär."* Eduard Emil Eckert,

Geschichte meiner persönlichen Anklage des Freimaurer-Ordens als einer Verschwörungs-Gesellschaft bei dem Ministerium in Berlin (Schaffhausen, 1858), p. 41. The newspaper was published until 1850 and printed anti-Masonic articles. See Wolfstieg, *Bibliographie*, no. 23821.

14. Eduard Emil Eckert, *Der Freimaurer-Orden in seiner wahren Bedeutung* (Dresden, 1852).

15. Eckert again described the ideal order as he imagined it to have existed before it was undermined by subversive forces and as he aspired to have it restored once the Freemasons had been suppressed. See especially his *Historisch-politische Zeitschrift in zwanglosen Heften zum Schutz der christlichen, ständisch-monarchistischen Staaten-Ordnung, des Welt-und Bürgerfriedens, der Familien-Bande und des Eigenthums* (Schaffhausen, 1860), I, 38–41.

16. Eckert introduced himself as a Protestant (*Geschichte meiner Anklage*, p. 11), but undertook the defense of all the Christian churches. According to the *Allgemeines Handbuch der Freimaurerei* (Leipzig, 1900), I, 215, he converted to Catholicism in Vienna, and committed suicide there in 1866.

17. One of Eckert's most confused works, *Die Mysterien der Heidenkirche* (Schaffhausen, 1860), dealt with this topic.

18. In support of his contentions, he cited many remarks by Jewish Freemasons whom we have previously encountered. See *Der Freimaurer-Orden*, pp. 253–263, and also Chapter X.

19. An excerpt from the subtitle of Eckert, *Der Freimaurer-Orden*.

20. The article was entitled "Die Freimaurerei und die Gegenwart" and appeared in *Historisch-politische Blätter für das katholische Deutschland*, 41 (1858), 756–800. The editors, at the time, were Edmund Jörg and Franz Binder. In the next issue, which continued the controversy with Eckert, it was admitted that one of the two had written the article (*ibid.*, 42 [1858], 564–565).

21. Excerpts from the articles appear in Karl Theodor August Wernicke, *Freimaurerei und Christenthum* (Berlin, 1854)—Vorwort von General von Selasinsky, pp. xiii–xiv.

22. "Das geistliche Amt und die Freimaurerei," *Evangelische Kirchenzeitung* (1843), 87–88, 689–699. This article was commented on favorably in General von Selasinsky's foreword to *Freimaurerei und Christenthum*, p. xiii.

23. *Asträa Taschenbuch für Freimaurer auf das Jahr 1853–1854* (Sonderhausen, 1853), p. 249.

24. Ernst Wilhelm von Hengstenberg, *Die Freimaurerei und das evangelische Pfarramt* (Berlin, 1854), pp. 26–27, 29–32.

25. Wolfstieg, *Bibliographie*, nos. 23640–23651.

26. *Zur Beurtheilung der Hengstenbergschen Schrift: Die Freimaurerei und das evangelische Pfarramt, Von einem Freimaurer mit Zustimmung seiner Bundes-Behörde* (Berlin, 1854), p. 21. In the pamphlet (p. 22), the

author speaks in the name of "unserer vaterländischen d.h. der Preussischen Freimaurerei."

27. An article published in the *Vossische Zeitung* of the November 2, 1855 issue. Excerpts also appeared in the *Freimaurer Zeitung* (1856), pp. 78–79. See Katz, "Samuel Hirsch."

28. R. Fischer, "Weitere Beleuchung des in der Berliner Evangelischen Kirchen-Zeitung erfahrenen Angriffs," *Freimaurer-Zeitung* (1854), pp. 9–13.

29. The *Freimaurer-Zeitung* (1856), pp. 78–79) reported that fifty-one clergymen in Pomerania had appealed to the Stettin Consistorium to prohibit clergymen belonging to the Freemasons. Some concrete action was taken. See Wolfstieg, *Bibliographie*, nos. 23650–23651.

30. "Das Freimaurerthum tritt daher nur da mit dem Christenthume in Widerspruch, wenn es . . . Heiden und Juden nicht minder als Christen in den Bund aufnimmt," *Freimaurer-Zeitung* (1856), p. 78. See also note 32 below.

31. *Zur Beurtheilung*, p. 22.

32. The restrictive defining clauses end with "und auch in dieser Hinsicht (ist) das christliche Prinzip gewahrt," *ibid.*

33. The address entitled *Der Tempel der Eintracht* delivered by a member of the lodge and quoted in *Latomia* (Leipzig, 1859), p. 30.

34. The account of the following astonishing occurrences is incorporated in the minutes of the Berlin Grand Lodges and is printed in the minutes of the Grossloge des Königreichs Hannover am 13 April 1863, p. 6.

35. *Ibid.*, p. 5.

36. Etzel, *Geschichte der grossen National-Mutterloge*, p. 235.

37. The minutes of the Grossloge des Königreichs Hannover, p. 5.

38. General testimony to this effect was presented by Theodore Merzdorf, a senior Mason. See *Die Freimaurer-Logen und die Annexion*, pp. 11–12. A concrete example is cited below, see note 62.

39. The printed minutes of the Mutterloge of May 23, 1861, p. 5; of December 5, 1861, p. 6.

40. Ten names are mentioned in the December minutes (see previous note). Seven were definitely Jewish and the other three may have been. Classified by occupation, three (all Jews) were physicians, six merchants, and one a stone-mason.

41. Rudolf Grosse, *Geschichte der Grossen Loge von Preussen, genannt Royal York zur Freundschaft* (Berlin, 1909), p. 51.

42. Adolf Widmann, "Brief an einen Juden und Freimaurer," *Zirkelcorrespondenz unter den St. Johannis-Logenmeistern der Grossen Landesloge der Freimaurer von Deutschland* (Berlin, 1872), I, 189–209.

43. *Mittheilungen aus dem Bunde der Grossen National-Mutterloge*, II, 91–93.

44. *Mittheilungen*, I (1870), 166–167.

45. The minutes of the deliberations of the commission of inquiry, *Mittheilungen*, I, 167–171. This commission had decided to defer its decision to the year set for the regular review of the constitution. In my analysis I have combined the remarks made on the two occasions.

46. The request of the daughter lodges that the proposal be brought to a vote was submitted on April 24, 1872. The results were handed to the commission on January 8, 1873. *Mittheilungen*, V (1874), 98–103, 136–143.

47. *Ibid.*, p. 99.

48. *Ibid.*, pp. 99–100.

49. *Ibid.*, p. 140; the speaker's place of residence is given on p. 142.

50. *Mittheilungen*, I, 170.

51. *Ibid.*, V, 101.

52. *Ibid.*, I, 170; V, 139. For the speaker's connections with Düsseldorf see p. 142.

53. *Ibid.*, V, 101–102, 136–137. The final tally is given on p. 143.

54. Etzel, *Geschichte der grossen National-Mutterloge*, pp. 273–275. A short summary of the discussion on the Jewish question appears on pp. 278–279.

55. *Mittheilungen*, V, 139–140, 142–143.

56. [Merzdorf], *Die Freimaurer-Logen und die Annexion*. The main arguments were also summarized in the article by the same author appearing in *Latomia* (1866), pp. 139–146.

57. This is evident from the recommendation (later withdrawn). See below.

58. The Morgenröthe had joined the Frankfurt Eclectic Covenant. See above, Chapter VI.

59. *Mittheilungen*, III (1871), 6–9.

60. *Ibid.*, I, 168–170; V, 140–141.

61. "So reich und umfassend äusserlich gebildet Jemand auch sein möchte, der dem christlichen Glauben nicht angehört, auf gleicher Stufe sittlicher Anschauung und Bildung werde er nicht angesehen werden können, und daher der inneren Gleichberechtigung mit den Brüdern des Bundes entbehren, welche als einer der Fundamentalsätze des Ordens mit Recht angenommen sei" (*ibid.*, I, 196).

62. *Ibid.*, V, 141.

63. *Ibid.*, I, 170.

64. This view was reiterated several times; *ibid.*, I, 168; V, 101, 139.

65. Minutes of the lodge meeting held on May 20, 1876; *ibid.*, VII (1876), 183–212.

66. The list (*ibid.*, VII, 183–188) shows that very many lodges were located in small cities where, as we have seen above, there was a stronger inclination to accept Jews.

67. *Ibid.*, VII, 194.

68. Many economic facts are adduced, out of anti-Semitic motives, by Otto Glagau in *Der Börsen- und Gründungs-Schwindel in Deutschland*

(Leipzig, 1877). See Paul W. Massing, *Rehearsal for Destruction* (New York, 1949), pp. 3–20. *Mittheilungen*, VII, 194.

69. The term made its appearance for the first time in the title of an anti-Semitic book: C. Wilmanns, *Die "goldene" Internationale und die Nothwendigkeit einer socialen Reformpartei* (Vierte, zum Theil veränderte Auflage, Berlin, 1876).

70. *Mittheilungen*, VII, 195–196.

71. Walter Frank, *Hofprediger Adolf Stöcker und die christlich-soziale Bewegung* (Berlin, 1928); Heinrich von Treitschke, *Ein Wort über unser Judenthum* (Berlin, 1880). The articles had appeared in the *Preussische Jahrbücher*, two already at the end of 1879.

72. *Freimaurer Zeitung* (1876), pp. 73–75, 93–95, 100–102, 137–140, 145–149, 181–183.

73. *Ibid.*, pp. 137–140, 145–149, 181–183.

74. Treitschke, *Ein Wort über unser Judenthum*, p. 18: "Seit vielen Jahren wird immer häufiger und immer leidenschaftlicher in den Gesprächen der guten Gesellschaft, ohne Unterschied der Partei, die Frage erörtert, wie wir unsere alte deutsche Art gegen die wachsende Macht und den wachsenden Uebermuth des Judenthums beschützen sollen."

Chapter X. The Source of "Jews and Freemasons"

1. The anti-Semitism of the period has been analyzed in the work by Sterling, *Er ist wie du.*

2. The first (no. 1) of the leaflets is dated July 1848. The place of publication appears in the twelfth issue, no. 12, dated July 1849. The title page of many of the leaflets states that the costs of the printing were defrayed by anonymous donors, whose initials only are given. See note 11 below.

3. No. 11 (May 1849).

4. No. 12 (June 1849), pp. 1–10.

5. See above, Chapter IV.

6. No. 12, p. 3.

7. No. 11, pp. 3–11.

8. See Chapter VIII.

9. No. 11, p. 3.

10. Börne's remarks expressing his confidence in the future triumph of the Masonic idea were printed in larger type (*ibid.*, p. 9)—the anonymous author thus indicating his interpretation of them.

11. I found a bound volume of the leaflets in the library of the Alpina Grand Lodge of Switzerland in Berne where I was allowed to pursue my researches in October 1965.

12. The passage is quoted by Eckert in his first work, *Der Freimaurer-Orden*, pp. 259–263, and afterward in abridged form in his *Historisch-politische Zeitschrift*, pp. 70–72.

267

13. *Der Freimaurer-Orden*, pp. 259, 261.

14. In the *Historisch-politische Zeitschrift*, Freemasonry is defined as an association for the restoration of the *Heidenkirche* (pagan church). Eckert's work, *Die Mysterien der Heidenkirche*, was designed to provide a historical basis for the theory.

15. *Der Freimaurer-Orden*, pp. 256–257; *Historisch-politische Zeit-schrift*, pp. 70–71.

16. *Der Freimaurer-Orden*, pp. 387–390.

17. Sterling, *Er ist wie du*, pp. 25–27. The sociological analysis of conditions prevailing during the first half of the century presented in this work also applies in large measure to the fifties and sixties.

18. *Historisch-politische Zeitschrift*, pp. 32–37.

19. Alban Stolz, *Akazienzweig für die Freimaurer* (Freiburg, 1863), pp. 29–30.

20. Pachtler's first published work on the Freemasons appeared in 1872. See Wolfstieg, *Bibliographie*, no. 27935.

21. He delineated his ideas for the most part in his two books: Georg Michael Pachtler, *Der stille Krieg der Freimaurerei gegen Thron und Altar* (Freiburg, 1873); *Der Goetze der Humanitaet oder das Positive der Freimaurerei* (Freiburg, 1875).

22. Pachtler, *Der stille Krieg*, pp. v, 44–53, 168.

23. *Ibid.*, p. 44.

24. Pachtler, *Der Goetze*, p. 613.

25. The text itself (*Der stille Krieg*, p. 44) speaks of restrictions still being in existence. In note 2, however, the author states that the last barriers had been removed and that, on November 28, 1872, four Jews were appointed to the Grand Lodge, the Mutterloge. Pachtler here had confused the Mutterloge with the Royal York. In his second work published in 1875 (Pachtler, *Der Goetze*, p. 613) he acknowledged that not all restrictions had been withdrawn.

26. *Der stille Krieg*, p. 170; *Der Goetze*, p. 613.

27. Eduard Emil Eckert, *La Franc-Maçonnerie dans sa véritable signification, ou son organisation, son but et son histoire* (Liège, 1854). The translation is not listed in Wolfstieg's catalogue.

28. *Bulletin du Grand Orient de France* (1848), p. 280.

29. This news was reported in the *Archives Israélites*, VI (1869), 187. Crémieux had been a Mason since 1812. Salomon Posener, *Adolphe Crémieux (1796–1880)* (Paris, 1934), pp. 168–173.

30. *Histoire doctrine et but de la Franc-Maçonnerie par un Franc-Maçon qui ne l'est plus* (Lyon and Paris, 1857), p. 97.

31. *Le monde maçonnique* (1859), p. 374. The author of the article pointed out how the *Histoire* had been influenced by Eckert, and established that Eckert's writings were the main source for the *Histoire*.

32. Gougenot de Mousseaux, *Le Juif, Le Judaisme et la judaisation des peuples chrétiens* (Paris, 1869).

33. On Gougenot de Mousseaux, see Robert Francis Byrnes, *Antisemitism in Modern France* (New Brunswick, N.J., 1950), pp. 113–114.

34. The first two sections of the book portray Jewish tenets and actions in the anti-Jewish perspective of the Church.

35. Paragraph 5 of ch. V (pp. 159–184) deals with this topic.

36. Chs. VI and VII (pp. 184–242) are devoted to this topic. De Mousseaux gives a lengthy account of the Damascus Blood Libel and lends full credence to the anti-Jewish accusations. See pp. 200–219.

37. Ch. IV (pp. 76–101).

38. Chs. VIII–IX (pp. 254–333).

39. Ch. XII (pp. 482–499).

40. Especially ch. VIII, paragraph 3 (pp. 262–272).

41. Pp. 72–76, 333–334. He also points to the B'nai B'rith as a Jewish organization uniting Jews for common action.

42. *Ibid.*, p. 271. He refers here to Eckert as *"le docte protestant Eckert."* See below, note 45.

43. ". . . sans oublier que les artisans de tous les désordres antichrétiens ou anti-sociaux qui agitent le monde, sous le couvert des sociétées occultes, se rattachent par le lieu secret et judaïque de la cabale a l'immense et universelle association que désigne le *nom récent* de franc-maçonnerie" (*ibid.*, p. 538). In support of this assertion he cites Eckert's "rare" volume.

44. *Ibid.*, p. 342. De Mousseaux quotes the remarks referred to in note 19 above as they appeared in the French and Belgian press.

45. "Depuis longtemps nous savions en effet, nous dit le docte *protestant,* Eckert, que dans les symboles de ses loges, la franc-maçonnerie . . . 'consacre le culte du matérialisme, et qu' elle y prêche une doctrine abominable, monstrueux mélange de *philosophie, de judaïsme* et de christianisme, qui se résourt, en dernière analyse au déisme le plus grossier' " (*ibid.*, p. 274).

46. See Richard H. Laarss, *Eliphas Lévi, der grosse Kabbalist und seine magischen Werke* (Vienna, 1922), for further details on him.

47. De Mousseaux devoted a supplementary chapter of his book (pp. 504–509) to the influence of the Cabala on Freemasonry. Lévi's works are quoted there and frequently in other places in the book. De Mousseaux's opinion is summed up in his introduction (Causerie): "Car la maçonnerie, issue des mystérieuses doctrines de la cabale, que *cultivait derrière l'épaisseur de ses murs* la philosophie du dix-neuvième siècle, n'est que la forme moderne et principale de l'occultisme, dont le Juif est de prince, parce qu'il fut dans tous les siècles le prince et le grand maître de la cabale" (p. xxiii; italics in original).

48. *Ibid.*, pp. xxiii–xxiv, 268–271.

49. De Mousseaux dealt with the Mortara incident and accused the Jews of being ungrateful to the Catholic Church (*ibid.*, pp. 275–279).

50. *Ibid.*, pp. 333–340.

51. "Résumons nous donc . . . : cette nation *universelle,* aidée de tout ce que notre monde contient et produit de mécontents et de mécréants . . . aidée par l'association *patente* de la maçonnerie *universelle,* dont les principaux directeurs du judaïsme sont l'âme et la vie; aidée par l'associa-

269

tion *patente de l'Alliance israélite universelle* . . . ; cette nation, disons nous, n'est-elle pas en voie, ne se trouve-t-elle pas à le veille de devenir la première force du monde?" (*ibid.*, p. 492; italics in original).

52. (C. C. de Saint Andrée) [E. H. Chabouty], *Franc-Maçons et Juifs, sixième age de l'église d'après l'Apocalypse* (Paris, Brussels, and Geneva, 1880). For the identity of the author, see Byrnes, *Antisemitism in Modern France*, p. 129.

53. *Ibid.*, pp. 70–77, 495, 707, 716, 718–735, and especially 260–354.

54. "De tous ces témoignages, venus par différents cotés, résulte la certitude absolue de ce fait, que les juifs inspirent et dirigent tout dans les deux mondes et surtout en Europe: politique, finances, commerce, industrie, économie, philosophie, science et arts; qu'ils sont en un mot 'les rois de l'époque.'

"Mais d'un autre côté, nous venons de nous convaincre tout a l'heure que la Franc-Maçonnerie inspire et dirige tout, elle aussi, dans le monde entier et principalement en Europe.

"Auquel des deux, au juif ou au franc-maçon, appartiennent véritablement la direction et la puissance? Nous sommes donc en présence de ce dilemme: ou c'est la Maçonnerie qui a saisi le juif et qui s'en sert et le pousse en avant; ou bien, c'est le juif qui s'est emparé de la Maçonnerie et qui s'en est fait un marchepied et un instrument de ses desseins" (*ibid.*, p. 539).

55. "C'est donc le juif qui par son or, autant que par son genie, a saisi le suprême pouvoir dans la Maçonnerie et les sociétés secrêtes," *ibid.*, p. 540.

56. *Ibid.*, pp. 487–488, 540, 647–668.

57. *Ibid.*, pp. 324–343, 632–633, 697. I have found no trace of this organization anywhere else.

58. Alphonse Toussenel, *Les Juifs, rois de l'époque. Histoire de la féodalité financière* (Paris, 1845).

59. [Chabouty] *Franc-Maçons et Juifs*, pp. 525–536.

60. E. H. Chabouty, *Les Juifs, nos maitres! Documents et developpements nouveaux sur la question juive* (Paris, 1882).

Chapter XI. The Extent and Limits of the Slogan

1. Joseph Lémann, *L'entrée des Israélites dans la société française et les états chrétiens* (Paris, 1886).

2. Lémann developed this thesis extensively. See especially, *ibid.*, pp. 298–336.

3. *Ibid.*, pp. 341–348, 355–356.

4. *Ibid.*, p. 341.

5. Scholars have endeavored to explain the extent of Drumont's influence and have pointed to his method of argumentation and his style. See Israel Schapira, *Der Antisemitismus in der französischen Literatur;*

Edouard Drumont und seine Quellen (Berlin, 1927) pp. 129–135; Byrnes, *Antisemitism in Modern France*, pp. 148–155.

6. Schapira, *Antisemitismus in der französischen Literatur*, p. 11.

7. Byrnes, *Antisemitism in Modern France*, pp. 159–167.

8. *Ibid.*, pp. 129–136.

9. Edouard Drumont, *La France juive*, 40th ed. (Paris [1886]), I, 217, 260; II, 347, 535–557.

10. He concentrates his attention on the Freemasons in II, 307–348, but the topic comes up time and again elsewhere, after Drumont's confused manner.

11. Edouard Drumont, *Nos maîtres, la tyranie maçonnique* (Paris, 1899), pp. 13–25.

12. Paul Desachey, *Bibliographie de l'Affaire Dreyfus* (Paris, 1905).

13. Nathaniel Katzburg, *Antisemitism in Hungary, 1867–1914* (Hebrew), (Tel Aviv, 1969), pp. 81–84.

14. On his own testimony, Gyözö Istoczy, *A magyar antiszemitapárt megsemmisitése s ennek következményei* (Budapest 1906), pp. 5–6; *Manifest*, p. 4 (see next note).

15. *Manifest an die Regierungen und Völker der durch das Judenthum gefährdeten christlichen Staaten . . .* (Chemnitz, 1882).

16. See Chapter XII.

17. See Chapter X.

18. *Geschichte der grossen National-Mutterloge*, pp. 331, 334–335. During the course of the proceedings, votes were taken several times, some more favorable to Jews; there is no satisfactory explanation for the fluctuations. See next note.

19. *Mittheilungen aus dem Bunde der Grossen National-Mutterloge*, 15, part 4 (1884), 138.

20. The history of the founding of the German B'nai B'rith lodges is recounted by Louis Maretzki, *Geschichte des Ordens Bnei Briss in Deutschland 1882–1907* (Berlin, 1907), pp. 5–20; Ismar Elbogen, *A Century of Jewish Life* (Philadelphia, 1944), pp. 192–193. According to Elbogen, Fenchel and his colleagues were members of the Odd Fellows, who were not considered proper Masons, but he gives no source for this assertion. Maretzki related that B'nai B'rith representatives approached this order to obtain information on Fenchel. He may have been a member there, yet there is no positive proof that he did not belong to an authentic Freemason lodge.

21. Maretzki, *Geschichte des Ordens Bnei Briss*, pp. 24, 44, 46, 115–127; see also *Geschichte der Frankfurt-Loge 1888–1928* (Frankfurt am Main, 1928), pp. 7–13.

22. *Fünfzigjährige Jubelfeier des Unabhängigen Ordens Bnei Briss in der Henry-Jonas-Loge*, XVIII, no. 367 (Hamburg, 1893), 24.

23. *Mittheilungen der Grossen Loge von Preussen genannt Royal York. 1885/86*, pp. 143–147. "Die religiosen Gedanken stehen in vollem Einklang mit dem geläuterten Christenglauben, aber sie sind auch in den reli-

giösen Ueberzeugungen solcher Nichtchristen enthalten, wie wir sie in die Logen aufnehmen" (*ibid.*, p. 146).

24. Unequivocal testimony on this point is furnished by Hermann Settegast himself in *Die deutsche Freimaurerei, ihr Wesen, ihre Ziele und Zukunft* (Berlin, 1892), p. 48, and in *Das Geheimnis, das christliche Prinzip und die Hochgrade in der Freimaurerei* (Berlin, 1893), p. 21. See Dr. I. Halevi's observations (*Bausteine*, III [Sept. 1894], pp. 17–18), which are based on a comparison between the Royal York membership list and the roster of the Jewish community, in which membership on the part of every professing Jew was compulsory.

25. Settegast, *Die deutsche Freimaurerei*, p. IV.

26. Settegast, *Das Geheimnis . . .* , pp. 21–22.

27. Settegast's struggle against the Prussian Mother Lodges is described at length in Pierre Marteau's *Politik und Zustände in den drei altpreussischen Grosslogen* (Frankfurt am Main, 1906), pp. 111 ff.

28. According to the *Verzeichnis der ordentlichen Mitglieder des Vereins Grosse Freimaurer-Loge von Preussen, genannt Kaiser Friedrich zur Bundestreue (Bis 10. August 1892)*. It contains a report of the founding meeting held on August 1, 1892.

29. Settegast, *Deutsche Freimaurerei*, pp. 54–55; Marteau, *Politik und Zustände*, p. 112.

30. Bausteine. *Mittheilungen der Grossen Freimaurer-Loge von Preussen, genannt Kaiser Friedrich zur Bundestreue, 1893*, II (June 1893), 58–60.

31. Marteau, *Politik und Zustände*, pp. 112–114.

32. Frank, *Hofprediger Adolf Stoecker*, p. 232.

33. Wolfstieg, *Bibliographie*, no. 15502.

34. This is evident from Josef G. Findel's remarks in *Der freimaurerische Kampf für die Juden und die Settegast'sche Grossloge* (Leipzig, 1894), p. 5.

35. Wolfstieg, *Bibliographie*, nos. 19526–19592.

36. Marteau, *Politik und Zustände*, pp. 116–117.

37. *Bausteine*, III (Sept. 1894), 17–18.

38. The composition of the executive committee is listed in the document referred to in note 28 above. Of the fifteen active executive members, ten bore distinctly Jewish names.

39. Josef G. Findel, *Die Juden als Freimaurer* (Leipzig, 1893), p. 25. Even though he is speaking as antagonist, the evidence is consistent with the prevailing state of affairs.

40. *Ibid.*, p. 25, 27.

41. *Ibid.*, p. 14.

42. The closest analogy is the history of the *Burschenschaften*.

43. Findel, *Die Juden als Freimaurer*, p. 6, 21.

44. On p. 21 of *Der freimaurerische Kampf* Findel asserts: "Die Juden wollen erst einen Finger, dann die ganze Hand."

45. *Ibid.*, pp. 6, 9–12.

46. Settegast, *Die deutsche Freimaurerei*.

47. The publisher was Emil Goldschmidt. His name appears in the list of founders of Settegast's lodge. The title page of Settegast's book contains a note stating that all the proceeds from the sale of the book would be devoted to the founding of a new lodge. Goldschmidt also published the lodge periodical, *Bausteine*. Findel alleged that the new lodge members had threatened a publisher refusing to accede to a specific request of theirs that they would issue a periodical to compete with one currently published by him. Goldschmidt was the only member in this business and he had a key function in the lodge.

48. The German version, *Das verjudete Frankreich,* appeared in Berlin in 1886.

49. See Chapter X.

50. Henri Rollin, *L'Apocalypse de notre temps* (Paris, 1939). John Shelton Curtiss, *An Appraisal of the Protocols of Zion* (New York, 1942), pp. 107–112, contains an extensive bibliography. Walter Laqueur, *Russia and Germany: A Century of Conflict* (London, 1965), pp. 79–104.

In addition to the books listed in the previous note, see also Herman Bernstein, *The Truth about "The Protocols of Zion"* (New York, 1935), especially pp. 20–25. Other books will be mentioned in the next chapter in connection with the exposure of the *Protocols* as a forgery.

52. Bernstein translated Joly's book into English. *Ibid.,* pp. 258–279. The chapter from Goedsche's book appears there too, pp. 265–284, and the *Protocols* themselves on pp. 295–359.

53. Byrnes, *Antisemitism in Modern France,* pp. 128–129. See also Rollin, *L'Apocalypse,* p. 472; Curtiss, *An Appraisal of the Protocols,* p. 62.

54. Bernstein, *The Truth,* pp. 307, 324, 332, 334, 335.

55. Curtiss, *An Appraisal of the Protocols,* pp. 79–82.

273

Chapter XII. Approaching Ostracism

1. Elbogen, *A Century of Jewish Life,* p. 457.

2. The developments can be deduced from the reactions of the *Mitteilungen aus dem Verein zur Abwehr des Antisemitismus.* The Verein kept close watch on all that transpired in this regard.

3. *Die Vernichtung der Unwahrheiten über die Freimaurerei* (Leipzig: Verein deutscher Freimaurer, 1928), p. 6.

4. Heinz Brauweiler, *Die Brüder im Weltkriege* (Cologne, 1916); Heinz Brauweiler, *Deutsche und romanische Freimaurerei* (Cologne, 1917); Pater Albuin, *Für Gott und Vaterland! Ein Weckruf an das christliche Volk zum Kampfe gegen die Weltmacht der Freimaurerei* (Münster, 1916); Wilhelm Ohr, *Der französische Geist und die Freimaurerei* (Leipzig, 1916). The last-named book is both scholarly and topical in its approach; see pp. 185–195.

5. *Historisch-politische Blätter* (Munich, 1915), II, 65–71; (1917), II,

553–556 ("Das internationale Judentum in der Freimaurerei nach maurerischen Quellen").

6. Johann Konrad Schwabe, *Freimaurerei und Presse im Weltkrieg* (Frankfurt am Main, 1916), vol. I. Here and in the two volumes published in 1918 and in 1926, Schwabe gathered a wealth of material on this topic.

7. *Der Hammer* (1915), pp. 302–303, 313–318.

8. Theodor Fritsch, *Verborgene Fäden des Weltkrieges* (Leipzig, 1917).

9. *Ibid.*, p. 17. See also Walter Rathenau, *Zur Kritik der Zeit* (1922), p. 207.

10. *Historisch-politische Blätter* (1915), p. 82.

11. As far as I know, history books have taken no account of the activities of the *Verband gegen die Überhebung des Judentums*. The names of its founders are listed in the Jewish monthly *Im Deutschen Reich* (October 1912), p. 468.

12. Otto Bonhard, *Geschichte des alldeutschen Verbandes* (Leipzig and Berlin, 1920); Alfred Kruck, *Geschichte des alldeutschen Verbandes, 1890–1939* (Wiesbaden, 1954). Some of the founders (such as Fritz Bley, Graf Ernst zu Reventlow, and N. Strantz are mentioned in the historical account of the *Alldeutschen*; see the indexes in both books.

13. Bonhard, *Geschichte des alldeutschen Verbandes*, p. 99; Kruck, *Geschichte des alldeutschen Verbandes*, pp. 130–131.

14. The *Vorposten*'s statements on Masonry are summarized in Schwabe, *Freimaurerei und Presse*, III, 48–49.

15. *Auf Vorposten*, 1 (1921), 12.

16. Several articles on Freemasonry appeared in 1914. See Schwabe, *Freimaurerei und Presse*, III, 48–49.

17. Schwabe (*ibid.* p. 58) mentions two other newspapers which took up this topic: *Mitteilungen des Wahrheitsbundes* and *Der Bahnbrecher*. I have not seen either of them.

18. Schwabe, *Freimaurerei und Presse*, pp. 58, 59–66. The subject was also covered in the Jewish press: *Allgemeine Zeitung des Judentums* (July 12, 1918), p. 338; *Mitteilungen des Vereins zur Abwehr des Antisemitismus* (August 7, 1918), pp. 67–68.

19. *Die Zukunft* (August 1918), pp. 156–172.

20. Friedrich Wichtl, *Weltmaurerei, Weltrevolution, Weltrepublik* (Munich, 1919). Karl Heise's *Entente-Freimaurerei und der Weltkrieg* (Basle, 1919) appeared at about the same time. The material of this book is similar to Wichtl's, but the style is heavy and rough. It was published in an enlarged edition in 1920.

21. See especially in ch. XXIII (ed. 1920), pp. 182–190.

22. [Paul Bang] (W. Meister), *Judas Schuldbuch; eine deutsche Abrechnung* (Munich, 1919).

23. I have the fifth, the February 1920 edition; see pp. 201, 202. Bang was an *Auf Vorposten* reader. Following its lead, he dealt already in his first edition (pp. 134–135) with international Jewish organizations: the Al-

liance and B'nai B'rith. It appears that he was close to, perhaps even a member of, the Prussian Freemasons, and it was difficult for him to swallow the accusations against them. At all events, he finally yielded to the prevailing opinion.

24. Fritz Bley, *Am Grabe des deutschen Volkes* (Berlin, 1919), pp. 195–211. Wichtl is quoted several times in this chapter.

25. Ludwig Langmann, *Der deutsche Zusammenbruch und das Judentum* (Göttingen: Selbstverlag, 1919).

26. The second edition was published by the Deutscher Volksverlag, Munich, 1919. See *ibid.*, pp. 45–56.

27. *Auf gut deutsch* (1919), pp. 148–151, 270–271, 401–416, 549–557, 706–707.

28. [Müller von Hausen] (Gottfried zur Beek), *Die Geheimnisse der Weisen von Zion* (Charlottenburg, 1919), pp. 7, 10. There were two editions, de-luxe and regular. The references here are to the regular edition.

29. *Auf Vorposten*, 8–9 (1921), 200.

30. *Die Geheimnisse*, p. 7; Norman Cohn, *Warrant for Genocide, The Myth of the Jewish World Conspiracy and the Protocols of the Elders of Zion* (London, 1967), pp. 126–130. He identifies the Russian emigres who brought the book to Berlin but has no real proof to substantiate his conjectures.

31. Rollin, *L'Apocalypse de notre temps*, p. 96.

32. Lucien Wolf, *The Jewish Bogey and the Forged Protocols of the Learned Elders of Zion* (London, 1920), p. 96, and in the declaration of the American Jewish Committee of December 1, 1920 reprinted in the *American Jewish Yearbook* (New York, 1921), p. 367. The subject is analyzed in the light of archive materials by Morton Rosenstock in *Louis Marshall: Defender of Jewish Rights* (New York, 1935) pp. 118–122.

33. Friedrich Wichtl, *Freimaurerei, Zionismus, Kommunismus, Spartakismus, Bolschewismus* (Hamburg, 1921). The definition appears on p. 5.

34. Kruck, *Geschichte des alldeutschen Verbandes*, pp. 136–137.

35. The letter was published in *Freiheit* (May 19, 1920). Müller reprinted it that same year in *Auf Vorposten*, 3–6, 77.

36. *Geheimnisse*, p. 251.

37. *Auf Vorposten*, 6–7 (1921), 176–177.

38. *Ibid.*, 3–6 (1920), 64; 1 (1921), 14.

39. *Mitteilungen* (April 10, 1920); *Im Deutschen Reich* (May 1920), pp. 50–52 ("Ein Stück aus dem Irrenhause").

40. Diedrich Bischoff, *Freimaurerei und Deutschtum; eine Auseinandersetzung zwischen Freimaurerei und Antisemitismus* (Leipzig, 1920).

41. *Auf Vorposten*, 1 (1921), 14.

42. Müller explained that the silence of the press was due to its preoccupation with other affairs. He was probably referring to the Kapp putsch of March 1920. Practical reasons may possibly have contributed to the *Protocols* being overlooked. At all events, since the first opportunity

275

to gain publicity had passed, no interest could have been awakened without some special contributing reason. Clearly Müller's statement reveals that he and his associates were disappointed at the time.

43. *The Jewish Peril, Protocols of the Learned Elders of Zion* (London, 1920).

44. *The Cause of World Unrest* (London, 1920). The American edition bears the same date of publication. There the author's name is given as H. A. Gwynne.

45. *The American Jewish Yearbook*, XXII (1922), 179.

46. The article was reprinted in *Auf Vorposten*, 3–6 (1920), 81–84.

47. Laqueur, *Russia and Germany*, p. 312. His conjecture is that the article was written by Robert Wilton, the *Times*'s Russian correspondent during the Revolution.

48. Wolf, *The Jewish Bogey*, p. 37.

49. Wolf himself referred to these circles (*ibid.*, p. 7) and was aware of their activities.

50. The article appeared in the *Deutsche Zeitung* (May 17, 1920), the official organ of the *Alldeutsche*.

51. *Auf Vorposten*, 3–6 (1920), 65.

52. Otto Friedrich, *Die Weisen von Zion, das Buch der Fälschungen* (Lübeck [1920]), p. 2.

53. Benjamin Segel, *Die Protokolle der Weisen von Zion kritisch beleuchtet. Eine Erledigung* (Berlin, 1924), pp. 37–38.

54. Laqueur, *Russia and Germany*, pp. 102–104.

55. Alfred Rosenberg, *Die Politik der Weisen von Zion und die jüdische Weltpolitik*, p. 5. The first edition appeared in 1923. For his attitude, see below.

56. In the introduction to the American edition.

57. Friedrich, *Die Weisen von Zion*, p. 2. Goedsche was designated as the source in the articles in *Mitteilungen* and *Im deutschen Reich* (see above, note 39) as well as by Lucien Wolf in *The Jewish Bogey*, pp. 28–32.

58. A new edition appeared in 1919: *Das Geheimnis der jüdischen Weltherrschaft* (Berlin, 1919).

59. Friedrich, *Die Weisen von Zion*, p. 8.

60. The articles in the *Times* were published in pamphlet form under the title, *The Truth about the "Protocols": a Literary Forgery. From the "Times" of London, August 16, 17 and 18, 1921.*

61. See above, note 53.

62. The subtitle of the book, *Eine Abrechnung*, gives clear evidence of its purpose. See the end of the book, pp. 231–233.

63. *Hammer* (June 15, 1920), p. 229: "Was die Anführungen aus den Zionisten-Protokollen anbetrifft, so muss man sagen, dass Protokolle so nicht auszusehen pflegen."

64. *Auf Vorposten* (1921), 14–15.

65. Theodor Fritsch, *Die zionistischen Protokolle* (Leipzig, 1924), pp. 4, 74–76.

66. During the first period of his activity, his most widely circulated book was *Antisemiten-Kathechismus* (Leipzig, 1888). Here societies as such are mentioned but not the Freemasons (see 1893 ed., pp. 202–209). This book reappeared in a new form as *Handbuch der Judenfrage*, the 1919 edition of which contains a chapter on the Freemasons (p. 439). Another pamphlet on the subject appeared in 1920. Theodor Fritsch, *Die unterirdische Macht* (Leipzig, 1920). These publications still spared the German Masons to some extent, but later all distinctions were erased.

67. Alfred Rosenberg, *Die Spur der Juden im Wandel der Zeit* (Munich, 1920), pp. 88–109; Alfred Rosenberg, *Das Verbrechen der Freimaurerei* (Munich, 1921), p. 9.

68. The article is reprinted in Alfred Rosenberg, *Kampf um die Macht* (Munich, 1943), pp. 20–30.

69. Alfred Rosenberg, *Die Protokolle der Weisen von Zion und die jüdische Weltpolitik* (Munich, 1923), pp. 5–9. I have used the fourth, the 1933, edition.

70. Adolf Hitler, *Mein Kampf* (1943), pp. 6–9, 337. The book was first published in 1925.

71. A. Stein, *Adolf Hitler, Schüler der "Weisen von Zion"* (Karlsbad, 1936). Hitler himself stated that he had learned how to wield power from the Protocols. See Herman Rauschning, *Gespräche mit Hitler* (New York, 1940), pp. 224–225.

72. *Mein Kampf*, p. 345.

73. Rauschning, *Gespräche mit Hitler*, pp. 226–227.

74. Erich Ludendorff, *Kriegsführung und Politik* (Berlin, 1922), p. 322.

75. The first book to deal with the subject is Eric Ludendorff, *Vernichtung der Freimaurerei durch Enthüllung ihrer Geheimnisse* (Munich, 1927).

76. The details appear in a sheet attached to the notices of the Verein, such as "Sind die Freimaurer Judenknechte und Vaterlandsverderber?" (1926).

77. The declaration of February 16, 1924 of the three Berlin Grand Lodges stated that they stood, "auf dem Boden deutscher und christlicher Anschauung." This declaration is reprinted in Ludwig Müller von Hausen's *Die altpreussischen Logen und der National-Verband deutscher Offiziere* (Charlottenburg [1924]), p. 2.

78. To be eligible for membership, candidates had to qualify as "die im deutschen Volkstum wurzeln und auf dem Boden christlicher Anschauung stehen." G. Pösche, *25 Jahre Freimaurerei 1906–1931* (Berlin, 1931), p. 61.

79. Müller von Hausen, *Die altpreussischen Logen*, p. 7.

80. Bischoff, *Freimaurerei und Deutschtum*, pp. 3–5.

81. *Latomia* (1919), pp. 100–103.

82. *Die Vernichtung der Unwahrheiten über die Freimaurerei* (4th ed.,

Leipzig, 1929), p. 32. The first edition appeared in 1928. The figures are given "nach sorgfältigen Ermittelungen" and are, in my opinion, reliable.

83. Steffens, *Freimaurer in Deutschland*, p. 346.

84. Bischoff, *Freimaurerei und Deutschtum*, pp. 19–20.

85. This is the pamphlet mentioned above in note 82, pp. 30–33.

86. Steffens, *Freimaurer in Deutschland*, p. 346.

87. Mülhausen's evaluation obviously did not carry the same weight as the Verein's. It is also inconceivable that within two years the number of Jewish Masons had been reduced to a third.

88. Pösche's remarks are enlightening (*25 Jahre Freimaurerei*, pp. 61–63). He had been raised in a Jewish neighborhood, had kind recollections of his boyhood friends, and was even grateful to Jews for helping him. Nevertheless, he justified the exclusion of the Jews from the lodges on ideological grounds.

89. Müller von Hausen claimed (*Die altpreussischen Logen*, p. 7) that Jewish converts had risen to leadership even in the Christian lodges. The remarks of the Verein indicate that the position of these converts was by no means secure ("In den christlichen Logen finden sich vereinzelt getaufte Juden oder Nachkommen von solchen"), *Vernichtung*, p. 32. Pösche, for his part, mentions an actual instance of discrimination against a convert in not appointing him to the "Innere Orient," the highest degree of the Royal York (*25 Jahre Freimaurerei*, p. 61).

90 Pösche, *25 Jahre Freimaurerei*, pp. 31–33. The same atmosphere is described in the memoirs of August Horneffer, *Aus meinem Freimaurerleben* (Hamburg, 1957), pp. 122–133.

91. *Ibid.*, pp. 122–135.

92. The Verein summed up the position in 1928 as follows: "Zahlreiche humanitäre Einzellogen zum Teil gar keine, zum Teil nur ganz wenige Nichtchristen haben" (*Vernichtung*, p. 32).

93. Müller von Hausen, *Die altpreussischen Logen*, pp. 1–4. He wrote another book, *Die Hohenzollern und die Freimaurer*, which I have not seen.

94. So the 1920 manifesto read, which was distributed among all citizens without distinction. See *Sind die Freimaurer Judenknechte?*, p. 5.

95. This stage of the process is described by Steffens, *Freimaurer in Deutschland*, pp. 371–383.

96. *Ibid.*, pp. 379–383.

97. Stein, *Adolf Hitler*, p. 18.

98. *Ibid.*, p. 37. French and Polish versions followed closely after the appearance of the German. A Roumanian translation of 1922 is in the National Library, Jerusalem. It is not known whether this is the first edition or not.

99. Bernstein, *The Truth about "the Protocols,"* pp. 54–58; Rosenstock, *Louis Marshall*, pp. 122–127. Rosenstock describes in detail the fate and influence of the *Protocols* in the United States.

100 First, excerpts of the *Protocols* were printed in a number of month-

lies, later a full translation was published. See R. Lamblin, *'Protocols' des sages de Sion* (Paris, 1921), pp. xii–xiv. This book is the third translation.

101. Eugen J. Weber, *Action française, Royalism and Reaction in Twentieth-Century France* (Stanford, 1962), pp. 200–201.

102. Mgr. Jouin, *Le Péril judéo-maçonnique* (Paris, [1920]).

103. How Jouin came to fight the Masons is described in *Discours de Monseigneur Jouin au Congrès de la Ligue anti-judéo-maçonnique, le lundi 26 novembre 1928* (Paris, 1929), pp. 1–2.

104. Jouin obtained the Russian version of the *Protocols* from Müller von Hausen. *Le Péril judéo-maçonnique*, p. 2.

105. *Ibid.*, p. 19. Jouin had published Goedsche's story in 1912 in *Revue*, I (1912), 11–16.

106. Jouin, *Discours*, p. 2.

107. *Ibid.*

108. Weber, *Action-française*, pp. 219 ff., 240–246, 259–275, 295–316.

109. The Wiener Library in London has a substantial collection of contemporaneous French propaganda pamphlets written by Paul Ganem, Léon de Poncins, Jean Bertrand, Henri Coston, and other anonymous authors.

110. One example is Franz Alfred Six, *Studien zur Geistesgeschichte der Freimaurerei* (Hamburg, 1942). Other works of the same nature have been referred to above.

111. The known authors are Friedrich Hasselbacher, Albert Steingrüber, Dr. Custos, and Robert Schneider. I saw these and other anonymous works in the Wiener library. The official agency for the dissemination of the material was the *Propaganda-Ausschuss des Instituts zum Studium der Freimaurerei*. See D. Schwartz, *Die Freimaurerei, Weltanschauung, Organisation und Politik* (Berlin, 1938). The introduction to the book was written by Reynard Heydrich, Chief of the Security Police.

112. The legal proceedings were reported in the Amsterdam Jewish Central Information Office news bulletins which were published while the trial was in progress. A copy is lodged in the National Library, Jerusalem, and bears the title *Der Berner Process und die "Protokolle der Weisen von Zion."*

113. Two of the experts afterward published their opinions: Ulrich Fleischhauer, *Die echten Protokolle der Weisen von Zion* (Erfurt, 1935); Carl Albert Loosli, *Die "Geheimen Gesellschaften" und die Schweizerische Demokratie* (Berne, 1935).

114. *Der Berner Process*, bulletin 23, p. 4. See Curtiss, *An Appraisal of the Protocols of Zion*, pp. 92–93. Laqueur, *Russia and Germany*, p. 97.

Chapter XIII. Historical Significance

1. It is difficult to obtain an authentic description of the lodge ceremonies. Even today Masonic writers deliberately hide the details of these

rites behind obscure language. See, for example, Fred L. Pick and G. Norman Knight, *The Freemason's Pocket Reference Book* (London, 1963), p. 137; Horneffer, *Aus meinem Freimaurerleben*, p. 22. It seems that the disrobing ritual was still common in the lodges by the beginning of nineteenth century. The Frankfurt *Morgenröthe* followed this practice as is shown by the account of an initiation ceremony and its interpretation in the speech delivered by the Master in 1809; *Reden gehalten in der . . . Loge zur aufgehenden Morgenröthe* (Frankfurt am Main, 1809), p. 65. And this lodge strove for simplicity in its ceremonies.

2. A. Horne, "King Solomon's Temple in the Masonic Tradition," *Ars Quatuor Coronatorum*, 72 (1962), 221–227.

3. Pick and Knight, *The Freemason's Pocket Reference Book*, pp. 39–40.

4. Jacob Katz, *Exclusiveness and Tolerance, Studies in Jewish-Gentile Relations* (Oxford, 1961), pp. 3–47.

5. G. Scholem, "Zur Geschichte der Anfänge der christlichen Kabbala," *Essays Presented to Leo Baeck on the Occasion of his Eightieth Birthday* (London, 1954), pp. 158–193.

6. Shohet, *Beginnings of the Haskalah*, pp. 51–52.

7. Egidus Günther Hellmund, *Christliches Bedenken von den sogenannten Frey-Mäurern etc.* (Wiesbaden, 1742), p. 22; also Jacob Katz, "Freemasons and Jews" in *The Journal of Jewish Sociology*, IX (1967), 140–141.

8. The literature exaggerates very much. The question has been dealt with most recently in Koseleck, *Kritik und Krise*, pp. 41–115. The author relies almost entirely on random sources and his generalizations are not substantiated.

Chapter XIV. Real Relations

1. See Graetz, *Geschichte der Juden*, XI (Leipzig, 1900), 59–76; Katz, "The Term 'Jewish Emancipation,' " pp. 1–25.

2. The history of Jewish emancipation is fully described in Martin Philippson, *Neueste Geschichte des jüdischen Volkes*, vol. I (Leipzig, 1907), and most recently in the relevant chapters of Raphael Mahler, *History of the Jews in Modern Times* (Hebrew), 4 vols. (Merhavya, 1954–1956), as well as its bibliography.

3. Friedrich C. Sell, *Die Tragödie des deutschen Liberalismus* (Stuttgart [1953]), pp. 151–171.

Chapter XV. Imaginary Relations

1. Cohn, *Warrant for Genocide*, pp. 26–29.

2. As we have seen in Chapter III, there were Cabalistic trends in Ma-

sonry. Other groups were suspected of such tendencies by their enemies, and sometimes without sufficient reason. See Alexis Schmidt, "Freimaurerei und Kabbala," *Zirkelcorrespondenz unter den St.-Johannis Logenmeistern* (Berlin, 1875), pp. 1–14.

3. Müller von Hausen, *Die altpreussischen Logen*, p. 12.

4. See Jacob Katz, "A State within a State—the History of an anti-Semitic Slogan," *the Israel Academy of Sciences and Humanities Proceedings*, IV, no. 3.

5. For the source of this thesis, see H. Lüthy, "Du 'complet protestant' ou 'juste milieu,' " *Le Passé présent* (Monaco, 1965), pp. 243–263.

6. Byrnes, *Antisemitism in Modern France*, pp. 110–125.

7. See Chapters XI and XII.

Index

289

291

293